POSITIVE PSYCHOLOGY

This book provides an accessible and balanced introduction to positive psychology scholarship and its applications, incorporating an overview of the development of positive psychology. *Positive Psychology: The Basics* delineates positive psychology's journey as a discipline, takes stock of its achievements and provides an updated overview of its core topics, exploring the theory, research and interventions in each.

Launched as a rebellious discipline just over two decades ago, positive psychology challenged the emphasis of applied psychology on disease and dysfunction and offered a new, more balanced perspective on human life. From its foundations in the late 20th century to recent "second-wave" theories around the importance of recognizing negative emotions, this compact overview covers the key ideas and principles, from research around emotional wellbeing, optimism and change, to posttraumatic growth and positive relationships. The first jargon-free introduction to the subject, Hart introduces the reader to a range of issues, including self-regulation and flow, character strengths and virtues and positive relationships, concluding with a chapter on how interventions can affect happiness and wellbeing.

Positive Psychology: The Basics is an essential resource for students, practitioners, academics and anyone who is interested in understanding the essence of a life well lived.

Dr Rona Hart is a senior lecturer in Applied Positive Psychology, and the former Programme Leader of the immensely popular MSc in Applied Positive Psychology Programme and the MSc in Applied Positive Psychology and Coaching Psychology Programme at the School of Psychology, University of East London, UK.

The Basics

The Basics is a highly successful series of accessible guidebooks which provide an overview of the fundamental principles of a subject area in a jargon-free and undaunting format.

Intended for students approaching a subject for the first time, the books both introduce the essentials of a subject and provide an ideal springboard for further study. With over 50 titles spanning subjects from artificial intelligence (AI) to women's studies, *The Basics* are an ideal starting point for students seeking to understand a subject area.

Each text comes with recommendations for further study and gradually introduces the complexities and nuances within a subject.

For a full list of titles in this series, please visit www.routledge.com/The-Basics/book-series/B

POSITIVE PSYCHOLOGY
THE BASICS

Rona Hart

Routledge
Taylor & Francis Group

LONDON AND NEW YORK

First published 2021
by Routledge
2 Park Square, Milton Park, Abingdon, Oxon OX14 4RN

and by Routledge
52 Vanderbilt Avenue, New York, NY 10017

Routledge is an imprint of the Taylor & Francis Group, an informa business

British Library Cataloguing-in-Publication Data
A catalogue record for this book is available from the British Library

Library of Congress Cataloging-in-Publication Data
A catalog record has been requested for this book

ISBN: 978-1-138-55193-0 (hbk)
ISBN: 978-1-138-55195-4 (pbk)
ISBN: 978-1-315-14785-7 (ebk)

Typeset in Bembo
by Swales & Willis, Exeter, Devon, UK

CONTENTS

ILLUSTRATIONS

FIGURES

TABLES

PREFACE

Consider a scientific scholarship that is as invested in promoting happiness, wellbeing, strength and resilience as much as it is concerned in alleviating stress and distress. A science that explores what makes a good life, and disseminates concepts, research findings and interventions that can help us flourish and grow. This is what positive psychology is about.

Launched as a rebellious discipline just over two decades ago, positive psychology challenged the emphasis of applied psychology on disease and dysfunction and offered a new, more balanced perspective on human life. Since its establishment it has seen remarkable progress, and has laid down solid theoretical and empirical foundations for its concepts and its applied work.

This books delineates positive psychology's journey as a discipline, takes stock of its achievements and provides an updated overview of its core topics, exploring the theory, research and interventions in each.

Chapter 1 delineates the background that has led to the establishment of positive psychology, and defines what it contains and where its focus lies. It also provides an overview of its development in the past two decades and discusses its future trajectory and the key debates and critique that emerged over the years around its concepts.

Chapters 2 and 3 review and discuss two core topics in positive psychology that have attracted significant public interest over the years: wellbeing and happiness. Chapter 2 reviews the mounting research on happiness and considers why happiness matters and what determines happiness. Chapter 3 opens with a distinction between hedonia and eudaimonia, and then reviews the leading models of wellbeing and the recent research on them.

Chapter 4 unpacks a key component of happiness and wellbeing: positive emotions. The chapter discusses the structure of emotions and their utility, and reviews the Broaden-and-Build Theory of positive emotions. The final section explores the leading models of emotional intelligence.

Chapter 5 explores two classic concepts in positive psychology: optimism and hope. The chapter describes the three leading models of optimism, summarises the concept of hope and reviews the empirical work on the upshots of optimism and hope for wellbeing and healthy functioning.

Chapter 6 explores two related concepts: goal pursuit and change. The chapter opens with a review of goal theory, and then considers the optimal parameters for setting goals. The chapter then offers a brief review of two leading models of behavioural change.

Chapter 7 focuses on a prominent component of performance that can lead to persistent goal pursuit and achievement: self-regulation. The chapter explores the concept, and considers the benefits of self-regulation and its costs when it fails. The chapter also summarises the concept of grit.

Chapter 8 explores the concept of flow: what it entails, the conditions under which it can occur and its upshots and dark side.

Chapter 9 examines meaning in life: a core component of wellbeing. The chapter addresses the question of what makes life meaningful, and reviews the empirical research on the benefits of meaning in life.

Chapter 10 reviews a key construct in positive psychology that has attracted significant public interest: character strength and virtues. The chapter describes the Values in Action (VIA) Character Strength and Virtues classification, and concludes with a review of the recent research on its applications.

Chapter 11 focuses on relationships and their impact on wellbeing, and offers some insights from recent research as to how relationships can be improved and strengthened.

Chapter 12 explores four interrelated topics: stress, coping, resilience and posttraumatic growth. The chapter examines how stress occurs and the upshots of stress, and reviews the leading coping strategies. The chapter then reviews the concept of resilience, and explores the factors that can promote resilience. The chapter ends with an exploration of the construct of posttraumatic growth.

Chapter 13 examines the applied side of positive psychology: positive psychology interventions. The chapter opens with an overview of this topic and makes a distinction between two types of interventions offered today: composite programmes and discrete exercises. The chapter then discusses the conditions for optimal delivery of these interventions, and the research on their impact.

Finally, on a personal note: positive psychology has unquestionably transformed my life and the life of those around me for the better, enabling us to lead a more meaningful, fulfilling life, as well as to weather the difficult times. Many of our students who undertook the MSc in Applied Positive Psychology or the MSc in Applied Positive Psychology and Coaching Psychology at the School of Psychology, at the University of East London assert the transformational power of the body of knowledge that constitutes positive psychology. I therefore wish the reader the best possible implementation of the knowledge shared in this book, and an insightful, enjoyable journey of growth.

ACKNOWLEDGEMENTS

It has been a long and intense journey to the completion of this book. I am grateful for the care and nurturing support that I have received from so many people whose love and encouragement have wrapped around me in the many hours of work.

I owe the deepest gratitude to my family who absorbed the burdens and stresses that this journey has put on our family life. To my husband Dan and my children Tal and Sharon, who have been my anchor and light through this project, thank you for your love, your belief in me and your infinite encouragement and support, particularly during my recent cancer journey. Thank you for keeping me centred and balanced.

I wish to convey my heartfelt gratitude to my friends for their interest, their care, love and immense encouragement.

To my colleagues at the University of East London, thank you for your kind, generous and supportive collegiality and for your guidance and inspiration.

To my students who I feel so blessed to work with: thank you for your enthusiasm, open-mindedness, kindness and love of learning.

THE DEVELOPMENT OF POSITIVE PSYCHOLOGY

These are exciting times for positive psychology! Launched in 1998 as a rebellious discipline, it has become, in a short space of time, an influential social movement, which has captured the interest and imagination of the scientific community as well as the general public. Since its inception it has grown exponentially in terms of publications and readership, research output, courses and studentship, media attention and public interest, and is predicted to continue to grow in popularity over the next decades. Conversely, however, it is also expected to disappear, and counter-intuitively, its impending dissolution would be considered by some as a sign of its success.

Alongside the exhilaration of its trailblazing activity and rapid growth, and the existential movement between the desire to carve its own space and the contradictory pull to assimilate into other applied psychology disciplines, some challenges emerged. These include a fierce critique of its existence and blurred boundaries, a dismissal of the merit of its concepts and scientific work, exclusionary practices by chartering organisations and internal fragmentation that threatens its intellectual integrity and progress.

We are therefore at the brink of a crucial period for positive psychology, one which will determine its fate. Will it sustain in its current form, change, integrate into other applied psychology disciplines or fade away?

This chapter delineates the background that has led to the establishment of positive psychology, defining its aims, contours and remit. It also offers an overview of its development in the past two decades and concludes by discussing its possible future trajectories, and addressing some of its common misconceptions and critique.

A BRIEF HISTORY OF POSITIVE PSYCHOLOGY

We begin our journey into the history of positive psychology at the 1999 American Psychological Association (APA) annual conference. In a powerfully articulated presidential mission statement, Professor Seligman reminded his audience of the three missions that psychology had committed to achieve before World War II: "curing mental illness, making the lives of all people more fulfilling, and identifying and nurturing high talent" (Seligman, 1999, p. 2). He then asserted that, while its remedial mission has taken centre stage in terms of research and applications for more than five decades, the two other missions of psychology – improving the lives of all people and cultivating talent – "were all but forgotten". As a result of this limited agenda, psychology has become mainly a curative discipline that is focused on misery, malady and malfunction, and based upon the medical disease model: diagnosing what is broken, and attempting to repair the damage.

While Seligman acknowledged the outstanding progress and success that psychology has seen over the years in healing mental illness and broken lives, he noted that the field has been sidetracked: "Psychology is not just the study of weakness and damage, it is also the study of strengths and virtues. Treatment is not just fixing what is broken, it is nurturing what is best within ourselves" (Seligman, 1999, p. 2). This unbalanced agenda has left the profession unable to draw on what is right with people – their strengths, courage, optimism, resilience and many other capacities – to offer preventive measures that can buffer against the emergence of mental illness.

With this recognition, Seligman resolved to use his APA presidency to redress the imbalance in psychology, by establishing a novel discipline that places the spotlight on the cultivation of wellbeing and preventive measures, thereby complementing the current pathological and remedial agenda in psychology. Seligman called this new discipline *positive psychology*. Importantly, the aim was not to accentuate positive aspects of life while denying or devaluing negative experiences, nor to observe them through rose-coloured glasses. Rather, the aim was to widen the scope of applied psychology so that it aptly captures the full range of human experiences.

Fortunately, many researchers and practitioners welcomed this opportunity to engage with the healthy side of human psychology, and since then research activity, teaching and practice have blossomed.

Maslow's critique of psychology

Maslow's (1987) famed critique of psychology's preoccupation with the dysfunctional side of human psyche is often cited as evidence for the prolonged imbalance in psychology:

> The science of psychology has been far more successful on the negative than on the positive side. It has revealed to us much about man's shortcomings, his illness, his sins, but little about his potentialities, his virtues, his achievable aspirations, or his full psychological height. It is as if psychology has voluntarily restricted itself to only half its rightful jurisdiction, and that, the darker, meaner half.
>
> (p. 354)

Prior to Seligman's presidential address, a series of scholarly meetings took place which shaped the early vision, conceptualisation and development of positive psychology. The early seeds of the new discipline were planted in a chance meeting between Seligman and Csikszentmihalyi during a beach holiday. In the days that followed the two eminent scholars exchanged ideas about the future of psychology. Their conversations highlighted the gap in mainstream psychology, and revolved around the good life, happiness and what makes life worth living. These early conversations inspired the revolution that followed. Within a year several key organisations were established, including the Positive Psychology Steering Committee and the Positive Psychology Center at the University of Pennsylvania. The first Positive Psychology Summit soon followed, which inspired the production of core publications, and funding was secured for research and teaching activities. All of these ventures gave the newly emerging discipline a sound organisational foundation, and the means to publicise its vision and accelerate its impact (Csikszentmihalyi & Nakamura, 2011).

The development of positive psychology was noticeably inspired and shaped by Seligman's transformational leadership and revolutionary vision. The enormity of the task that Seligman and his leadership team embarked on, and the moral courage to challenge an establishment that one belongs to and rebel against its agenda, should not be underestimated.

WHAT IS POSITIVE PSYCHOLOGY?

Since its inception positive psychology has undergone several phases of defining and redefining its core philosophy, mission and remit, which is a common practice in newly established disciplines.

Defining positive psychology

The term "positive psychology" was originally coined by Maslow (1987). He defined positive psychology as

> the study of psychological health ... the study of the good man, of the secure and of the confident, of the democratic character, of the happy man, of the serene, the calm, the peaceful, the compassionate, the generous, the kind, of the creator, of the saint, of the hero, of the strong man, of the genius, and of other good specimens of humanity.
>
> (p. 318)

Following the launch of positive psychology, Seligman and Csikszentmihalyi (2000) offered the following definition:

> The field of positive psychology at the subjective level is about valued subjective experiences: Wellbeing, contentment, and satisfaction (in the past); hope and optimism (for the future); and flow and happiness (in the present). At the individual level, it is about positive individual traits: the capacity for love and vocation, courage, interpersonal skill, aesthetic sensibility, perseverance, forgiveness, originality, future mindedness, spirituality, high talent, and wisdom. At the group level, it is about the civic virtues and the institutions that move individuals toward better citizenship: Responsibility, nurturance, altruism, civility, moderation, tolerance, and work ethic.
>
> (p. 5)

In line with this depiction, Gable and Haidt (2005) defined positive psychology more concisely as *"the study of the conditions and processes that contribute to the flourishing or optimal functioning of people, groups, and institutions"* (p. 104).

Finally, Lomas, Hefferon, and Ivtzan (2014a) concentrated on its applied side and defined positive psychology as *"the science and practice of improving wellbeing"* (p. ix).

As can be seen from these definitions, there are repeated core themes around which there is consensus among scholars, particularly regarding its focus on wellbeing, its scientific grounding, and targeting people who are considered psychologically healthy.

However there are also some variations in emphasis, mainly around the depiction of its remit, which is still an area of disagreement.

THE MISSION OF POSITIVE PSYCHOLOGY

The grand vision of positive psychology was highly ambitious: "To catalyse a change in the focus of psychology from preoccupation only with repairing the worst things in life to also building positive qualities" (Seligman & Csikszentmihalyi, 2000, p. 5).

In order to advance this change, several key objectives have been identified (Seligman, Parks, & Steen, 2004):

- To place a new set of topics and questions high on the scientific agenda, focusing on the healthy aspects of human psychology.
- To create a shared language that enables communication and understanding of the new topics under the umbrella of positive psychology.
- To create and empirically test interventions that are geared to enhance wellbeing.
- To integrate positive and negative lenses in therapeutic work.

Mental health is not the absence of illness

The philosophical stance underlying the quest for integration within psychology communicates a powerful message. It indicates that mental health is not merely the absence of illness or dysfunction, and therefore should be assessed by the presence of psychological wellness and flourishing (Seligman, 1999).

THE REMIT OF POSITIVE PSYCHOLOGY

One of the challenges that positive psychology faced lies in the attempt to define its remit and draw the discipline's contours. In other words, what does the term "positive" stand for? This is an essential endeavour for a new discipline which enables researchers and practitioners to characterise it, differentiate it from other disciplines and highlight its originality. Below are several aspects of positive psychology that key authors have placed under the "positive" banner.

- *Positive assumptions about human nature*: Applied work in psychology often draws on particular assumptions about human nature, which are value-laden, yet often implicit. Seligman (2005) noted that mainstream psychology was dominated by Freudian perception of human nature, which views people as corrupt and driven by aggressive or pleasure-seeking sexual instincts. In contrast, positive psychology rests on Aristotelian and humanistic approaches which view people as inherently good, moral, and driven by a desire to grow and fulfil their potential.
- *Holistic ideology*: Consistent with the assumptions about human nature, the work of clinical psychology is rooted in illness ideology – a set of principles that describe the mission, target population and "jurisdiction" of clinical psychology, that is, what is defined as normal and abnormal, clinical and non-clinical problems, and how psychopathology, dysfunction and disease are diagnosed and treated (Maddux, 2005). In challenging the dominance of the illness ideology and the medical model, positive psychology presented a more holistic model of psychology and a new ideological agenda: one which aims to go beyond remedial work to promote flourishing.
- *Positive language*: The language of the illness ideology consists of terms such as disorder, pathology, symptom, diagnosis, treatment, patient and clinician. In order to create a more balanced psychology, positive psychology scholars and practitioners needed to create a different linguistic depository, one which can facilitate thinking about, describing and discussing the positive side of human psychology. "In this new language, ineffective patterns of behaviors, cognitions, and emotions are construed as problems in living, not as disorders or diseases" (Maddux, 2005, p. 66).
- *Positive aim and orientation*: This category reflects a key aim of positive psychology as anti-thesis to the clinical, illness-focused orientation of mainstream psychology. It highlights positive psychology's focus, and its priorities in research, teaching and applied work (Pawelski, 2016).
- *Positive outcomes*: Positive psychology aims "to provide an empirical vision for understanding and cultivating the good life"

(Pawelski, 2016, p. 343). This suggests that its applied work is intentionally designed to achieve particular outcomes on an individual or group level: the cultivation of positive states (such as happiness and flow) and the development of positive traits (such as optimism and wisdom).

- *Positive target population*: This point represents the key target population that positive psychology aims to benefit, which is predominantly non-clinical (Pawelski, 2016).
- *Positive processes*: These refer to the mechanisms or processes that positive psychology aims to operate (that are often embedded within positive psychology interventions). These processes are designed to cultivate, use or develop capacities that can help people and groups achieve their desired outcomes (Pawelski, 2016); for example, the use of character strengths, mindfulness practice or gratitude.
- *Positive topography*: These are the key topics that can be seen as "belonging" to the discipline (for example, happiness, strengths, optimism, wisdom) (Pawelski, 2016).
- *Positive value position*: Positive psychology scientists and practitioners acknowledged that terms such as "the good life" or "positive traits" are value-laden: they contain judgements about what is good and worthy. This stands in contrast to the imperative that science should be value-neutral, and hence these terms are open to debate and scrutiny. As a scientific discipline, positive psychology explicitly takes a facilitative and non-prescriptive position. It does not dictate how people should lead their lives. Instead, it provides the means that can help people achieve their desired objectives (Linley, Joseph, Harrington, & Wood, 2006).

Positive vs. negative psychology?

The use of the term "positive" in its title triggered a semantic challenge: if there is a positive psychology, then other disciplines of psychology can be seen as "negative psychology". This unintentional association is unfortunate, since no one wishes to see themselves as a "negative psychologist". To clarify, positive psychology authors often refer to the disciplines situated on the opposite side of the applied therapeutic spectrum as "clinical psychology", "mainstream psychology", "psychology as usual" or "business-as-usual psychology".

In an extensive mapping exercise Rusk and Waters (2013) detailed the array of topics that are currently being researched under the umbrella of positive psychology. The authors found 233 topics (Figure 1.1) that can be clustered into 21 broad themes, namely: life satisfaction, happiness, positive emotions, mood, self-efficacy, motivation, self-regulation, creativity, optimism, resilience, hardiness, mental toughness, posttraumatic growth, behavioural change, relationship, altruism, leadership, citizenship behaviour, education, mindfulness and gratitude.

It is noteworthy that, among these topics, 30% are novel topics that were not explored prior to the launch of positive psychology. Examples include: positive emotions, character strength, gratitude, mental toughness and psychological capital. However, since 70% of topics (including, for example, optimism, self-efficacy, self-determination, resilience, self-regulation, mindfulness and wisdom) were studied long before positive psychology was inaugurated, this raises questions around ownership. To what extent do these topics fit with the definition and key aims of positive psychology? As it stands

Figure 1.1 A Wordle showing the 233 key positive psychology research topics (Rusk & Waters, 2013).

today, the remit of positive psychology has been cast widely, therefore capturing within its contours these established concepts that are seen as allied with positive psychology, rather than originated by the new discipline.

Importantly, while these topics have been explored prior to the establishment of positive psychology, some have not been fully developed, nor assembled into a coherent body of knowledge, and consequently this knowledge has remained unappreciated and underutilised. Hence, one of the key missions and challenges that positive psychology faced at the outset was the effort to collate, appreciate, build on, integrate and further develop this corpus of knowledge and offer it "a conceptual home" (Linley & Joseph, 2004b, p. 3).

THE ROOTS OF POSITIVE PSYCHOLOGY

It is evident that scientific work into some of the topics that are currently assembled under the umbrella of positive psychology did not originate with the launch of the new discipline. Indeed, there is a substantial body of knowledge on positive topics that is associated with Western and Eastern philosophical and theological traditions.

For example, Ancient Greek philosophers Aristotle and Epicurus explored ideas around the "good life", paying particular attention to the concepts of happiness, hedonia and eudaimonia, and the importance of virtues for good life (Waterman, 1990). Utilitarian philosophers Mill and Bentham (1987) introduced the principle of utility, also known as the "greatest happiness principle". It suggests that government policies or actions should aim to promote happiness for the largest number of people, and should not be endorsed if they induce unhappiness or pain.

Within the discipline of psychology, research into positive themes is often traced back to James' (1890/1950) exploration of healthy mindedness and happiness. James considered happiness as one of life's important concerns and urged scholars to explore how to achieve and maintain it.

Humanistic psychology is often considered a strategic forerunner of positive psychology (Waterman, 2013) due to their shared philosophical assumptions about human nature and focus on the healthy side of human psychology. Led by prominent researchers and practitioners, including Maslow and Rogers, a key principle of humanistic psychology is that people are motivated by a desire to grow and fulfil their potential – a need to self-actualise.

Unfortunately, during the first phase of its establishment, positive psychology leaders have not sufficiently acknowledged the origins of the new discipline, hence attracting significant critique of this omission (Taylor, 2001). However, today there is apt recognition of this lineage, and an appreciation of this rich tradition and its contribution to positive psychology (see review by Snyder, Lopez, & Pedrotti, 2011).

POSITIVE PSYCHOLOGY: TAKING STOCK

How well has positive psychology progressed in establishing itself as a discipline and in achieving its goals? Looking back, we can revere with awe its many outstanding achievements.

As a scientific discipline, positive psychology has certainly established itself, with all the essential operational components now in place. There is an impressive and continually growing body of research conducted and published by hundreds of scientists in 46 countries (Donaldson, Dollwet, & Rao, 2015). Rusk and Waters (2013) assessed that around 18,000 research papers were published in the first 15 years since its launch. Additionally a record number of academic books, handbooks and textbooks on positive psychology generally or on one of its core topics were published since it was established.

There are currently seven international positive psychology journals and six regional journals, though the majority of the research papers in positive psychology were published in other psychology journals. In addition, 25 positive psychology associations (both national and international) promote and publish research, and hold periodic conferences that bring scientists together (Kim, Doiron, Warren, & Donaldson, 2018).

As a result of this impressive research activity and knowledge exchange, our understanding of the structure and content of psychological wellbeing and what makes life worth living, and the factors that can promote or undermine wellbeing has vastly expanded and deepened. Research has now moved beyond basic and exploratory research, as new conceptual models, research methodologies, empirically tested interventions and measurement tools were developed and tested.

An additional expansion of positive psychology research and practice has occurred through the establishment of several sub-branches:

positive education, positive organisational scholarship, positive psychiatry, positive ageing, positive psychology coaching and several others.

In terms of teaching, currently 18 universities offer postgraduate degrees (Masters and PhD programmes) in positive psychology in English, and 13 offer degrees in other languages. Numerous universities offer certificate courses or modules on positive psychology topics at undergraduate or postgraduate level.

Additionally, several Massive Open Online Courses (MOOCs) on positive psychology topics are currently offered as certificate courses by leading universities, and these are attracting millions of participants. An additional development, offered by universities as well as private institutions, is non-certificate courses, often involving psychoeducation and positive psychology interventions, most of which are online or provided through phone applications.

Notably, today the questions and topics that positive psychology explores are positioned high not only on the scientific agenda, but also on the global and national social policy and health agendas. In response to calls made by positive psychology leaders (Diener, 2000), many countries (particularly in the West) have incorporated measures of wellbeing (including satisfaction with life, happiness, meaning in life, relationship, mental illness, quality of life and more) into their national and international surveys (see, for example, OECD, 2017; ONS, 2019), hence offering policy makers vital data to assess the impact of policies on people's wellbeing, as well as to make comparisons across time and geographical locations.

The self-help industry has also been transformed since the launch of positive psychology. Numerous self-help book have been written by renowned positive psychology scholars who can provide scientific evidence for the concepts and interventions described in their books (see, for example, Fredrickson, 2010; Lyubomirsky, 2011; Seligman, 2006). This has enabled the new discipline to disseminate its research findings widely and expand its reach.

Media attention around positive psychology as a philosophy, scientific venture and movement has been extensive, and research findings from positive psychology scholars regularly receive media attention.

Positive psychology also features strongly across the Internet and in social media sites. A recent Google search of the term "positive psychology" returned more than 291 million web-pages, while "wellbeing" and "happiness" returned 117 million and 676 million results respectively. A YouTube search found 45 million entries with the term "positive psychology", while a similar search on Facebook found 148 million pages. These search findings serve to demonstrate the popularity, spread and indeed impact of positive psychology around the globe.

This extensive public attention suggests that positive psychology has had extensive semantic influence, hence achieving the goal of creating a common language that enables communication around its topics.

Positive psychology 2.0

One of the distinct developments that took place in recent years is the emergence of the second wave, which encourages positive psychology scholars and practitioners to embrace the dark side of life (Ivtzan, Lomas, Hefferon, & Worth, 2015). Born out of critique of the first wave, the leaders of the second wave claimed that, in its desire to carve a distinctive space for itself and become an anti-thesis to clinical psychology, the first wave of positive psychology may have taken an extremist position: it ignored and to some degree even rejected the difficult and distressing aspects of life. The second wave aims to move away from this extremist position, calling for a more complete, more realistic existential synthesis between the light and dark sides of life in its scholarship.

The most challenging goal that positive psychology aspired to achieve was to integrate the positive aspects of human psychology within applied therapeutic practice. A search of the literature to assess the progress made in this area revealed impressive advances, as practitioners advocate and share ideas as to how to integrate positive psychology concepts, models or interventions into counselling and clinical therapeutic work, health psychology, forensic psychology and psychiatry.

In clinical and counselling psychology substantial evidence demonstrates the efficacy of positive psychology concepts and interventions in alleviating a variety of mental disorders, including depression, anxiety, trauma, schizophrenia and addiction (Ruini, 2017). In psychiatry, the term *positive psychiatry* has been coined to capture the wealth of positive concepts and interventions that can be included in psychiatric work (Palmer, 2015). Similarly, in health psychology researchers have incorporated positive psychology interventions, typically including gratitude, optimism, hope, kindness and mindfulness, into health psychology practice, with some promising outcomes in patients with a variety of illnesses, including cancer, cardiovascular disease and diabetes (Macaskill, 2016).

Is positive psychology a discipline, a collective identity, an ideology or a social movement?

In the early years following its launch Linley and Joseph (2004b) debated whether positive psychology is a new sub-discipline within psychology, and argued that positive psychology should be seen as a "collective identity" that brings under its auspices researchers from varied disciplines who are interested in "the brighter sides of human nature" (p. 4). As such, it can be seen as an ethos and a set of concepts and tools that can be adopted and applied by scholars or practitioners in any psychological field.

However, in view of the progress described above, Lomas and Ivtzan (2016) assessed that positive psychology has become a distinct applied discipline within psychology, which requires appropriate recognition and accreditation that will signify the professional identity of those who conduct research, teach and facilitate its interventions.

Another common description of positive psychology is that of movement which aims to challenge the status quo, and hence carries an ideological stand-point as to what psychology should focus on (Peterson & Park, 2003). In line with this perception, Biswas-Diener, Linley, Govindji, and Woolfston (2011) described positive psychology as a force for social change, and positive psychology practitioners as transformative activists.

Since a key goal of positive psychology was to redress the imbalance in applied psychology, the explosion described here in scholarly work, teaching activity, publications, media and public attention to positive psychology concepts suggests that indeed the balance has been substantially restored.

In an early paper assessing the progress of positive psychology, Linley et al. (2006) wrote:

> it is clear from many perspectives that positive psychology has arrived. Yet in our view, this is just the beginning, and what has been achieved so far, while both laudable and remarkable, may be just an historical footnote to what is to follow.
>
> (p. 8)

Today these words still hold true with added mileage, reach and impact. Positive psychology now stands at a critical milestone in its journey, one which will determine its fate. In the next section, several possible future avenues for positive psychology will be discussed.

THE FUTURE OF POSITIVE PSYCHOLOGY

In an early paper Linley et al. (2006) bluntly asked: "Does positive psychology have a future?" (p. 8). The authors attempted to address this question by predicting the possible future paths that positive psychology may take, arriving at three prospective avenues:

- *Complete integration within other psychology disciplines which will ultimately lead to the disappearance of positive psychology as a separate field.* Having achieved its key mission, whereby the principles of positive psychology are ordinarily incorporated into psychological research, teaching and professional practice, the disappearance of positive psychology would in fact be a sign of its success. Diener (2003) explained: "My hope is that positive psychology will eventually disappear because it becomes part of the very fabric of psychology. Thus, it will fade as a campaign precisely because it has been so successful" (p. 120).
- *Partial integration with other psychology disciplines with continued specialisation.* Viewed against the full integration model described above, a partial integration may be interpreted as failure to achieve its central goal. Linley et al. (2006) considered that, in this scenario, positive psychology will continue to pursue its mission to redress the imbalance in psychology. However, other authors (Lomas, Hefferon, & Ivtzan, 2014a) seem to consider this option as a preferred path for positive psychology. While still advocating

the incorporation of positive psychology concepts and interventions within all areas of psychology, they call for a professional chartered status and accreditation to be developed for positive psychology practitioners, that is comparable to, but separate from, other applied psychology disciplines.

- *Little or no integration, with continued specialisation.* Linley et al. (2006) considered that this mode of operation would indicate that positive psychology has failed to bring about the anticipated integration, and hence may "continue as a specialist, but increasingly marginalised area, locked out of the major psychological agendas" (p. 10). The main challenge with this state of affairs is that positive psychology would then face the same critique that instigated its launch: that in focusing solely on the positive side of human experience, it has become biased and imbalanced.

Placing these possible future avenues against the progress and achievements detailed in the earlier section, it seems that positive psychology has taken the second route – partial integration with continued specialisation – and has already made significant strides in both.

Who is a positive psychologist?

Currently positive psychology is an unregulated and unaccredited field of practice. This means that there are no established principles, standards or guidelines as to how its concepts and interventions can be applied in client-facing settings. Consequently positive psychology training and interventions can be offered by anyone, through any means, including books, internet sites or phone applications.

However as the field matures, requests are mounting to professionalise the field through regulation and accreditation. Lomas and Ivtzan (2016) suggested two accreditation routes: one for a "positive psychology practitioner" – which is a master level accredited professional practice, and "positive psychologist" – a doctorate level professional accreditation (already offered by Claremont University) leading to chartered status as a psychologist. Presently efforts to create these accreditation routes are well under way, and it is expected that these will be in place shortly.

CHALLENGES AND CRITIQUE

In the years since its launch, positive psychology has faced substantial challenges and has attracted some intense critique, some of which is briefly reviewed below.

Challenging the key goal of positive psychology

In an early paper titled "Does the positive psychology movement have legs?" Lazarus (2003) launched a fierce critique on the principal objective of positive psychology: to prioritise the healthy side of life in its scholarship. The key point made by Lazarus (and other adversaries) is that attending to the sunny side of life is elitist and selfish, and must not come at the expense of relieving suffering, which should remain the main priority of psychology.

In response to this critique Peterson and Park (2003) wrote:

> Does the positive psychology movement have legs? We think so. We believe that it also has a heart, a brain, and considerable courage in challenging the status quo. However, the positive psychology movement is not a trip over the rainbow to Oz ... What positive psychology should not have is an imperialist attitude that prescribes one way to the good life or that dismisses the grim realities experienced by all members of our society.
>
> (p.146)

They also highlighted the cost of the pathology-focused agenda in psychology: wellbeing is taken for granted, the study of healthy people is deplored as a scientific indulgence, and crucially, the professional and scientific void was filled by the self-help industry.

Old wine in new bottles

Positive psychology has been criticised for exaggerating its novelty, and failing to acknowledge its lineage. As described earlier, the title "positive psychology" and the criticism of psychology for being one-sided were expressed several decades earlier by Maslow, and the study of good life and the call for psychology to focus on the brighter side of life also predated the launch of positive psychology.

In addressing this critique Peterson and Park (2003) noted:

> Positive psychologists do not claim to have invented the good life or even to have ushered in its scientific study. As we see it, the contribution

of positive psychology has been to provide an umbrella term for what have been isolated lines of theory and research and make the self-conscious argument that the good life deserves its own field of inquiry within psychology, at least until that day when all of psychology embraces the study of what is good along with the study of what is bad.

(p.144)

Positive psychology as happiology

In its early days positive psychology was often described as "happiology" – a science of happiness (Held, 2005) – and scorned for offering what critics saw as naïve and superficial answers to weighty questions. Some compared its content to "self-help" products: saleable and accessible quick fixes which have been "repackaged and given the veneer of respectable science" (Miller, 2008, p. 3).

Hart and Sasso's (2011) content review, which captures the core topics that are now explored under the banner of the discipline and the developments that occurred in the field, can help "dispel the myth that positive psychology is an elite endeavour solely concerned with Pollyanna-style 'happiology' in people who find themselves in idyllic circumstances" (p. 82).

The public face of positive psychology

Several authors fiercely condemned the public (smiley) face of positive psychology (see Figure 1.2). Lazarus (2003) mockingly described the movement's prime message in the media as: "You have to accentuate the positive, eliminate the negative, latch onto the affirmative, and don't mess with Mr in-between" (p. 93), which he slammed as

Figure 1.2 The smiley public face of positive psychology

"popular slogans designed to whip up enthusiasm for a vague and old-hat ideology that so far has had little new to say" (p. 107). He then went on to note that positive psychology is "in danger of being just another one of the many fads that come and go in our field" (p. 93). Similar critique on its public image was voiced by other authors (Held, 2004), who questioned the ways in which positive psychology research is broadcasted and promoted, and warned that its smiley-face image, together with the flood of dubious products, severely undermines the credibility of its scientific enterprise.

In response, Hart and Sasso (2011) noted that positive psychology scholars were highly frustrated with the overly eager media attention and with the simplistic interpretation of its philosophy, concepts and research findings. However they also acknowledged that they have little control over this state of affairs.

Positive psychology as a new religion

Positive psychology is often described as a movement, by both proponents and opponents (Lazarus, 2003); however, some critics compared it to a secular religion or a cult that advocates Pollyannaism.

In response, Peterson and Park (2003) noted:

> Positive psychology is not an ideological movement or a secular religion. Our world has enough of these. To be sure, many will provide some insights into the good life that positive psychologists should explore, but the emphasis has to be on the exploration of these insights with the tools of science to see which square with the facts of the matter and which do not.
>
> (p. 145)

The tyranny of positivity

One of the most heated critiques on positive psychology is that it generates social pressure to be positive, optimistic or happy under all circumstances. Held (2002) described this as the "tyranny of the positive attitude" and claimed that the scientific findings of positive psychology are often communicated through the media as highly prescriptive: "We must think positive thoughts, we must cultivate positive emotions and attitudes, and we must play to our strengths to be happy, healthy, and wise" (Held, 2004, p. 12). This message also insinuates that unhappiness is unbearable, socially unacceptable and harmful.

In response, Linley and Joseph (2004b) acknowledged that

> in talking of "the good life", "good citizenship", "positive individual trait", and "valued subjective experiences", we inevitably presuppose a value position ... in assuming a value position, we also explicitly note that this position should not be prescriptive in dictating to individuals the specific ways in which they should lead their lives.
>
> (p. 5)

Blame the victim

An extrapolation of the tyranny of positivity, particularly in individualistic cultures, is that individuals are responsible for their own happiness (Held, 2002). This implies that wellbeing or the good life is largely within individuals' control. Therefore, if people are unhappy, the "blame" lies with them (rather than their circumstances). Coyne and Tennen (2010) warned that positive psychology ideas and interventions may lead to a "blame the victim" ethos whereby sufferers of harsh circumstances who fail to exhibit the necessary traits or states – optimism, resilience, wellbeing or happiness – are blamed for their misery.

However, a counter-argument could be made that this is not the only psychological model which claims that people have some control over their mental states. Cognitive behavioural therapy (CBT), one of the leading therapeutic models today, in effect relays a similar message: it teaches clients to identify and challenge negative automatic thoughts and replace these with more realistic, adaptive interpretations (Beck, 2011). However, by encouraging clients to examine their own emotional states, challenge their cognitions and modify them, CBT implies that people's mental health is to some degree in their control. Notably, CBT has been studied extensively and proven to be highly effective in treating a large range of psychological disorders (McMain, Newman, Segal, & DeRubeis, 2015). Hence, similar to the cognitive behavioural movement, positive psychology indeed conveys a message that wellbeing is to some degree in people's control, but it does so without judgement or blame, and while acknowledging what is not in people's control.

Challenging the conceptions of positive and negative

A long-standing critique of positive psychology challenged its definition and use of the terms "positive" and "negative". Lazarus (2003) argued that the aspiration to study the positive aspects of life separately from the negative aspects is a questionable scientific endeavour:

> This polarity represents two sides of the same coin ... One would not exist without the other. We need the bad, which is part of life, to fully appreciate the good. Any time you narrow the focus of attention too much to one side or the other, you are in danger of losing needed perspective.
>
> (p. 94)

A related question is: what counts as positive or negative experiences, traits, behaviours or emotions? Larsen, McGraw, and Cacioppo (2001) argued that people can experience both types of emotions at the same time; for example, hope can bring about positive anticipation together with concern or even anxiety. Behaviours considered as positive such as passion can become obsessive, and hardship can lead to personal growth. Hence what seems to be a positive experience or trait can culminate into a negative outcome and vice versa.

In response, Kashdan and Steger (2011) acknowledged that "to date positive psychology researchers have had little to say on the yin and yang of positive and negative, and the dialectical tension between stress and growth" (p. 10). This recognition also prompted the emergence of the second wave which embraces the full range of human experience, and brought about a more nuanced understanding of positive and negative experiences and processes (Ivtzan et al., 2015).

Bad science

In a paper titled "Positive psychology in cancer care: Bad science, exaggerated claims, and unproven medicine", Coyne and Tennen (2010) mounted a fierce attack on positive psychology research and applications in behavioural medicine. In particular, they challenged the scientific grounds and methods of studies which claimed to have found significant associations between a positive outlook (such as optimism, hope and acceptance) and recovery in cancer patients. They also challenged findings from experiments that assessed the effects of positive psychology intervention on health outcomes, dubbing these findings "exaggerated claims".

Interestingly, positive psychology leaders warned of "the temptation … to run ahead of what we know" (Peterson, 2005, p. xxiii). They therefore stressed that "Positive psychology is psychology – psychology is science – and science requires checking theories against evidence … positive psychology will rise or fall on the science on which it is based" (p. xxiii). It should be noted however that similar weaknesses in research methodologies can be found not only in all psychology sub-disciplines but also in other social sciences.

Too WEIRD

An early critique of positive psychology was that it is mainly Western in its cultural orientation, and to a degree elitist (Becker & Maracek, 2008). This is a likely outcome of the fact that positive psychology was established in the USA and hence much of its early research was conducted in US universities, and was tested initially mainly on students. Hendriks et al. (2019) described these research populations as WEIRD – Western, educated, industrialised, rich and democratic. The upshot of this narrow cultural perspective is that its research cannot be straightforwardly applied to other cultures.

This limitation was recognised by positive psychology authors who acknowledged its "cultural embeddedness" (Linley & Joseph, 2004a, p. 719), but also noted that this state of affairs is typical in all disciplines in psychology. Furthermore, recent reviews suggested that, as the discipline matures, its global reach is expanding and its cultural perspective is becoming more inclusive. Kim, Doiron, Warren, and Donaldson (2018) found that, while 41% of positive psychology research was conducted and published in the USA, 52% was conducted and published in other countries (Europe, Asia, the Americas, Oceania and Africa), and 7% includes multi-national research.

CONCLUSION

The journey that positive psychology has embarked on since its launch may be best described as a rollercoaster ride: fast to begin with and gathering momentum, at times bumpy, risky, breath-taking and hair-raising, yet at the same time inspiring and exhilarating. As seen in this chapter, the development that positive psychology has seen in merely two decades is nothing short of phenomenal. Importantly, and counter to the expectation of some scholars, it seems that positive psychology is here to stay. While it has integrated with other psychology disciplines to some degree, it has also carved its own space and specialisation, soon to be recognised by a professional chartered status and accreditation. In the following sections of the book, positive psychology's fascinating journey unfolds through the exploration of the developments that occurred in several of its core topics.

In many ways what Gable and Haidt (2005) earlier noted still holds true today:

Those of us involved in positive psychology are often amazed at how fast the train has been moving. However, scholars who are not involved in positive psychology may be skeptical about both the cargo and the destination of the train.

(p. 103)

Given the dizzying pace of its scientific development, educational reach and public recognition, it is perhaps to be expected that a rebellious new discipline that challenges the psychological establishment at core level, will come under attack and attract ferocious critique. While it can be argued that some of this critique is misplaced, or exaggerated, oftentimes there is some validity to it, which deserves attention and, at times, appropriate action.

Looking back, having to address both the challenges and critique facilitated reflection, new learning and modification and consequently prompted significant developments in positive psychology in its underpinning philosophies, theories, research agenda, methodologies and interventions. Indeed scepticism, critical awareness, reviewing, re-thinking and questioning are essential for healthy development of the discipline, and we continue to welcome these.

HAPPINESS

The pursuit of happiness is a valued and celebrated life-goal for many people today. In the USA, the Declaration of Independence (1776) granted citizens certain constitutional rights that governments are committed to protect. Among these, the key rights are "life, liberty and the pursuit of happiness". Since then, surveys across a variety of cultures and across generations found that people rate happiness as a highly desired commodity that is worth pursuing, and perceive happiness as attainable and sustainable (Diener, Suh, Smith, & Shao, 1995). However, some authors considered the prominence of happiness in the political and public spheres and people's desire for it a modern obsession (Burnett, 2011). Unfortunately, the theory and research into happiness advanced by positive psychology scholars have been accused of inadvertently reinforcing this obsession (Held, 2005).

With this critique in mind, this chapter opens with a definition of happiness, and considers why happiness matters. The chapter then briefly reviews the research into happiness, particularly the factors that can increase or diminish happiness.

Defining happiness

Happiness is often referred to as *hedonic* or *subjective wellbeing* (SWB) in the academic literature.

SWB consists of:

- *A cognitive component*: Our general *satisfaction with life* (SWL), in which we evaluate how well we are faring in the key domains of our lives (for example, health, relationships, work and money).
- *An emotional component*: The frequency of *positive affect* (such as excitement, joy or love) and *negative affect* (such as fear, anger or disgust) that we experience during a defined period of time.

The following formula is often used to represent SWB:

$$SWB = SWL + Positive\ affect - Negative\ affect$$

By definition, people with high levels of SWB will likely be satisfied with their lives, experience pleasant emotions frequently and experience negative emotions infrequently (Diener, 2000).

Research on SWB has begun more than 30 years ago, but has shown an exponential increase recently. Diener, Lucas, and Oishi (2018a) estimated that about 170,000 articles and books were published on the topic just in the past 15 years.

What do people mean when they say "I'm happy"?

There are three different associations that people commonly attach to the phrase "I'm happy" (McMahan & Estes, 2011):

- *Happy in the moment*: This indicates that a person is experiencing particular positive emotions in this moment, that they interpret as happiness.
- *Happy with life*: When people use this connotation of happiness, they are giving an indication that they are generally doing well in terms of their wellbeing and SWL. Much of the research on happiness has explored this interpretation of happiness.
- *Happy person*: This use of the term refers to happiness as a personality trait that suggests that a person is typically cheerful and upbeat.

MOST PEOPLE ARE HAPPY

In an early paper titled "Most people are happy", Diener and Diener (1996) reviewed substantial research evidence (916 large-scale surveys involving more than a million participants from 45 countries), which showed that in most countries the majority of people (70%+) reported positive levels of happiness (the average score was 6.7 on a scale from 0 to 10). These happiness levels remained stable for several decades, and included disadvantaged groups, who showed similar levels of happiness to others. The authors therefore concluded that most people are "pretty happy". Later the authors noted that "the data do not indicate that everyone is ecstatic. Instead, most people are mildly happy and satisfied" (Biswas-Diener, Vitterso, & Diener, 2005, p. 205).

Two decades later the authors updated their data (Diener, Diener, Choi, & Oishi, 2018b). They concluded that, in economically developed countries, most people continue to be modestly happy on average; however, in countries where basic needs are not met, both SWL and emotional states are negatively affected. This indicates that macro-level circumstances indeed matter and can impact happiness levels under conditions of privation. However, once needs are met *at a basic level*, personal circumstances ranging from illness to income seem to have a fairly modest impact on happiness.

Measuring happiness

Research into happiness often uses self-report questionnaires to measure the two components of SWB: SWL and people's emotional experience.

The Cantril Self-Anchoring Scale (Cantril, 1965) and the Satisfaction With Life Scale (SWLS) (Diener, Emmons, Larsen, & Griffen, 1985) are often used for measuring life satisfaction. The Cantril scale features a single life satisfaction question, and the SWLS includes five items.

To measure participants' emotional experience researchers often use the Positive and Negative Affect Schedule (PANAS: Watson, Clark, & Tellegen, 1988) or the Scale of Positive and Negative Experience (SPANE: Diener et al., 2010). The PANAS requires participants to assess to what extent they experienced 20 emotions (10 positive and 10 negative) in a defined period. Similarly, the SPANE contains 12 broader emotions.

An important point to note is that in some studies happiness is assessed by using only one of these scales – either SWL or a measure of emotions.

An additional scale developed by Lyubomirsky and Lepper (1999) directly measures subjective happiness. The scale has four items.

Another way to measure happiness is to gather similar information from participants' family and friends, which provides external validation for the self-reported measures (Diener et al., 2018a).

An alternative method to measure happiness that avoids the usual drawbacks of questionnaires is the Experience Sampling Method (ESM) (Pavot, 2018). It prompts research participants at random times to record their thoughts and emotions on a mobile device. By sampling people's ongoing experiences, ESM can offer an average score for each person, and can analyse changes in people's happiness across time, locations and circumstances.

Other methodologies for measuring happiness include interviews, physiological measures (brain activity and hormone levels) and ratings of emotional experiences as these are manifested in people's facial expressions (Diener et al., 2018a).

All the above-mentioned measures have been widely used and show robust psychometric capacities (Pavot, 2018).

THE BENEFITS OF HAPPINESS: DOES HAPPINESS LEAD TO SUCCESS?

A substantial body of research has examined the benefits of happiness by comparing between people with varying levels of SWB, conducting longitudinal studies on the outcomes of earlier levels of happiness, and through the use of experimental research designs that examine the effectiveness of positive psychology activities that can enhance happiness. Pavot and Diener (2004) underscored the importance of this body of research: if the research does not show any significant, distinct beneficial outcomes that derive from experiencing happiness, which extend beyond merely feeling good, "then the importance of SWB as a desirable goal is significantly diminished" (p. 684).

In summarising the findings of these studies Lyubomirsky, King, and Diener (2005b) queried: does happiness lead to success? Drawing on our own life experiences, many of us would likely argue that success leads to happiness, and contest the opposite direction of causality. Yet as the review below demonstrates, *happiness is beneficial* and can lead to numerous successful outcomes in key life domains, including longevity, physical and mental health, work, income, family and social life.

Health and longevity

Happy people consistently report better health and fewer ailments compared to less happy individuals, and therefore require fewer doctor appointments and hospital visits, fewer medications and fewer sick leave days. Happy people are also more health-conscious, and tend to engage with physical activity, and less likely to engage in unhealthy behaviours. These lifestyle choices seem to pay off: happiness is associated with better quality of life and physical functioning. It is also correlated with longevity (Steptoe, 2019).

The nuns' study

In one of the most renowned studies that linked happiness and longevity, Danner, Snowdon, and Friesen (2001) assessed whether the life expectancy of 180 elderly Catholic nuns could be predicted by the levels of happiness that they had expressed nearly six decades earlier. To measure their early levels of happiness, researchers analysed autobiographical essays that the nuns wrote in their 20s, upon entering the convent.

Strikingly, the authors found that happier nuns lived nearly 10 years longer on average than unhappy nuns, thus providing an indication that happiness levels can impact longevity. These findings are given further credibility due to the fact that nuns lead a relatively uniform lifestyle, whereby their diets, daily routines, physical and social activities and exposure to risks are fairly similar, hence removing environmental differences that can impact longevity.

Wellbeing

Happiness is considered a strong criterion for assessing people's mental health. This is because a number of mental illnesses (such as depression and anxiety) are diagnosed through the prolonged presence of negative emotions. Therefore, by definition the experience of sustained SWB can offer a sound indication of the absence of mental illness. Accordingly, people at the top of the happiness scale show fewer symptoms of psychopathology compared to others. They also score high on other measures of wellbeing, including low levels of stress and rumination. On the positive side they report feeling rested, experiencing personal growth and having personal autonomy and free time (Diener, Seligman, Choi, & Oishi, 2018c).

During difficult times happy individuals tend to experience lower levels of stress, and use more adaptive coping mechanisms (such as solution-focused strategies) compared to others. They also show higher levels of hardiness and resilience, and maintain their positive attitude (Luhmann, Hofmann, Eid, & Lucas, 2012).

Personality

In terms of personality traits, happy people seem to display positive temperament, conscientiousness, self-esteem, confidence and self-efficacy, and low levels of neuroticism. They seem to set higher goals for themselves compared to their less happy peers, and display more optimism, competence, self-control and perseverance when pursuing these goals. They also make better decisions, and tend to optimise (look for a good-enough option), rather than maximise (aiming to achieve the best result). They also tend to be more grateful, savour life pleasures and are often spiritual or religious (Lyubomirsky et al., 2005b).

Work and income

When seeking employment, happier individuals are more likely to apply to more positions, be invited to more job interviews and secure higher-paying and prestigious jobs, compared to unhappy job seekers. Once employed, they perform well (in most, though not all, types of tasks), often beyond the call of duty, and display high levels of engagement, effort and productivity. They also demonstrate creativity and flexibility, and experience flow frequently (Walsh, Boehm, & Lyubomirsky, 2018).

When working on long-term goals they show persistence, and resilience when facing hurdles. They also exhibit less counterproductive, risky or retaliatory work behaviours, and seem to show high standards of work in terms of attendance, punctuality, usage of resources and time, and adherence to rules. Hence, they are evaluated more positively by their managers and customers, and are less likely to lose their jobs and become unemployed. They are also more satisfied with their jobs, experience less job burnout, absenteeism or other withdrawal behaviours compared to their unhappy colleagues, and hence show high commitment to their organisations and are less likely to leave (Walsh et al., 2018).

In their work relationships, happy employees show goodwill, citizenship and prosocial behaviours, and are more altruistic, cooperative, helpful and courteous towards others. They also experience more cohesion and trust, and engage in fewer conflicts. In return they seem to receive both emotional and tangible assistance from colleagues and managers compared to their less happy peers (Walsh et al., 2018).

Happy leaders and managers seem to receive high ratings from their employees, who assess their workplace climate positively, and report being happier and healthier than those working with unhappy leaders. There is also evidence to suggest that companies with happy employees are more profitable (Walsh et al., 2018).

These findings gave rise to the "happy–productive employee" assertion, which posits that it is worthwhile for organisations to invest in their employees' happiness, as this can lead to a more productive and profitable work environment (Cropanzano & Wright, 2001).

Do happy doctors make a better diagnosis?

Research suggests that experiencing positive emotions, even briefly, can impact performance. Estrada, Isen, and Young (1997) attempted to explore this association by inducing positive emotions in 44 medical doctors prior to making a diagnosis. The researchers aimed to assess whether positive emotions could influence the accuracy of the diagnosis, and anchoring (a thinking mode that can lead to errors due to decreased flexibility).

Participants in the study were randomly assigned to two experimental groups and a control group, all of which received materials describing a case that they were required to diagnose. One experimental group received a small pack of chocolates and candies tied in a bag, with a thank you note. They were asked to put the candy away however and not eat it. The second experimental group were asked to read phrases related to sources of satisfaction in medical practice, such as: "I can relieve my patients' anxiety." The control group received only the materials. Transcripts of their diagnoses were then scored.

The findings indicated that doctors in the candy and statement groups achieved a correct hypothesis significantly earlier, and showed less anchoring compared to controls. This suggests that positive emotions briefly induced in several ways can improve cognitive organisation, flexibility, reasoning and decision making.

"What good is happiness? It can't buy money." This pun made by comedian Youngman (1998) is in fact incorrect: studies suggest that happier people are able to meet their basic financial needs, and more. In fact, the majority of them fare better than their less happy peers financially. Longitudinal studies have shown that happier young adults were more likely to earn higher income decades later, compared to less happy individuals. Ultimately their constructive work ethic and performance lead to enhanced employability and stronger career profiles, which can explain the higher income (Walsh et al., 2018).

Social life

Studies have reported on strong associations between happiness and social life. Happier people are more likely to be extroverts, and have relatively larger networks of close, high-quality social ties and organisational affiliations compared to their less happy peers. They engage more often in social activities, are more sociable and report higher levels of satisfaction and value from the companionship and support that their social ties offer them. Hence, they rate their family and friends more positively, are less jealous of others and feel that they are treated with respect. Happiness can also affect the trajectory of relationships: young adults who are highly satisfied with their life are more likely to get married in the following years, and be more satisfied with their partnerships, and therefore less likely to separate or divorce (Pavot & Diener, 2004).

In contrast to the common myth, happy individuals are not selfish. In fact research suggests that happy people are interested in current affairs, view others more positively, hold a prosocial outlook and are likely to be more cooperative, altruistic, compassionate and charitable than unhappy individuals.

In turn, others tend to rate happy individuals as more intelligent, competent, confident, assertive, energetic, friendly, socially skilled, articulate, well mannered, socially active, warm, moral and supportive, and even physically attractive and likeable, and less selfish. Research has also shown that happiness is infectious: happy people seem to spread happiness to others, resulting in happier communities, organisations and nations (Lyubomirsky et al., 2005b).

In sum, happiness is not just a pleasurable experience. In fact, in becoming happier, we can improve key aspects of our lives, including our health and longevity, psychological wellbeing, our work, career, income, and our relationships. Importantly, when we become happier, we also benefit others – our families, communities and societies.

In view of these impressive findings, there is a strong argument to be made that understanding happiness, its determinants and outcomes, and developing interventions that can increase people's happiness levels is a worthy scientific objective (Lyubomirsky, Sheldon, & Schkade, 2005a). Given that most people are modestly happy, the main objective of these interventions is to lessen chronic unhappiness, to heighten happiness when it is consistently low and to help individuals recover from testing life events and regain their positive outlook and emotional balance. On this note, Diener et al. (2018a) cautioned that "more is not always better. Just because high SWB is associated with benefits in some domains does not mean that increasingly high levels of SWB will always result in gains" (p. 27).

Another caveat to bear in mind regarding the research on the benefits of happiness is that some (though not all) of the findings cited above are drawn from correlational studies. These can show a relationship between variables but cannot detect causation.

WHAT DETERMINES HAPPINESS?

An intriguing question that researchers endeavoured to answer is: why are some people happier than others? In other words, what are the factors that determine people's happiness, and what accounts for the variations between them?

In an early paper Lyubomirsky et al. (2005a) drew on the extent research to present the *Sustainable Happiness Model*, which outlined the main determinants of enduring happiness. Recently several papers (Diener et al., 2018a; Nes & Roysamb, 2015; Sheldon & Lyubomirsky, 2019) revisited the model and both endorsed and challenged different aspects of it. In the summary that follows, the original model and some of the recent updates on it are presented.

The Sustainable Happiness Model

According to Lyubomirsky et al.'s (2005a) Sustainable Happiness Model (also known as the Happiness Pie), three key factors can explain individuals' levels of happiness:

1. Genetics and personality
2. Life circumstances
3. Intentional activities.

Genetics and personality

Research suggests that a substantial proportion of people's happiness levels can be explained by their genetic lineage. In recent reports the percentage was estimated to be around 30–40% (Nes & Roysamb, 2015) (while the earlier model proposed a higher figure, around 50%). This suggests that we have a happy or unhappy hereditary predisposition, which can explain some of the variations between individuals in happiness levels. Research evidence, mainly obtained from twin studies, suggests that this genetic imprint is difficult to deviate from. The inborn factors that shape happiness are manifested in people's temperament and affectivity, as well as in several happiness-relevant personality traits, such as extraversion, optimism, hope and neuroticism.

Happiness set point

Ample research has indicated that most people show considerable stability in their happiness over time. Consistent with the notion that happiness is partly hereditary, researchers suggested that people may have a "happiness set point" (or set range) which can explain the observed stability in their happiness. The set point can be described as a person's typical level of happiness. Lyubomirsky et al. (2005a) noted that it is "genetically determined and is assumed to be fixed, stable over time, and immune to influence or control" (p. 13). Although life events can trigger temporary increases or decreases in people's happiness, research suggests that most people show an involuntary tendency to return to their baseline sooner or later.

It is worth noting that some scholars challenged the merit of set-point theory (Diener et al., 2018a) in the face of evidence which revealed that some people change their set point over the life course, and do not always return to set point, particularly following adverse events. On the other hand, recent genetic research seems to provide more robust evidence for the hereditary component of happiness, though the authors noted that "genetic and environmental factors transact and interplay" in the development of happiness (Røysamb, & Nes, 2018, p. 13).

Life circumstances

According to Lyubomirsky et al.'s (2005a) model, a fairly modest percentage of happiness can be explained by life circumstances (on average 10%, but with significant variability around this figure). Circumstances include a wide array of factors that can impact happiness: demographic factors (such as age, gender and ethnicity), people's personal history and life events that can impinge on happiness, whether people's basic needs are met, macro-social structures (such as country and culture), as well as circumstances that people have some control over (such as health, education, marital status, occupation and work, income and lifestyle).

Although circumstances certainly influence happiness, the small percentage of SWB that these account for suggests that achieving desired changes in circumstances (such as getting a rise in income, moving to a warmer climate, getting married or having a child) may not bring about the lasting happiness that people desire. These findings puzzled researchers and prompted them to conduct further inquiries into this point. One explanation for the weak impact of circumstances on happiness levels is the process of hedonic adaptation.

Hedonic adaptation

Consider the experience of buying your first car. You worked hard to pay for it, and after weeks of shopping around and completing the required paperwork, the car was parked in your driveway. The first days of driving it were filled with excitement as you explored the new car and appreciated the benefits of owning a car. However, what happened to your happiness level a few months down the line? For the majority of people the answer is: the initial happiness levels dwindled as they got used to having a car.

This phenomenon is known as "hedonic adaptation" (or habituation). It suggests that when we experience positive or negative events in our lives, these typically bring about a temporary increase or decrease in our happiness levels. However, over time, we become accustomed to our new circumstances, and eventually we return to our happiness set point. This suggests that any gains in happiness that people may achieve following a positive change in their circumstances are short-lived. In due course people will adapt to it and no longer derive the same amount of happiness that they experienced initially. Research has also suggested that the "hedonic adaptation is faster and more likely to be 'complete' in response to positive than negative experiences" (Lyubomirsky, 2011, p. 203).

The process of habituation provides some explanation as to why circumstances often show a marginal impact on people's long-term level of happiness. It also became a source of pessimism for researchers who are searching for interventions that can generate enduring happiness:

> The notion of an individual fighting against the effects of adaptation brings to mind an image of a pedestrian walking up a descending escalator. Although the improving circumstances of her life may propel her upward toward ever greater happiness, the process of adaptation forces her back to her initial state.
>
> (Layous, Sheldon, & Lyubomirsky, 2015, p. 186).

This can lead to a perpetual search for the next, short-lived happiness-boosting event, which is known as the "*hedonic treadmill*".

Similar to the critique on the set-point theory, the universality of the hedonic adaptation model has been challenged, since researchers observed that some events typically take longer to adapt to, while other events commonly result in quicker adaptation. Circumstances that are prone to quicker adaptation include marriage, gaining higher income and making lifestyle changes. Circumstances that show slower pace of adaptation include immigration and cosmetic surgery. Some life circumstances, particularly adverse events (such as the onset of disability and widowhood) can exert a long-term negative impact on SWB, indicating a slower adaptation process. Among these, unemployment seems to have a detrimental long-term impact on people's happiness. The "scarring effect" of unemployment can persist even after becoming re-employed.

Researchers also found that people differ in the ways in which they perceive and interpret life events, which shape their initial reaction to the event. They also vary in their propensity to adapt to events. This indicates that life circumstances can impact happiness, but the strength and duration of their effect vary depending on people's personality and the events considered.

Intentional activities

The last component in Lyubomirsky et al.'s (2005a) model refers to people's day-to-day choices of thoughts, activities and behaviours. The authors claimed that this component is "arguably the most promising means of altering one's happiness level" (p. 15), since these activities and behaviours are in people's control. The term "intentional" suggests these activities require a degree of will, deliberate effort and commitment. Examples of intentional behaviours include engaging in physical exercises, socialising and being kind to others. Examples of cognitive activities include setting and pursuing life goals, expressing optimism or gratitude and avoiding social comparison. Some of these intentional activities have been examined in the form of structured positive psychology interventions to assess their impact, and the results suggested that these exercises can produce moderate improvements in SWB (see further details in Chapter 13).

In the original model the authors approximated that these intentional positive activities can predict about 40% of people's happiness. However, in a later paper (Sheldon & Lyubomirsky, 2019), drawing mainly on experimental research that tested the efficacy of happiness interventions, they considered that this figure could be lower (around 15% but with significant variation around this figure).

Happiness interventions

Positive psychology interventions that are geared to increase happiness are exercises that have been tested for their efficacy in empirical research, and hence they are considered evidence-based. They are designed to increase positive emotions, life satisfaction or both. They may include brief, ad hoc exercises such as writing about your best possible self, or setting life goals. Some activities necessitate some repetition to maintain their impact for longer, such as writing a gratitude diary, engaging in physical activity, savouring, or conducting acts of kindness. There are also some happiness group-based programmes involving several meetings. Examples include the Fundamentals for Happiness Programme (Fordyce, 1983) and The Happy Life: Voyages to Wellbeing programme (Cloninger, 2006) (see details in Chapter 13).

Sheldon and Lyubomirsky (2019) developed several models that can help boost and sustain happiness levels over the long term:

- *The Eudaimonic Activity Model* suggests that engaging in intentional behaviours that are eudaimonic in nature can increase our happiness levels as a byproduct. Eudaimonic activities are geared to satisfy our basic needs and increase our psychological wellbeing through optimal functioning. They may include activities such as the pursuit of valued life goals, engaging in meaningful undertakings, connecting with others, and seeking growth-promoting activities.
- *The Positive Activity Model* aims to facilitate the choice of activities and behaviours that can enhance happiness levels, and more importantly, it offers several ways to help maintain these happiness levels with some consistency. The model identifies evidence-based interventions that can reliably raise happiness levels, and suggests how best to enact them. It also offers the person–activity fit diagnostic – a tool to help us assess which intervention may suit us best (see Chapter 13).
- *The Hedonic Adaptation Prevention Model* posits that hedonic adaptation is not inevitable. One way to prevent or slow down the adaptation process is to continue to interact with new positive life circumstances, appreciate and savour them. Another way to slow adaptation is to avoid social comparison and the desire to acquire

more or a better version of what we have, which may trigger the "hedonic treadmill" phenomenon.

- *Prioritising positivity*: Another way to habituate volitional happiness-boosting techniques is by "prioritising positivity" (Catalino, Algoe, & Fredrickson, 2014). It requires people to organise their day-to-day lives in a way that naturally increases opportunities to experience positive emotions. It involves spending time doing things that we genuinely enjoy, such as walking, gardening or socialising. It also involves considering the emotional implications of actions and decisions. The authors reported that people who pursued happiness in this way were indeed happier than those who did not, hence suggesting that habituating and weaving happiness-raising activities in daily life are worthwhile endeavours.

Social comparison

Social comparisons, or "keeping up with the Jones", are highly common and are weaved into the way that we judge and interpret life events and circumstances (Gerber, Wheeler, & Suls, 2018). At times we may compare our current situation to previous circumstances, and in other times, we may compare ourselves to others. The comparisons can pertain to a variety of aspects, from health and marital situation to income and lifestyle.

Upward social comparison occurs when people compare themselves to others who are doing better than they are, while *downward comparisons* take the opposite direction. Researchers have observed that some upward comparison is useful as it may inspire us to take action, for example to pursue an ambitious goal. However persistent upward social comparison can be self-defeating and can lead to jealousy, insecurity and unhappiness. In line with this observation, research has reported that happy people engage more in downward social comparisons.

PREDICTORS OF HAPPINESS

A sizable body of knowledge has accumulated over the years regarding the key predictors of happiness, some of which fit into the "circumstances" or "intentional activities" categories in Lyubomirsky et al.'s

(2005a) happiness pie. Among these, six predictors have received the majority of researchers' attention. These are: social ties, wealth and lifestyle, education and work, health, demography, and macro-social structures (country and culture).

Relationships

A theme that has repeatedly featured in the happiness literature is that social relationships can strongly impact people's happiness (Diener et al., 2018a). Close and supportive family, friendships and collegial relationships are considered a key source of happiness. Research on the happiest individuals revealed that having a close, positive and supportive social circle, and spending a substantial portion of their time socialising, was a distinctive feature of this group.

Longitudinal studies on marriage revealed that newly married people experience initially a significant rise in their happiness; however they seem to return to baseline after 2 years on average due to adaptation. Despite this decline, research on the association between marriage and happiness consistently reveals that happily married people show higher SWB levels compared to unmarried, divorced or separated people. This was found across all age groups, educational levels, racial groups and different cultures. Moreover, those who described their marriages as unhappy showed the lowest levels of happiness, suggesting that the quality of marriage heavily influences happiness levels. Both married and single people show a decrease in their happiness in their 30s (that is considered to be age-related); however, single people showed steeper decreases in their SWB. This suggests that marriage can buffer against the age-related declines in happiness (Grover & Helliwell, 2019). In the past decades the correlation between happiness and marriage has been weakening in the West, and researchers considered that this is due to the decrease in marriage rates, as more couples choose to cohabit instead. However, the data on cohabitation suggests that it does not increase happiness as much as marriage does (Mikucka, 2016).

Research on friendships shows that they significantly impact happiness. However here too, relational quality is the key predictor of happiness, and matters much more than quantity (Demir & Weitekamp, 2007). Rath and Harter (2010) provided evidence that happiness spreads through social networks: the odds of a person being happy increase by 15% if their friends are happy. More compellingly, the odds increase even more if their friends are surrounded by other happy friends. The authors concluded that access to happy social networks has more influence on our happiness than a $10,000 pay rise!

Are children truly "bundles of joy"? Research on the association between parenthood and happiness shows mixed findings (Nelson, Kushlev, & Lyubomirsky, 2014). Some studies suggested that parents are slightly happier than non-parents, while others found no difference. Research that followed parents over long periods reported increased happiness prior to the birth of the first child, which returned to baseline shortly after. However, other studies found that happiness decreased with the birth of each child. This is explained by the stresses of parenthood (sleep deprivation, worry and decrease in marital satisfaction). The relationship between children and marital satisfaction is described as curvilinear, which in turn impacts SWB. A significant drop has been registered in marital satisfaction at the birth of the first child, which further declines when children reach adolescence, but it increases once children have left home (Gorchoff, John, & Helson, 2008). A study by Kahneman, Krueger, Schkade, Schwarz, and Stone (2004) reported that working mums had fewer positive emotions and rated taking care of their children as slightly more enjoyable than commuting and chores. Further research suggested that parents' happiness is linked to the child's characteristics (such as temperament), while others suggested that the parent's age, gender and attachment style can affect their happiness. Socioeconomic status and the support available for parents are also factors that impinge on parents' SWB (Nelson et al., 2014).

Do we know what makes us happy?

Wilson and Gilbert (2005) argued that people find it difficult to accurately judge what can make them happy or unhappy. The concept of "affective forecasting" suggests that people tend to predict how much a life event is likely to impact them. However the authors found that people are not very accurate in their predictions. They recover much quicker from negative events than the prediction, and don't derive as much happiness from positive events compared to the prediction. The conclusion is that we may not really know what makes us happy, increasing the chances that the pursuit of happiness will be misdirected.

Wealth and life-style

Can money buy happiness? Many people associate money and happiness and often consider wealth as a key source of happiness. Lyubomirsky (2014) claimed that this perception is one of the biggest myths around happiness, but is it a myth?

A robust body of research indeed shows a moderate relationship between happiness and money – in particular income, cash availability, spending and giving (Tay, Zyphur, & Batz, 2018). However more thorough exploration of these findings revealed that there is a positive association between earnings and happiness, but it ceases to exist once a certain (fairly modest) level of income is reached. That is, money can lead to an increase in happiness levels, but mainly for those who are on the poor side of the scale. Once elementary needs are met, more monetary assets do not make people happier. Higher income is associated with lower occurrence of negative emotions, in particular sadness, fear, worry and stress, but this effect also fades once a certain (basic) level of income is reached.

Interestingly, cash in the bank was strongly associated with happiness (Ruberton, Gladstone, & Lyubomirsky, 2016). Going from 0 to $1,000 (from nothing to sufficiency) was associated with significant gains in happiness, but increasing financial assets from $1,000 to $10,000 produced fewer increases in happiness and therefore appears to be subjected to diminishing returns. The findings highlight the importance of holding a minimal monetary buffer that can be used in times of urgency or hardship, but also the relative unimportance of having wealth above sufficiency levels. In line with these findings, financial losses seem to have a larger effect on happiness than income gains (Tay et al., 2018).

Higher incomes are associated with more time spent at work or in managing assets and less time in doing activities that boost happiness, such as socialising. According to the research, money can also impede prosocial behaviour (Vohs, Mead, & Goode, 2008) and can increase attention to oneself, hence undermining social connection. More money brings the luxury of choice because a person can afford a larger variety of items. While it may seem that having more options to choose from is more enjoyable, research has demonstrated that too much choice may impede happiness (Lyengar & Lepper, 2000).

On the poor side, the inability to meet one's economic responsibilities and basic needs is often accompanied by stress, depression and anxiety. Money struggles reduce self-worth, sense of personal control, independence and self-determination (Haushofer & Fehr, 2014) which in turn undermine happiness. Additionally, money is a source of conflict for many families, which hampers social relations, adding more stress to financial worries, and weakens social support. Financial difficulties predict reduced marital satisfaction, intensified marital conflict and higher prospects of divorce (Papp, Cummings, & Goeke-Morey, 2009).

Does living in California make people happier?

Many people hold a perception that living in a sunny location will make them happier. But would it? Schkade and Kahneman (1998) examined this question by comparing the life satisfaction levels of 1,993 students studying at universities located in Midwest USA and in Southern California. The participants were asked to rate their SWL for themselves and for students living in one of the two regions, as well as to rate how important certain factors are for their happiness.

The results revealed that overall life satisfaction was similar in both regions. However participants expected students residing in California to be happier than students residing in colder climates. Climate was rated as an important factor for life satisfaction, although Midwestern students attached higher levels of importance to it than those living in California. The authors concluded that, although living in a sunny location is a seductive idea, it does not seem to improve happiness in the long run.

Similar to other domains of life, hedonic adaptation indeed occurs in the financial and life-style domains. Research has shown that, after an income rise people experience a short-term boost in their happiness, although they tend to rapidly adapt to their new income and their new standard of living. There is also evidence to suggest that, as people earn more money, they tend to consume more, which may lead to increases in materialism (Tay et al., 2018).

To mitigate the effects of adaptation researchers suggest spending money on things that are resistant to adaptation. Spending money on ourselves (bills, mortgage, material goods) makes people less happy than spending money on others (family, friends, charity). Happiness from buying stems from how and on whom we spend money, not how much money we have or spend. Spending money on possessions makes us less happy than spending money on experiences and memories. When shopping, focusing on products that either meet basic needs or alleviate pain or discomfort could be a more effective acquisition than purchasing luxury items. Importantly, happiness seems to be less about life's costly highs (expensive gifts, vacations or celebrations) and more about enjoying small everyday pleasures (Dunn & Norton, 2013).

Lottery studies

In a renowned study Brickman, Coates, and Janoff-Bulman (1978) examined retrospectively the effects of a lottery win on happiness. They reported that, after an initial brief increase in happiness, lottery winners returned to baseline and were not significantly happier than a comparison group. However, a common critique on this study is that it included few lottery winners.

A larger-scale study reported that lottery winners and people receiving substantial inheritances showed higher levels of happiness than others (Gardner & Oswald, 2007), which remained stable for about 2 years and then diminished.

Materialism

Materialism is defined as the belief that the acquisition of material goods leads to life satisfaction (Richins & Dawson, 1992). A meta-analysis conducted by Dittmar, Bond, Hurst, and Kasser (2014) found a modest negative association between materialism and happiness, and more. Individuals who are more materialistic reported decreased sense of security, poor need satisfaction and lower physical and psychological health (compulsive buying, anxiety, depression and substance abuse). Diener and Oishi (2000) conducted a study among 7,000 college students in 41 countries, and found that placing high importance on wealth correlated negatively with life satisfaction, while placing high value on love correlated positively with life satisfaction. Financial security and sensible money management (living within means) correlated with happiness more strongly than income.

The Easterlin paradox

The Easterlin paradox (Easterlin, 1974) has captured considerable attention across social sciences. The paradox suggests that over the past decades people (particularly in the West) have become richer, yet happiness levels have remained stable. Easterlin (2005) suggested that this is mainly due to hedonic adaptation and social comparison.

Accordingly, Tay et al. (2018) reported that income inequality was associated with lower happiness and this association was particularly strong for poorer respondents.

Demographic factors

Significant research has focused on patterns of happiness over a lifetime. Research has suggested that there is a U-shaped association between happiness and age (Blanchflower & Oswald, 2008): young adults are relatively happy, but happiness reaches a low point around the age of 30–40, which improves in older adults, but then declines again in very old age. However there is some controversy around the U-shaped trajectory, with some authors (Steptoe, Deaton, & Stone, 2015) suggesting that the U-shaped curve occurs mainly in the West and that in other countries SWB declines with age.

Reports on gender differences in happiness suggest that these are small, though there are some differences between genders in the emotional component of happiness: women show higher levels of both happiness and unhappiness compared to men. However in countries with high levels of gender equality, smaller gender differences in happiness were found (Zuckerman, Li, & Diener, 2017).

Education and work

Levels of education are moderately associated with happiness, as well as with work and income, both of which moderately impact happiness (Michalos, 2008). However analyses at country level suggested that national averages in educational attainment were one of the strongest predictors of happiness (Lawless & Lucas, 2011).

Employment is a strong predictor of happiness, with employed people showing higher happiness than unemployed people, and those holding skilled professional jobs being happier than those who perform unskilled jobs (Argyle, 2013). In a large-scale review McKee-Ryan, Song, Wanberg, and Kinicki (2005) found that unemployed people showed lower psychological and physical health and had suicidality risk. Similarly, Lucas, Clark, Georgellis, and Diener (2004) reported that the impact of job loss on wellbeing and happiness lasted years after the event, and the unemployed did not return to their earlier levels of SWB. The authors therefore suggested that unemployment has a "scarring effect", that can alter the happiness set point. Additionally, unhappiness due to unemployment seems to spill over to other people – notably the unemployed person's significant others. However, the unemployed were not equally unhappy. Those who were healthier and wealthier and had good social support and weaker desire to work were found to be slightly happier than others.

Country-level unemployment can predict the nation's average levels of happiness (Argyle, 2013). Among employed people, job satisfaction and overall happiness were found to be moderately linked (Diener, Suh, Lucas, & Smith, 1999) and this is explained by the fact that work provides not only financial rewards but also purpose and meaning, affiliation, interest and opportunities to perform, achieve and develop, which are predictors of happiness. Warr (2007) reported that jobs that offer a good person–job fit are more satisfying. However, a long commute to work seems to decrease happiness (Stutzer & Frey, 2008).

Health

Intuitively many of us would predict that health plays a prominent role in happiness. However research suggested that, with the exception of extreme circumstances, most objective health measures correlate weakly with happiness, apart from sleep quality, which shows a strong correlation with happiness. People's subjective assessments of their health is strongly associated with SWB (Diener et al., 2018a). Studies have also shown that people adapt to some acquired disabilities and return to their happiness set point in time, with the exception of severely disabling conditions (Lucas, 2007).

Macro-level factors

Over the last 20 years, national and cultural differences have become a major focus of happiness research (Diener et al., 2018a), supported by large-scale national and international surveys that routinely collect data on happiness. Culture shapes how people define happiness, what values they hold and what expectations they have from life, and also how they convey emotional experiences. Nations also vary in their capacity to provide services and support their citizens, hence influencing life priorities and lifestyles. Studies which examined differences between nations in SWB found that people are happier in richer and economically developed nations (most of which tend to be individualistic) compared to less developed countries. Countries that are lawful, with lower corruption, crime, discrimination and unemployment and higher government efficiency, equality, progressive taxation, effective welfare systems, stronger social bonds, higher levels of trust, freedom, autonomy and choice, and stronger environmental control (clean air and water and green spaces) show higher levels of happiness.

Scholars also noted that religious individuals have higher SWB than the non-religious (Hackney & Sanders, 2003). These findings can be explained by the sense of meaning and spirituality that people derive from religious beliefs, the psychological benefits of praying or attending religious services and the sense of belonging, identity and social support that comes from affiliation to a religious community. In a global study, Tay, Li, Myers, and Diener (2014) found that all four major religions were related to higher happiness, but this effect was stronger in poorer countries. They also found that non-religious people experienced lower happiness levels than their religious peers if they lived in a highly religious nation.

CONCLUSION: IS THE PURSUIT OF HAPPINESS FUTILE?

Research on happiness has exploded since positive psychology was established. As the review provided in this chapter shows, happiness is much more than just a pleasant experience; it is in fact highly beneficial and, as Lyubomirsky et al. (2005a) argued, can lead to success in several life domains.

According to the research, there are three core determinants of happiness: genetics and personality, which shape people's happiness set range; life circumstances, many of which are prone to hedonic adaptation; and volitional activities. Given that relative stability of the happiness set point, and the potency of hedonic adaptation, researchers have been debating a critical point: is the pursuit of happiness worthwhile or is it "as futile as trying to become taller" (Lykken & Tellegen, 1996, p. 189)? Some scholars argued that pursuing happiness can backfire, resulting in disappointment, which indicates that a better strategy might be to accept our happiness levels (Gruber, Mauss, & Tamir, 2011). In contrast, Sheldon and Lyubomirsky (2019) argued that, with some attention to our thinking habits and the choices that we make regarding how we spend our time, and the activities that we engage with, and indeed with some intentional effort, attaining higher happiness levels is possible, and these can be maintained over the long term.

WELLBEING

Wellbeing is an innate human goal, a desire to lead "a good life" and for our lives to evolve as we aspire. The experience of a "life well lived" involves both feeling good and functioning well. In line with these two aspects of life, the scientific study of wellbeing draws on two major philosophical traditions: *hedonia* and *eudaimonia*. Hedonia is defined as the pursuit of pleasure. Eudaimonia on the other hand indicates functioning well, which can be interpreted as performing well, or doing what is right or worthy (Huta, 2016). These schools of thought shaped the direction of contemporary research into wellbeing, and hence they represent a fundamental divide in positive psychology scholarship.

But what does the term "good life" mean? This question has been a point of significant debate for decades, and scholars still differ in what they consider the optimal combination of factors or properties that epitomise wellbeing.

On the back of this age-old debate, this chapter begins by clarifying the main differences between hedonia and eudaimonia. It will then go on to review the major theoretical models of wellbeing that are commonly used in positive psychology scholarship.

HEDONIA AND EUDAIMONIA

The distinction between hedonia and eudaimonia can be traced back to Aristotle's observation that wellbeing is felt not only from satisfying basic needs and desires, but from enacting virtues and doing what is morally worth doing. Aristotle coined the term "eudaimonia" to portray a life that is worth living, and as such, it represents a way of life, as opposed to hedonia, which is a state or a feeling, and therefore an outcome of a person's way of life (Huta, 2016).

Contemporary psychological perspectives define hedonia as an orientation or specific behaviours or actions that are geared to engender the experience of pleasure, comfort or gratification (Huta, 2016). The experience of positive emotions is therefore at the core of hedonia. The models of happiness reviewed in Chapter 2 are central in the hedonic tradition, with the term hedonia and happiness often used as synonyms.

Current conceptions of eudaimonia often equate it with wellbeing, with the term wellbeing often used interchangeably with eudaimonic wellbeing, positive mental health, flourishing, optimal experience, wellness or thriving, resulting in some confusion.

Empirical research into the correlation between hedonia and eudaimonia consistently shows a strong positive association between them (Goodman, Disabato, Kashdan, & Kauffman, 2017; Seligman, 2018). Hence, like the proverbial iceberg, the hedonic (feel-good) facets are often seen as an indicator of a person's eudaimonic (function well) wellbeing elements, though they do not offer a complete picture of what lies below the waterline. Hence the two concepts are indeed distinct.

Defining wellbeing

Although the definition of wellbeing has been debated for decades, a growing number of scholars seem to endorse the World Health Organization's description of positive mental health:

> A state of wellbeing in which the individual realises his or her own abilities, can cope with the normal stresses of life, can work productively and fruitfully, and is able to make a contribution to his or her community.
>
> (WHO, 2001, p. 1)

MODELS OF EUDAIMONIC WELLBEING

Over the years several wellbeing models have been developed that correspond with the characterisation of eudaimonia. These include early work by humanistic scholars such as Maslow's (1987) and Rogers' (1963).

Hierarchy of human needs

Maslow's (1987) conception of wellbeing highlights people's instinctive need to develop and fulfil their potential, thereby leading to self-actualisation and self-transcendence (a later development in Maslow's work – see Koltko-Rivera, 2006). Maslow placed "deficiency needs" (physiological needs, safety, love and belonging, and esteem needs) at the bottom of the needs pyramid, and "growth needs" (self-actualisation and self-transcendence) at the top, and argued that once people satisfy their deficiency needs, they are motivated to fulfil growth needs.

Self-actualisation

Self-actualisation is defined as a stage of personal growth whereby individuals are able to fulfil their needs, express themselves, pursue their interests and valued goals, and realise their talents. This stage culminates in peak experiences, meaningful life and self-fulfilment, which are considered key aspects of eudaimonic wellbeing.

Self-actualisation involves:

- The continual actualisation and self-expression of potentials, talents and capacities;
- Pursuing valued goals or a mission (or calling, vocation or destiny);
- A deeper knowledge of, and acceptance of, one's intrinsic nature;
- The development of morality and virtues;
- An inclination toward harmony, integration or synergy within the person.

Self-transcendence

Self-transcendence is defined as an "inherent, gradual developmental process, resulting in increased awareness of dimensions greater than the self and expansions of personal boundaries within intrapersonal, interpersonal, transpersonal, and temporal domains" (McCarthy, Ling, & Carini, 2013, p. 179).

It involves a shift in our experience of selfhood as we endeavour to connect to a larger context. It therefore entails a decrease in attachment to our own perspectives, viewpoints and truths, and an extension of care, compassion and concern toward others.

While self-actualisation is concerned with oneself – fulfilling one's potential and self-expression – self-transcendence is a desire to transcend one's self-interest and to strive toward a goal that is bigger and beyond oneself.

The fully functioning individual

Similar to Maslow, Rogers (1963) proposed that people have an innate actualising tendency. Rogers believed that every individual can achieve self-actualisation, by pursuing and realising their goals and desires. Rogers identified five characteristics of the fully functioning person:

- *Openness to experience*;
- *Existential living* – ability to be fully present with our experiences;
- *Trusting ourselves*;
- *Creativity*;
- *Fulfilled life* – pursuing valued goals and experiencing satisfaction with life.

It is noteworthy from these descriptions that eudaimonia requires individuals to engage, at times, in effortful and challenging activities that may not be pleasurable, since they require us to exert effort, express our virtues, grow and contribute to a wider context, which is a point of departure from the hedonic principle. Later wellbeing models followed this line of thought and include the Psychological Wellbeing Model (Ryff, 1989), Self-Determination Theory (Ryan & Deci, 2000) and the Social Wellbeing Model (Keyes, 1998).

Psychological wellbeing (PWB)

Ryff's (1989) model of Psychological Wellbeing consists of six capacities that are seen as facilitators of optimal wellbeing:

- *Life purpose*: A sense of purpose, direction and meaning in life which often emerges from setting and pursuing valued goals;
- *Autonomy*: Having the capacity to make decisions and take action in accordance with our own convictions. It necessitates being self-determined and responsible for our actions;
- *Personal growth*: A desire and capacity to realise our potential through authentic self-expression and seeking new experiences;

- *Environmental mastery*: The ability to choose, create or manage the varied environments in which we live. It involves the ability to control both internal and external factors;
- *Positive relationships*: The capacity to connect with others, develop relationships, care for others, express empathy and affection, and experience love and intimacy;
- *Self-acceptance*: Knowing, liking and ultimately accepting ourselves, including our weaknesses and dark sides.

Psychological wellbeing measures

The initial version of the Psychological Wellbeing scale (Ryff, 1989) included 120 items. In several revisions that followed, shorter scales were tested (Ryff & Singer, 1996), with the shortest including 18 items. The scales are available in 30 languages, and were used in more than 650 publications (Ryff, 2014).

Self-Determination Theory (SDT)

Ryan and Deci (2017) defined wellbeing as "thriving" or "being fully functioning". Similar to humanistic eudaimonic theories, Self-Determination Theory claims that people have an innate drive to grow, express their interests and talents and realise their potential. The desire to self-actualise is often manifested through the pursuit of valued, self-congruent goals.

Self-Determination Theory suggests that there are three innate, elementary psychological growth needs (as opposed to deficit needs) that people seek to satisfy through their interaction with their environments:

- *Competence*: Feelings of effectiveness and confidence in our ongoing interactions with our environment, and having opportunities to express our capacities;
- *Autonomy*: Being able to follow our true interests and values, and having choice and control over our actions;
- *Relatedness*: Feeling connected and caring for others, having a sense of belonging to a family or other groups or institutions.

Figure 3.1 Self-Determination Theory: three basic needs
(adapted from Ryan & Deci, 2017).

According to Self-Determination Theory, wellbeing is attained when individuals meet these needs, while need frustration can significantly diminish wellbeing.

Self-Determination Theory measures

Several wellbeing scales evaluate the degree to which basic needs are met. A nine-item measure developed by Sheldon, Elliot, Kim, and Kasser (2001) is highly used in a variety of studies.

There is substantial overlap between the Psychological Wellbeing Model and Self-Determination Theory. Both models consist of individual features (such as competence, autonomy and purpose) and both include a social dimension. Additionally, both models refer to the avenues through which a person can attain and maintain optimal wellbeing. However there is also a point of departure between the models: in Self-Determination Theory the path to wellbeing is through meeting basic needs, while the Psychological Wellbeing Model offers a more complex roadmap which contains a set of conditions and behaviours that can foster wellbeing.

An additional wellbeing model that complements the models reviewed above, and focuses solely on the connection between individuals and their social environments, is the Social Wellbeing Model (Keyes, 1998).

Social Wellbeing Model

The Social Wellbeing Model considers the quality of a person's relationships with others. It assesses how people interact with individuals, groups and institutions around them (such as their neighbourhoods, workplaces and communities), and how these interactions impinge on their wellbeing. According to Keyes (1998) the rationale for creating a model of wellbeing that focuses on the social domain is that "individuals remain embedded in social structures and communities, and face countless social tasks and challenges" (pp. 121–122).

The model encompasses five dimensions of social life:

- *Social integration*: The quality of an individual's ties with their community and society. This is often manifested through a person's affiliation with and sense of belonging to institutions and identification with a collective, based on shared features, and social cohesion.
- *Social acceptance*: People who demonstrate social acceptance hold positive views on human nature, convey trust in others and believe that people are capable, kind and industrious. They therefore accept others, and feel comfortable with them.
- *Social contribution*: Being a part of multiple social systems comes with social responsibilities. A person's contribution to the groups and institutions to which they belong amounts to their social value.
- *Social actualisation*: This concept represents the idea that, similar to individuals, institutions and societies have a potential for growth that can be realised through their members' actions.
- *Social coherence*: A concern for gaining knowledge and understanding of current affairs, caring about our world, and understanding how things work. It involves making sense of events and circumstances, and deriving coherent meaning from them.

Social wellbeing measures

Two measures have been developed and tested for this model. The first measure contains 50 items, and a second shorter version includes 15 items (Keyes & Shapiro, 2004).

COMBINED MODELS OF WELLBEING

Some models of wellbeing incorporate both hedonic and eudaimonic features, therefore combining "feeling good" and "functioning well" to offer more holistic theories of wellbeing. Conceptually, they envision hedonia and eudaimonia as paired psychological functions, and assert that people require both to flourish. These models include Seligman's (2002) Authentic Happiness, an early model which was later revised to develop PERMA (Seligman, 2011), the mental health continuum (Huppert, 2009; Keyes, 2002), the Happiness and Meaning Orientations Model (Wong, 2011) and the Gallup Wellbeing Global Survey (Rath & Harter, 2010).

The Authentic Happiness Model

Seligman's (2002) Authentic Happiness framework is a wellbeing model that contains both hedonic and eudaimonic features. Seligman suggested in this initial model that there are three pathways to "the full life":

- *The pleasant life*: The first pathway to optimal wellbeing focuses on positive emotions, which is the hedonic aspect of the model. The model recommends that we engage more often (though with moderation) with pleasurable activities that can prompt the experience of positive emotions with their numerous associated benefits. Basic pleasures include touch, food, sex, dance, walk, sleep, and many others. More sophisticated pleasures may include enjoying art, music, a film, reading and shopping. There are also social pleasures: good conversation, a party or a trip. Pleasures can provoke many emotions: cheerfulness, joy, bliss, euphoria, delight, excitement. In fact, the key reason why we engage with these types of activities is to provoke these emotions. Though it may sound superficial, researchers have recognised that the capacity to feel these emotions is critical for wellbeing.

  Actions that provoke pleasure, however, have some drawbacks. It is not realistic to expect to continuously be in a state of emotional "high"; ups and downs are normal and human. Another point is that the emotional upshots of pleasurable activities do not last long. Therefore if we do not engage with the activity, we cannot feel pleasure. This means that there is an element of addiction in these activities. We are drawn to repeatedly engage with these activities to derive pleasure. Also, larger amounts of the activity do not always make it more pleasurable. For example, if we offer someone 10 portions of chocolate one after the other, the first one would be pleasurable, the second may still be tasty, but the last one would not even be nice to have! Additionally, some pleasure-seeking activities can be harmful in the long run. Importantly, people require different levels of pleasure in their lives: for one person going to a social event once a month would be sufficient, but another person may need to engage with similar activities twice a week to derive the same levels of positive emotions. Individual differences are therefore important and need to be respected.

- *The engaged life*: The second route to wellbeing is through the experience of engagement, or in its premier form, flow (see details in Chapter 8). The model suggests that seeking opportunities to engage with tasks that we find interesting, which necessitate the use of strengths, skills or talents, and which we can perform with some level of mastery, can elevate our wellbeing. The outcome is heightened absorption, concentration, focus, dedication and ultimately peak performance, which invokes a sense of self-efficacy and accomplishment.

  The activity can be of any type: sport, art, math exercise, computing, writing, reading, video games, and many others. Flow and the idea that effort and concentrated performance can lead to wellbeing may be surprising for some. It speaks to the fact that a life that requires no effort and no challenge may not be very fulfilling. Flow therefore contributes to long-term wellbeing through the cultivation of interest, skill development and mastery. An important caveat to bear in mind is that flow can occur when engaging with activities that can be harmful and at times addictive (for example, gambling).

- *The meaningful life*: The final pathway to optimal wellbeing proposed by Seligman is meaning in life (see details in Chapter 9). It epitomises what we authentically value and care for, and generates a sense of mattering and being worthy. The model recommends that we engage with activities that generate meaning which are often associated with pursuing valued goals, or contributing to a transcendent purpose that is greater than ourselves.

Belonging to a community, volunteering and joining a social movement are examples of the types of activities that generate meaning. Paradoxically, however, the activities may not be necessarily pleasurable. The types of experiences that we expect to generate from this category of activities are sense of purpose and direction, meaning and value, spirituality and belonging. These are much more sophisticated emotional states than pleasure. Also, in contrast to pleasure and flow, they are not addictive: The sense of meaningfulness that we gain from these activities remains even when we are not engaging with the activity.

It is noteworthy that the model entails both a set of desired outcomes, as well as a means to achieve them through voluntary behaviours. Each pathway is necessary but not sufficient for achieving optimal wellbeing, and hence all three are required to gain the experience of "the full life".

PERMA

In 2011 Seligman revised the Authentic Happiness Model and proposed an expanded model – PERMA (Figure 3.2). Similar to the original model, PERMA incorporates *positive emotions, engagement* and *meaning in life*. The additional components include:

- *Positive relationships*: This component is captured aptly by Peterson's (2006) often-quoted assertion that "other people matter". It is akin to the relational feature embedded within

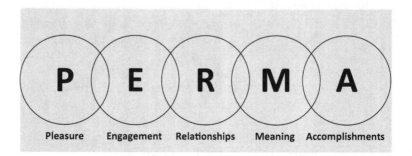

Figure 3.2 The PERMA model
(adapted from Seligman, 2011).

the models reviewed earlier (Psychological Wellbeing, Self-Determination Theory and Social Wellbeing), and its repeated inclusion in wellbeing models underscores scholars' reasoning that "there is no denying of the profound influences that positive relationships or their absence have on wellbeing" (Seligman, 2011, p. 21). The model recommends that people engage with others purposefully, and for its own sake, acknowledge the importance of relationships for their wellbeing and consider how to create, nurture and maintain their relationships.

- *Accomplishments*: The final pathway to wellbeing is through the pursuit and achievement of tasks or objectives that require us to apply our skills, effort and time, with the intent of achieving specific goals. The model therefore suggests that people set goals and progress towards the realisation of goals that are aligned with their genuine interests and values. This pathway is linked with the engagement route, though it focuses on the goal being pursued, and the sense of gratification that follows when one reaches the goalpost, rather than process or mastery required for pursuing it.

The PERMA scale

The PERMA-Profiler (Butler & Kern, 2016) includes 23 items, of which 15 items pertain to the PERMA domains, and eight additional items assess overall wellbeing, negative emotions (sadness, anger and anxiety), loneliness and self-perceived physical health. Several large-scale surveys with over 30,000 participants were conducted to test the questionnaire, which revealed that average scores in the five PERMA domains ranged between 6.7 and 7.2.

The Happiness and Meaning Orientation Model

Wong (2011) argued that there are four pathways to happiness that together create a life that is worth living:

- *Hedonic happiness* represents the sensory or experiential route to happiness: being satisfied with life and feeling good.
- *Prudential happiness* is akin to Seligman's "engaged life" category. It represents an active pathway to happiness, since it involves

performing optimally in activities that we are genuinely interested in, resulting in a sense of fulfilment and achievement.

- *Eudaimonic happiness* is a way of life characterised by "the pursuit of virtue/excellence, meaning/purpose, doing good/making a difference, and the resulting sense of fulfillment or flourishing" (Wong, 2011, p. 70). It is a conduit to happiness through the expression of character and virtue.
- *Chaironic happiness* is a spiritual pathway to happiness. It is an attitude toward life that entails being attuned to the transcendent aspects of reality. It can manifest itself though meditation, peak experiences, awe and spirituality.

Meaning in life is central in Wong's approach to wellbeing, and accordingly he defined eudaimonia as "meaning plus virtue" and argued that "eudaimonia can be understood from a meaning perspective because of its emphasis on purpose, understanding, responsibility, and enjoying the fruit of the good life. Eudaimonia can also be viewed as rooted in both inner goodness and the common good" (Wong, 2011, p. 75).

In line with this view, Wong clustered the four routes to happiness into two categories:

- *A happiness orientation* which entails the hedonic and prudential happiness categories.

    Wong observed that people with a happiness orientation tend to seek and optimise positive experiences. They focus on pursuing success, feeling happy, experiencing gratification and avoiding pain or discomfort. They often exhibit high self-confidence, self-efficacy, achievement motivation and competence. They are interested in external sources of happiness, tend to put their self-interests first, and may show at times low compassion or altruism. When facing challenges or hardship they may give up. They also tend to prioritise gain above moral principles, and therefore are less likely to challenge other people's unethical behaviours.
- *A meaning orientation* which includes the eudaimonic and chaironic happiness categories.

    Wong found that people with a meaning orientation display a drive to actualise their purpose, and are interested in pursuing worthy ideals, even if these bear personal costs. They are concerned with leading a good life, and their focus lies in nurturing their inner life (inner peace or joy or spirituality). They prioritise responsibility, show high levels of compassion and altruism towards others, and have a strong capacity to self-regulate, endure and persevere. They are willing to sacrifice their own desires for others, and show moral courage in speaking up against unethical actions.

The Gallup Wellbeing Global Survey

Gallup research into wellbeing began in the 1930s and is considered one of the largest global surveys. It includes samples from more than 150 countries (representing 98% of the world's population), and involves millions of participants. Drawing on the vast data collected over the years through these surveys, Rath and Harter (2010) defined five distinct dimensions that together make up wellbeing:

- *Career wellbeing*: This represents what we engage in on a daily basis and the sense of purpose and satisfaction that we derive from this engagement;
- *Physical wellbeing*: Being healthy and experiencing vitality to enable day-to-day functioning, and get things done on a daily basis;
- *Financial wellbeing*: Managing effectively our finances, to reduce economic stress and increase our sense of security;
- *Social wellbeing*: Having strong relationships, including love in our lives;
- *Community wellbeing*: Being engaged and involved with local affairs, in particular where we live.

Gallup measures

Career wellbeing, physical wellbeing, financial wellbeing, social wellbeing and community wellbeing are measured continuously by the Gallup's wellbeing finder which enables individuals and organisations to assess their wellbeing.

In addition, Gallup presents a daily experience tracker which enables participants to gain a better understanding of their emotional experiences. The daily tracker includes 10 domains (five positive and five negative) that participants can assess themselves on:

- Feeling well rested;
- Being treated with respect;

- Learning or feeling interested;
- Experiencing enjoyment;
- Smiling or laughing;
- Sensing physical pain;
- Worrying;
- Feeling sad;
- Experiencing stress;
- Being angry.

These are considered the key elements of life that matter to us most, and also those that we have some control over. Rath and Harter (2010) asserted that if we're struggling in any of these domains, it can significantly hamper our wellbeing and drain us.

Wellbeing benchmarks

To facilitate action that is directed toward the improvement of wellbeing, Rath and Harter (2010) created a set of "wellbeing benchmarks" that individuals and organisations can use to assess how they are faring, detect areas of poor functioning and consider ways to improve them. Gallup produces a 0–100 score for each of the wellbeing areas (physical, career, social, community and financial) and defines cut-off points for optimal and sub-optimal wellbeing. Based on these scores, the authors defined three categories of wellbeing:

- *Thriving*: People who are doing well on all dimensions as well as experiencing wellbeing on a daily basis (feeling restful, enjoyment, comfort). Cut-off point for thriving is a score of 70+.
- *Struggling*: Individuals who report moderate functioning on all or some of the dimensions, and report daily hassles and stressors. Struggling is identified in a score of 40–69.
- *Suffering*: Individuals in this category are considered suffering as they rate their functioning and daily experiences below 40 on all or most dimensions. Gallup found that these individuals are often unable to meet basic needs and experience both poor physical health and psychological distress.

The mental health continuum

The mental health continuum model developed by Keyes (2002) originated from the idea that, similar to the diagnosis of mental illness, wellbeing should be conceptualised as a constellation of "symptoms" that together demonstrate "flourishing" – a state of complete mental health, which entails emotional wellbeing, psychological wellbeing and social wellbeing.

Keyes (2005) therefore defined the following symptoms of flourishing:

- *Continuous positive affect*: Being cheerful or in good spirits, happy, zestful, calm or peaceful.
- *Life satisfaction*: Being satisfied with life overall or with particular domains.
- *Positive functioning*: Scoring high on the following criteria:
    - *Positive attitudes* toward ourselves and self-acceptance;
    - *Positive attitude* toward others and social acceptance;
    - *Personal growth*: Understanding our own potential, willingness to grow and openness to new experiences;
    - *Social actualisation*: Believing that people, groups, organisations and communities can evolve positively;
    - *Purpose in life*: Setting life-goals, and having a sense of direction, purpose and meaning;
    - *Social contribution*: Feeling that our life has value, and that we can contribute and make a difference to others;
    - *Environmental mastery*: The ability to manage or navigate our environments;
    - *Social coherence*: Taking an interest in society, and the ability to comprehend society and culture;
    - *Autonomy*: Being self-directed according to internal standards;
    - *Positive relationships*: Having close, nurturing, trusting and satisfying relationships;
    - *Social integration*: Experiencing a sense of belonging to a group or community.

At the heart of this approach lies the question: how does mental health relate to mental illness? On this point researchers' conceptions differ: Huppert (2014) argued that mental health and illness are the opposite sides of the same spectrum (Figure 3.3), whereas Keyes (2002) claimed that mental health and mental illness are two axes that are orthogonally linked (Figure 3.4).

Figure 3.3 The mental health spectrum
(Adapted from Huppert, 2014).

Drawing on the mental health spectrum and remaining true to their assertion that wellbeing and ill-being are two sides of a single axis, Huppert and So (2013) went on to define 10 components of flourishing:

Positive appraisal (hedonic):

- Positive emotion and satisfaction with life

Positive characteristics:

- Emotional stability;
- Vitality;
- Optimism;
- Resilience,
- Self-esteem;

Positive functioning:

- Engagement;
- Competence;
- Meaning;
- Positive relationships.

The dual continua model (Keyes, 2002) on the other hand differentiates between five groups, based on their scores on both wellness and ill-being:

- *Flourishing* is a state in which "an individual feels positive emotion toward life and is functioning well psychologically and socially"

(Keyes, 2003, p. 294). In addition, flourishing individuals are identified as people with low occurrence of mental illness.

- *Flourishing with some mental illness symptoms / moderately healthy* is a group within the flourishing category that are functioning well despite having a moderate illness.
- *Languishing* is described as a state of "quiet desperation" whereby "an individual is devoid of positive emotions toward life, is not functioning well psychologically or socially, but has not been depressed. In short, languishers are neither mentally ill nor mentally healthy" (Keyes, 2003, p. 294).
- *Mental illness* is a category in which people meet the criteria for mental illness.
- *Languishing with mental illness* is a group of people who show symptoms of mental illness, as well as poor psychological wellbeing and functioning.

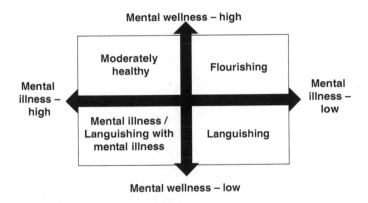

Figure 3.4 The dual continua model
(adapted from Keyes, 2005).

The dual continua model therefore reasons that mental health requires more than the absence of mental illness: it requires the presence of social, emotional and psychological fitness. At the same time, the occurrence of mental illness does not necessarily lead to poor wellbeing according to the model.

Findings from a national US survey (Keyes, 2005) suggested that only 17% were flourishing, 50% were moderately healthy, 10% were languishing, which Keyes (2003) described as a "silent and debilitating epidemic" (p. 294), and the rest met the criteria for mental illness (23%).

As can be seen from the review presented above, there is substantial overlap between the components of the wellbeing models, and currently there is no sign of consensus between scholars as to which components carry more weight than others. It's noteworthy that the "relationship" aspect is repeatedly included in several models.

One of the challenges of wellbeing theories, noted by Huta and Waterman (2014), is that there is often a different rationale underlying them. Some models focus on people's *orientations* (their motives or goals), others focus on the *behaviours* that people choose to engage with, while other models centre on the *experiences* that people seek or derive, and some models elicit people's day-to-day *functioning* (their abilities, habits and achievements). This makes it difficult to compare them or to integrate them. As can be expected, due to the similarities between these models there is also significant correspondence between their empirical research findings, which are briefly reviewed next.

PREDICTORS OF WELLBEING

Much of the research conducted on wellbeing (however it is defined or measured) attempted to explore what shapes wellbeing, and therefore it examined the degree to which demographic features, personality characteristics, health, work and relationships can affect wellbeing. Recent reviews assembled and synthesised this sizeable body of research, and key points are summarised below. It is worth mentioning that some of the findings reviewed below closely resemble those reviewed in Chapter 2 regarding happiness. This is because some wellbeing concepts and measures incorporate happiness items in their scales, and that, as noted earlier, the hedonic and eudaimonic aspects of wellbeing tend to show strong associations (Huta, 2013).

Health

A robust body of research explored the association between wellbeing or its components and a wide range of health conditions using self-report questionnaires, biological examinations and brain scans. They reported a circular relationship between physical health and wellbeing: poor physical health and disability, particularly later in life, are linked to low psychological wellbeing. Social support, resilience and spirituality seem to mediate this link (Ryff, 2018). Insomnia also seems to predict poor wellbeing (Ryff, 2018). However, in turn, adults with healthy levels of psychological wellbeing showed more conducive health behaviours (healthy eating, exercising, not smoking), resulting in fewer physical and psychological health conditions across the different age and gender groups, and ultimately lower mortality rate (Ryff, 2018).

Personality

Studies using the Big Five personality traits found that they predicted wellbeing: openness, agreeableness, extraversion and conscientiousness were found to be strongly linked with psychological wellbeing (Ryff, 2018). Satisfaction of psychological needs, goal orientation, optimism, optimal self-esteem, identity development, emotion regulation, coping, life management strategies and spirituality seem to predict higher levels of psychological wellbeing. Interestingly, low weight and positive body image were found to predict wellbeing, particularly among young women. Religiosity and spirituality also predict higher psychological wellbeing, particularly among older adults (Ryff, 2018).

Work, income and lifestyle

Higher levels of education and employment status predict enhanced wellbeing (Ryff, 2018). Similarly, high socioeconomic status is associated with both low rates of disorder and higher levels of wellbeing. However this effect shows diminishing returns as income increases (Huppert, 2009). Additionally, status and particularly income inequality are linked with poorer wellbeing (Huppert, 2009).

Paid work is associated with improved psychological wellbeing for men more than women (Ryff, 2018). The Gallup survey (Rath & Harter, 2010) revealed that only 20% of people actually like what they do, suggesting that only a minority of people enjoy optimal career wellbeing. Similarly, engagement at work has a profound impact on wellbeing: people who are disengaged are more likely to experience depression. People who have opportunities to use their strengths in their jobs are highly engaged and report high performance outcomes which in turn affects their overall wellbeing (Rath & Harter, 2010). Having a best friend at work can also increase engagement at work (Rath & Harter, 2010). As can be expected, employment discrimination and harassment in the workplace predict low wellbeing (Ryff, 2018).

Unemployment is consistently associated with high prevalence of mental disorders as well as poor wellbeing. However where unemployment is common, its effects on ill-being are not as strong (Huppert, 2009). Rath and Harter (2010) reported that people's overall wellbeing recovers more quickly following the death of a spouse than from a prolonged period of unemployment. This may explain why living in a wealthy country increases wellbeing, as the chances of unemployment are smaller in these countries, and there are more safety nets provided by the state to protect people from poverty.

As for spending money, we seem to spend the most when we feel low. Spending money on others impacts our wellbeing more positively than spending on ourselves. Spending on experiences increases wellbeing more than spending money on luxury items. Financial security – the sense that we have enough money to pay for necessities and not having money worries – influences wellbeing more than income.

Relationships

Rath and Harter (2010) argued that on average people require about 6 hours of social time per day to function well. On the health side they reported that having friends who are obese increases the chances of becoming obese by 57%. Marriage benefits both men and women's wellbeing, and accordingly, married people showed higher wellbeing compared to the never married, divorced or widowed, although this is mediated by socioeconomic resources. Single and widowed women showed better wellbeing compared to men in similar marital situations. However some studies found that divorced or separated women experience higher levels of autonomy compared to the never married (Ryff, 2018).

Findings on parenting have been mixed. In some studies parents showed lower wellbeing compared to non-parents, but in others the findings showed higher or similar levels. Nelson et al. (2014) found that parents reported higher levels of meaning in life compared to non-parents, and having a child living in the home was associated with meaning in life. Ryff (2018) reported however that parenting young children seems to be more challenging for women than for men. This improves when parenting adult children, particularly if the children are well adjusted and have left home. Time spent with children is highly rewarding, and similarly, engaging in family activities and helping others is linked to enhanced wellbeing across the life span. People with improved psychological wellbeing levels are more likely to engage in volunteering, which in turn boosts their wellbeing, particularly in old age (Ryff, 2018).

Demographic features

Is wellbeing predicted by demographic features such as age, gender and ethnicity?

Huppert (2009) found no difference between men and women on the positive side of wellbeing; however, on the ill-being side, women showed higher levels of depression and anxiety compared to men. The association between wellbeing and age is often described as U-shaped: younger and older people seem to enjoy better wellbeing than the middle-aged, who are also showing the highest levels of ill-being. Older men show low distress symptoms, but also have the lowest scores on positive wellbeing (Huppert, 2014).

Wellbeing interventions

There are various positive psychology interventions that are evidence-based and shown to be moderately effective in promoting particular aspects of wellbeing (for example, engagement, relationships, personal growth or meaning in life) as well as in increasing overall wellbeing.

Wellbeing interventions may include ad hoc exercises such as setting life goals, or practising forgiveness, though most wellbeing-boosting activities require repeated practice in order for them to have an impact, and to sustain their effect long-term. Examples include engaging in physical activity, using character strengths, developing an optimistic explanatory style or savouring. There are also some group-based wellbeing intervention programmes, such as mindfulness, wellbeing therapy (Fava, 2016) and quality of life therapy (Frisch, 2006), that have shown promising results both in clinical and non-clinical groups (see further details in Chapter 13).

CONCLUSION

Research on wellbeing has begun centuries ago, and has blossomed since the launch of positive psychology. As the review provided in this chapter shows, wellbeing as an outcome of "a good life" involves both feeling good and doing well, and as several authors have argued – doing good: contributing to a wider context. While scholars seem to agree that wellbeing is best captured by models that combine hedonic and eudaimonic features, and that wellness amounts to more than the absence of illness, there is less agreement as to the factors that can lead to optimal wellbeing, and these are laid out in the plethora of models reviewed in this chapter.

The large number of wellbeing models is indeed confusing; however, it is also enriching, as it has led to some of the most profound debates around what makes life worth living, with significant progress made. Perhaps one way of making best use of the richness of models and data in this area is to consider which models and measures fit more aptly to particular settings or circumstances, therefore making more nuanced use of the this body of knowledge.

The science of wellbeing aims to support people in their journeys towards flourishing. In line with positive psychology's philosophical tenets, it focuses on people's assets and the actions that people can take to improve their wellbeing. Nevertheless it does not turn a blind eye to human weaknesses and the dark side of human existence. It is a constructive area of research which conveys an optimistic message: we have some power to shape our wellbeing despite genetic, childhood and contextual influences. Importantly, understanding how to improve our wellbeing is not a selfish endeavour, since our wellbeing and indeed our ill-being spill out to others and affect our families, organisations and societies.

POSITIVE EMOTIONS AND EMOTIONAL INTELLIGENCE

In the earlier chapters we have seen that positive emotions are a defining feature of happiness, and a key component of several well-being models. Accordingly, scholars consider positive emotions as an indicator of people's psychological wellbeing. In the past two decades the study of positive emotions has taken centre stage in positive psychology, resulting in remarkable gains in our understanding of how positive emotions operate, what functions they serve and their many outcomes (Fredrickson & Cohn, 2008). In acknowledging the impressive progress made in this area, it is noteworthy that much of the research that predated the establishment of positive psychology examined negative emotions. The reason for this limited agenda is that negative emotions, when prolonged, intense or inappropriate, are regarded as indicators of psychopathology (Oatley & Johnson-Laird, 2014). Hence, compared to the ominous implications of negative emotions, researchers tended to belittle the merit of positive emotions and viewed them as "nice to have", but not very consequential.

On the back of this critical change in the perception, agenda and focus in emotions scholarship, this chapter aims to review the latest theoretical and empirical work on positive emotions. At the centre of this chapter is the Broaden-and-Build Theory of positive emotions, developed by Fredrickson (2013b) and her colleagues, which illuminates the key functions of positive emotions.

EMOTIONS

The nature and function of emotions have intrigued psychology researchers and practitioners for decades, with early thinking taking the view that emotions are wild, uncontrollable and at times dangerous, primal impulses. Compared to reasoning, they were often considered as an inferior, less sensible and hence less dependable function. Accordingly, early work on emotions considered how they can be controlled or channelled (Solomon, 2008). However, much has changed since this early conception of emotions. Today scholars consider emotions as fundamental psychological experiences that reflect and communicate our inner reactions to life events, and prompt us to act. Hence they have several beneficial functions. But what are emotions?

Conceptualising emotions

Scholars vary in how they define emotions but in recent years some convergence between definitions seems to be emerging. Oatley and Johnson-Laird (2014) offered the following key points that capture the essence of emotions:

- Emotions are *brief* conscious mental states which involve distinctive subjective sensations.
- They are activated in response to particular stimuli.
- The stimuli can be external (including events, people or objects), internal (for example, body sensations, memories) or both.
- Emotions are triggered by people's appraisals of the stimulus, in which the meaning and significance of the stimulus are construed.
- Once the stimulus is acknowledged, several systems operate in tandem to create what we recognise as "emotions". These vary in accordance with the particular emotion that is experienced:
  - *Physiological reactions* are triggered instinctively. These may include changes in heart rate, facial expressions, breathing, hormone secretion, muscle tightness, voice and more.
  - *Cognitive reactions* arise, including for example changes in cognitions, attention, self and social awareness.

- *The subjective experience* involved in emotions can be described along two dimensions:
  - *Emotional valence*: The extent to which an emotion is *positive* (pleasant) or *negative* (unpleasant). Positive emotions (such as joy, contentment or love) are therefore those that generate a positive valence, while negative emotions (such as anger, fear or sadness) are negatively vallanced.
  - *Arousal*: The *intensity* of the emotion can vary between low and high intensity. For example, joy is considered high arousal, while serenity is considered low arousal.

  All emotions can be described as a combination of valance and arousal. Depression for example is a negative affect combined with high arousal, while cheerfulness is a positive high arousal emotion. Boredom is considered a negative and low arousal emotion, while calm is a positive low arousal emotion.
- *Behavioural response*: Emotions are associated with *action tendencies* (Frijda, 1986), since they motivate and prepare us to act. The emotional valence and intensity that are sensed prompt an inclination to *approach* or to *avoid* the stimulus. For example, joy prompts a desire to continue to engage with the stimulus, while fear induces an urge to escape. Positive emotions are therefore considered as facilitators of approach behaviours, while negative emotions tend to trigger avoidance behaviours.

Emotional literacy

Scholars often differentiate between basic and complex emotions, as well as make a distinction between emotions, mood, feelings and affect.

- *Basic and complex emotions*: Ekman's (2003) work on facial expressions of emotions proposed that there are six basic emotions: anger, sadness, fear, disgust, joy and surprise. However other authors offered different accounts of basic emotions. Izard (2009), for example, argued that there are 10 basic emotions: anger, fear, distress, contempt, guilt, shame, disgust, interest, joy, and surprise. Keltner, Sauter, Tracy, and Cowen (2019) explained that basic emotions are distinct from other emotions due to evolutionary influences: they enabled our ancestors to respond in adaptive ways to everyday hazards and opportunities. As such, they are inborn and detectable from a very young age in humans as well as in some mammals, and also have particular brain signals. They can arise as a result of habitual appraisals, some can be felt without the presence of particular stimuli and their non-verbal expressions can be recognised cross-culturally (Ekman, 2003).

Complex emotions, on the other hand, such as empathy, jealousy, pride or embarrassment, integrate several basic emotions together with conscious and often highly intricate cognitive appraisals. As such, they are less universal, develop with maturity, and their manifestations vary across cultures according to "display rules".

- *Feelings* are a by-product of emotions that occur when we assign meaning to an emotion that is present. They are therefore cognitive inputs in the form of mental associations (usually subconscious) that are prompted in reaction to emotions. They are shaped by our personal experiences, memories, values and beliefs (Damasio & Dolan, 1999).
- *Mood*: Emotions are often confused with moods, but researchers view them as distinct concepts. Compared to emotions, moods tend to be more stable, not tied to a particular stimulus, long-lasting, less intense and "occupy the background of consciousness" (Fredrickson & Cohn, 2008, p. 778).
- *Affect* is a broader term which refers to the valance of both moods and emotions, and can offer an evaluation of a person's overall emotional experience (positive affect versus negative affect) during a defined time period.
- *Affective styles*: People differ in their emotional styles along several criteria, including the thresholds that trigger emotions, the type and valence of affect typically felt, the strength and duration of the emotion and recovery time. Affective styles tend to be fairly stable over time and moderately heritable (Hofmann & Kashdan, 2010).

Managing and communicating emotions

Once emotions are felt and noticed people tend to manage them or act on them. The following concepts explore these choices:

- *Restoring affective equilibrium*: Karasu (1992) argued that people aim to maintain a degree of affective balance in their life. When events (external or internal) disrupt this equilibrium, they will likely be followed by behaviours that aim to restore the balance. For example, self-soothing may follow after experiencing anger or fear.
- *Managing emotions and acting on emotions*: Once emotions are activated, people face a choice as to how to manage or regulate them, and the action tendencies that they prompt. A person can choose to express or display the emotions being felt fully or to some extent, or to mask or suppress them. One can also act partially or fully in accordance with the action tendency that is triggered, or not (Plutchik, 2001).
- *Communicating emotions*: Emotions can be communicated to others, through verbalisations as well as through non-verbal communication (gestures, postures and facial expressions). With the exception of basic emotions, the communication of emotions varies across cultures.
- *Emotional contagion*: When people communicate emotions, emotional contagion often occurs, whereby one person experiences the emotions imparted by another person (Hatfield, Cacioppo, & Rapson, 1992). Researchers considered that this occurs in part due to "mimicry", which is an automatic mirroring of other people's non-verbal cues.

THE FUNCTION OF POSITIVE EMOTIONS

Positive emotions certainly feel good! But, do they have any useful function?

In the past 20 years research around this question has blossomed, providing strong evidence that positive emotions are highly advantageous: they broaden our thoughts and actions, thereby facilitating optimal functioning; they build lasting resources, including resilience, hence fostering flourishing; and they can undo the effects of negative emotions, thus restoring affective balance.

These remarkable findings prompted an intriguing question known as the paradox of positive emotions: "How is it that fleeting experiences of joy, interest, or love – which can be so easily squelched or dismissed

– produce lasting gains in strengths and wellbeing?" (Fredrickson & Cohn, 2008, p. 777). Much of the insight into the function and consequences of positive emotions emerged from the Broaden-and-Build Theory of positive emotions, developed by Fredrickson and her team, and the extensive empirical research that underpins the model.

Can positive emotions buffer against colds?

Unhappy people by definition regularly experience more negative emotions than positive emotions, and according to the research, this places them at a higher risk for mental and physical illness compared to happier individuals.

In a groundbreaking study Cohen, Doyle, Turner, Alper, and Skoner (2003) examined whether happiness can buffer against a common cold. The researchers assessed 334 healthy adults for their inclination to experience positive emotions and negative emotions. Subsequently, participants were given nasal drops comprising rhinoviruses and were observed in isolation for the development of common cold symptoms.

Intriguingly, the main finding was that happiness was significantly associated with lower probability of developing a cold.

THE BROADEN-AND-BUILD THEORY OF POSITIVE EMOTIONS

The Broaden-and-Build Theory evolved from a desire to capture the uniqueness of positive emotions, and free the study of positive emotions from some of the restrictive assumptions and models that are commonly used for exploring negative emotions. The theory posits that "positive emotions *broaden* people's momentary thought–action repertoires and lead to actions that *build* enduring personal resources" (Fredrickson & Cohn, 2008, p. 782). In contrast, negative emotions *narrow* people's thought–action repertoires, and prompt particular types of actions (confront, escape or dismiss). When facing danger, the narrowed thought–action repertoire facilitates a swift and resolute action, which enabled our ancestors to survive in harsh environments. Fredrickson and Joiner (2018) noted that "just as negative emotions both characterise depression and also promote it … positive emotions appear to both characterise optimal functioning and promote it" (p. 196).

The yearbook study

Can emotional tendencies of young adults predict their wellbeing and life trajectories decades later? Harker and Keltner (2001) examined the physical and psychological wellbeing and marital life of 141 women who varied in their smiles in their college yearbook photos (age 20).

The researchers found significant differences between those who expressed a genuine (Duchenne) smile and those who expressed a fake smile in their photos. Those who expressed a genuine smile were rated more favourably by observers, and importantly, Duchenne smile predicted better physical and psychological wellbeing and more stable marriages 30 years later.

Table 4.1 (adapted from Fredrickson, 2013b) presents a sample of 10 positive emotions that are experienced most frequently in people's daily lives, showing the appraisal patterns that prompt each emotion, the broadened thought–action repertoire that these emotions lead to and the durable resources that they build. The table demonstrates how the theory can be applied for exploring particular emotions.

The broadening effect

According to the Broaden-and-Build Theory, when we experience positive emotions, our thought–action repertoire broadens. Positive emotions therefore produce a capacity to see the "big picture", a global-level view, while negative emotions often produce the opposite: a capacity to focus on a particular detail.

Empirical research has documented the broadening effect in a variety of cognitive functions. It is manifested in flexible, variable, expansive and inclusive thinking, creativity, problem solving, reasoned decision making, perseverance and capacity to handle more challenging tasks. These ultimately lead (in most, but not all, tasks) to improved performance. In the social domain, broadening takes the form of attentiveness to others, reduced divisions and increased overlap between oneself and others, higher trust and reduced tension between groups (Fredrickson, 2013b).

Table 4.1 Ten positive emotions, their appraisal, action tendencies and the resources they build

Positive emotions	Appraisal	Thought–action tendencies	Durable resources built
Love	Arises when positive emotions are felt in a safe relational context	Creates a desire for social connection, care and self-expansion	Builds or strengthens social bonds and community
Joy	Emerges when people receive good news or experience good fortune or a welcome surprise	Generates an urge to play or engage with the event	The skills acquired through the experiential learning
Gratitude	Felt when people receive a gift or benefit and acknowledge others for it	Creates a desire to be prosocial, kind or generous	Builds skills for showing care, loyalty and connecting
Serenity/ contentment	Occurs when people feel at ease and interpret their current circumstances as gratifying	Produces a desire to savour the current state and integrate them into new priorities or values	A refined sense of self and new priorities
Interest	Arises when novelty is present and people feel safe to explore it	Prompts a will to explore, learn or immerse oneself in the novelty and expand the self	The knowledge gained
Hope	Can arise in harsh circumstances where a person fears the worst, but wishes for a better outcome	Prompts a desire to act to turn things around	Builds optimism and resilience
Pride	Emerges when one accomplishes an important goal or takes credit for a good outcome	Creates a desire to achieve more/bigger accomplishments	Generates achievement motivation
Amusement	Occurs when one encounters a non-serious social incongruity	Prompts an urge to share a laugh or continue the glee	Builds or solidifies social relationships
Inspiration	Arises when people witness excellence	Creates a desire to excel	Fosters motivation for personal growth
Awe	Emerges when people encounter beauty or goodness on a grand scale	Urges people to absorb and accommodate this new experience	Creates new worldviews

(Adapted from Fredrickson, 2013b.) The emotions presented in the table are ordered starting with the positive emotions people feel most often to those that they feel less frequently.

The building effect

A large body of research shows the beneficial effects of positive emotions (as a component of happiness) on varied life domains (see Chapter 2). Summarised briefly, the research reveals that positive emotions can build intellectual resources (problem solving, learning capacity, resourcefulness and openness to learning), physical resources (cardiovascular health, optimal immune function, healthy lifestyle), social resources (interacting, playing, building trust, pro-social actions) and a variety of psychological resources (coping, resilience, goal pursuit). These findings suggest that positive emotions build a variety of resources, which in turn increase our health, longevity and wellbeing, our performance and relationships (Fredrickson, 2013b). An important point to highlight is that these personal resources are durable, and can outlast the transient nature of the emotional states that led to their attainment. Hence people can draw on them in later times, and while experiencing different emotional states.

The "upward spiral" efect

As people accumulate resources, cycles of "upward spirals" occur, whereby the newly accumulated resources and capacities induce more positive emotions. These continue to broaden and build further resources, thereby producing perpetual upward cycles of transformation in our emotional states and our resources. Recent evidence for the upward spirals emerged from studies in which the upward spiral theory was used to explain the ways in which positive emotions can prompt steady improvements in people's health behaviours (Fredrickson & Joiner, 2018).

The undoing effect

The undoing hypothesis proposes that positive emotions can undo the psychological and physical effects of negative emotional states (such as anger, anxiety, sadness or stress). Particularly in relation to chronic stress, which poses a high health risk (see Chapter 12), positive emotions "clearly stood out in their ability to 'undo' lingering cardiovascular activation" (Fredrickson, 2013b, p. 10). In the health domain, positive emotions are associated with less pain, and the capacity to fight off or recover more quickly from illness or injury. Fredrickson and Cohn (2008) attributed these findings to the undoing effect of positive emotions, which can attenuate the negative emotions that often accompany illness and injury. Positive emotions can also restore self-regulation and willpower following depletion.

In the clinical domain, the literature suggests that people with depression experience downward spirals, in which the low mood and the pessimistic thinking lead to a worsening in their condition, culminating in clinical depression. Fredrickson's (2013b) work provides evidence that positive emotions can interrupt these downward spirals, and trigger an upward spiral. And finally, even under harrowing circumstances, such as the September 11, 2001 terrorist attack in New York, positive emotions have been found to promote posttraumatic growth.

Bad is stronger than good

Baumeister, Bratslavsky, Finkenauer, and Vohs (2001) argued that negative psychological phenomenon are more powerful than positive psychological occurrences. For example, negative events (such as losing money) have a stronger impact on us than positive events of the same magnitude (winning or finding money). Similarly, negative information, problems in relationships, losses and negative emotions attract much more attention than positive information, pleasant relationships, gains or positive emotional states.

The authors proposed that this is due to evolutionary reasons. For our ancestors, being able to quickly attend to dangers was essential for survival. Accordingly, negative emotions essentially convey "a signal that something in our environment is awry and needs addressing" (Oishi & Kurtz, 2011, p. 106). Once triggered, they narrow people's minds, focusing attention on the source of danger and prompting appropriate action.

The positivity ratio

The undo principle of the Broaden-and-Build Theory suggests that positive emotions can undo the effects of negative emotions. However, Baumeister et al. (2001) argued that

> when equal measures of good and bad are present ... the psychological effects of bad ones outweigh those of the good ones... This is not to say that bad will always triumph over good, spelling doom and misery for

the human race. Rather, good may prevail over bad by superior force of numbers: Many good events can overcome the psychological effects of a single bad one.

(p. 323)

In line with this view, Fredrickson and Losada (2005) proposed a positivity ratio − a numeric value that represents the optimal ratio of positive to negative emotions that can bring about an affective equilibrium (ratio of 3:1) and can be used as a mark of flourishing (ratio of up to 12:1). Later on, due to critique on the mathematical equation that underlies the model, they retracted the numeric values, though the principle remained (Fredrickson, 2013b).

Measuring emotions

Most of the research into emotions uses self-report questionnaires to assess emotions. As noted in Chapter 2, the Positive and Negative Affect Schedule (PANAS) (Watson et al., 1988) and Scale of Positive and Negative Experience (SPANE) (Diener et al., 2010) are two of the most highly used scales.

Fredrickson and colleagues (2003) developed the Modified Differential Emotions Scale (mDES), which offers an assessment of how much people experience 10 clusters of positive and 10 negative emotions in a defined period.

Facial electromyography (EMG) has also been used in Fredrickson's work to capture the frequency of Duchenne smiles (Johnson, Waugh, & Fredrickson, 2010).

EMOTIONAL INTELLIGENCE

In the earlier section we have seen that emotions serve a function. They are a part of a feedback system that alerts us about events in our environment. As such, it is essential that we acknowledge and attend to them, decipher and comprehend the information that they transmit and learn to manage them. The ability to recognise emotions, engage with them, manage them, act on them and utilise them is seen as a set of capacities that make up emotional intelligence.

In recent research emotional intelligence has been strongly associated with wellbeing, health, positive relationships, performance, self-regulation and resilience (Cherniss, 2010).

Defining emotional intelligence

The concept of emotional intelligence was developed by Salovey and Mayer (1990), who defined it as *"the ability to monitor one's own and others' feelings and emotions, to discriminate among them, and to use this information to guide one's thinking and action"* (p.189).

It is based on the following premises (Cherniss, 2010):

- Emotions play a central role in life.
- People vary in their capacity to recognise, comprehend, utilise, communicate and manage emotions.
- These differences influence people's performance in a variety of contexts, including relationships and work.

Spector and Johnson (2006) observed that "there is perhaps no construct in the social sciences that has produced more controversy in recent years than emotional intelligence" (p. 325). Exaggerated claims about the merit of the concept have led to a backlash of cynicism. While some supporters argued that emotional intelligence is more important than IQ for individual wellbeing, relationships and performance, the opponents argued that it is just a new umbrella term for concepts that have been around for many years. Despite the ongoing debates, several models have been developed, and highly utilized in scholarly work. These are briefly described below.

THE EMOTIONAL INTELLIGENCE ABILITY MODEL

The Ability Model was developed by Mayer, Caruso, and Salovey (1999). It considers emotional intelligence as a set of competencies or skills that are malleable and can be developed. According to Mayer and his colleagues, emotional intelligence is a distinct type of intelligence.

They therefore considered it a mental ability. The model presents four domains or "branches" through which a person can become emotionally intelligent:

- *The ability to perceive emotions:* This category involves the ability to recognise emotions in ourselves and in others, express emotions accurately and communicate needs that are associated with these feelings. It also involves the capacity to distinguish between authentic and inauthentic expression of feelings.

- *The capacity to use emotions to facilitate thinking:* Utilising emotions involves the capacity to engage with our emotions and use them to facilitate cognitive activities, such as thinking, prioritising, decision making and problem solving. It also includes the ability to produce particular emotions in order to assist cognitive functions or to motivate us to act.

- *The ability to understand emotions:* This category involves the ability to understand emotional language, and be able to label emotions, and discern how certain emotions are linked. It also requires the capacity to recognise the causes and effects of feelings, to comprehend complex emotional states (such as contradictory feelings) and understand changes in emotional states.

- *The ability to manage emotions:* Managing emotion is the fourth component of emotional intelligence. It involves being open to feelings, both positive and negative, and the capacity to observe, reflect, engage or disengage from emotional states. These skills enable us to maintain or repair mood through a variety of strategies. It also entails the capacity to manage emotion in others.

The Ability Model measures

Several questionnaires were developed to measure the construct. The most popular is the Mayer–Salovey–Caruso Emotional Intelligence Test (MSCEIT; Mayer, Salovey, Caruso, & Sitarenios, 2003), which includes 141 items.

THE COMPETENCY MODEL OF EMOTIONAL INTELLIGENCE

The Competency Model was developed on the basis of the Ability Model by Goleman (1995) and his colleagues, and has been applied mainly in the work domain, and in the context of leadership. It is considered a "mixed model" since it includes both skills and personality traits.

It consists of four key components (Goleman, 2001):

- *Emotional self-awareness:* The ability to identify and understand our own emotions.
- *Emotional self-management:* The capacity to regulate our own emotions, particularly negative, high-intensity emotions (such as anxiety or rage) and constrain impulsive reactions.
- *Social awareness:* The ability to recognise emotional states in others and respond appropriately. Empathy is a key competency in social awareness.
- *Relationship management:* The capacity to accommodate or adjust our behaviours to influence other people's emotional states; for example, to calm or comfort someone when stressed or distressed.

The four key components are manifested through 20 competencies that can be learned and developed. These are:

- *Self-awareness*: Emotional self-awareness, accurate self-assessment and self-confidence;
- *Social-awareness*: Empathy, service orientation and organisational awareness;
- *Self-management*: Self-control, trustworthiness, conscientiousness, adaptability, achievement drive and initiative;
- *Relationship management*: Developing others, influence, communication, conflict management, leadership, change catalyst, building bonds, teamwork and collaboration.

However, Goleman also suggested that the capacity to develop these competencies is determined by people's emotional intelligence, which is considered an inborn aptitude.

The Competency Model scale

The primary scale developed for this model is the Emotional Competence Inventory (ECI) (Boyatzis, Goleman, & Rhee, 2000), which includes 110 items and matches the key components of the model.

THE EMOTIONAL–SOCIAL INTELIGENCE MODEL

The Emotional–Social Intelligence Model was developed by Bar-On (2006). It focuses mainly on individuals' social ability – the traits and skills that help people interact and connect with others. Similar to Goleman, it involves social skills as well as personality traits. Bar-On's work suggests that these capacities include:

- The ability to be aware of emotions, understand emotions and to communicate emotions;
- The capacity to be aware of other people's emotional states, understand them and use this knowledge to interact with others;
- The ability to handle intense emotions and control them when necessary;
- The capacity to use emotions to adapt to change and solve problems.

The five key components in Bar-On's model are:

- Intrapersonal abilities;
- Interpersonal capacities;
- Adaptability;
- Stress management;
- Mood.

The Emotional-Socoal Intelligence scale

Bar-On's model can be measured via the Emotional Quotient Inventory (EQ-i), a self-report measure with 131 items (Bar-On, 2004).

THE TRAIT EMOTIONAL INTELLIGENCE MODEL

The most recent model of emotional intelligence was developed by Petrides and his team (2007). It is considered a "second-generation" model since it incorporates some of the qualities included in the earlier models. The model consists of four components:

- *Wellbeing*: Entailing confidence, optimism and happiness;
- *Sociability*: Encompassing social competence, assertiveness and the capacity to manage other people's emotions;
- *Self-control*: Including stress management, low impulsivity and emotion regulation;
- *Emotionality*: Entailing emotional perception of oneself and others, emotion expression and conveying empathy.

The Trait Emotional Intelligence Questionnaire

The Trait Emotional Intelligence Questionnaire (TEIQue) includes 153 items which measure this model (Petrides, 2009).

Emotional intelligence training

There are several evidence-based training courses that are geared to increase emotional intelligence. The interventions are typically group-based and entail several weekly workshops that consist of mini-lectures, group discussion, exercises, case studies and homework assignments. Some of these are offered as part of university courses, while others are offered as workplace training, in particular leadership or management courses.

The topics discussed and practised in these courses cover the core competencies of emotional intelligence, and include social skills, motivation, coping, emotional reasoning, emotion recognition and emotion regulation (Mattingly & Kraiger, 2019).

CONCLUSION

Some critics have argued that positive psychology scholarship into positive emotions tends to "pathologise negative emotions, ignore situations where feeling good is inappropriate, or tacitly endorse an unsophisticated hedonism or a Pollyanna-like disregard for life's difficulties" (Fredrickson & Cohn, 2008, p.781). It is therefore important to reiterate the significance of negative emotions for our wellbeing, particularly when facing hostile environments and when managing losses. Crucially, in order to experience a full life, it is essential to experience both the yin and yang of life, rather than attempt to ignore or eliminate negative experiences and the emotions that they trigger. From a positive psychology perspective, and in line with positive psychology 2.0 (Ivtzan, Lomas, Hefferon, & Worth, 2015), all emotions, positive and negative, are seen as key parts of our feedback system, and are therefore ordinary, useful and meaningful. More critically, positive emotions are certainly not a panacea for all of life's challenges, and we should not expect nor seek to experience positive emotion at all times and in all situations. Since the function of emotions is to signal our inner reactions to life events, psychologists recommend acknowledging the presence of particular emotions, and attending to the messages that they convey, as this enables us to be more discerning when acting on emotions. It is therefore beneficial for us to cultivate positive emotions as a groundwork for our emotional lives, while responding appropriately – at times positively or negatively – to meaningful occasions as they transpire (Fredrickson & Cohn, 2008).

OPTIMISM AND HOPE

OPTIMISM

Nearly 50 years ago a paradigm shift occurred in psychology, and the construct of optimism was at the heart of it. Until the late 1960s, decades of scholarly research into mental health, including the work of Freud (1966) and Fromm (1955), reasoned that being realistic, that is, having an accurate perception of reality, is a critical component of mental health. In line with this logic, optimism was perceived as a cognitive distortion, a type of self-deception, or a defence mechanism, that entails illusions or delusions that distort people's perception of reality and can lead them to irrational judgements and poor functioning. Optimism was thus perceived as an indicator of a mental disorder.

These perceptions of optimism began to change in the 1970s, in the light of several strands of research into optimism that contested the notion that optimism is dysfunctional. One strand of scholarly work claimed that the majority of people are optimistic, and that optimism permeates human thought (Taylor & Brown, 1988). The other strand of research claimed that optimism is useful and adaptive, and that it promotes psychological wellbeing (Seligman, 2006). Although no claim has been made to propose that optimism is a *necessary* condition for mental health, the implications of these studies were groundbreaking. This is because their findings challenged the established definitions of what constitutes mental health by indicating that realistic perceptions of oneself and the reality in which one lives cannot be deemed as the hallmark of mental health; otherwise, most people would be considered mentally ill.

The examination of what constitutes mental health, and the centrality of optimism in demarcating the boundaries between healthy and unhealthy functioning, has prompted further research into optimism. In the past five decades a sizeable body of scholarly work has been published on the topic emerging from diverse disciplines, including health psychology, education, business and neuroscience, to name a few.

To summarise this abundant research field, this chapter opens with a definition of optimism, and then presents the three leading strands of research into optimism, and examines their theoretical stance and evidence on the benefits and disadvantages of optimism.

Defining optimism

Optimism and its parallel construct pessimism are described as *expectancies* regarding *future* outcomes (Carver & Scheier, 2009). The research on optimism originated from the psychology of expectancies, and is therefore linked to the exploration of estimations and predictions, and to goal-directed behaviours, such as decision making and planning.

Optimism is defined as *a generalised expectation that good things will happen* (Carver & Scheier, 2009) or *"the overestimation of positive events and the underestimation of future negative events"* (Sharot, Korn, & Dolan, 2011, p. 1)

While these definitions do not clearly state whether optimism is a trait or a state, nor whether it is a cognitive outlook or an emotional disposition, over the years three leading lines of research have emerged which distinguish between optimism as an *attributional style* (Seligman, 2006), a *trait* (Carver & Scheier, 2009) and an *inherent human characteristic* (Sharot, Riccardi, Raio, & Phelps, 2007).

In line with these definitions, pessimism is described as a tendency to expect negative outcomes (Seligman, 2006). The commonly held perception among researchers is that optimism and pessimism occupy the opposite sides of a single axis (Seligman, 2006), and this is reflected in most of the measurement tools currently being used. However, these views have been challenged by researchers who claimed that the two concepts are independent, and that optimism is more than the absence of pessimism (Norem & Chang, 2002). It has also been argued that optimism and pessimism are not mutually exclusive, and that people can experience them at the same time (Peterson, 2000). In view of this debate and for the sake of simplicity, the following sections will focus solely on the construct of optimism.

MODELS OF OPTIMISM

There are currently three leading strands of research into optimism. These vary in their theoretical perspectives and measures, and in their analysis of the benefits and costs of optimism.

Learned optimism: optimism as an explanatory style

One of the intriguing questions in the study of optimism is: what explains its occurrence? Peterson and Seligman's (1984) work uncovered a cognitive mechanism which can explain the emergence of optimism or pessimism in people's thinking. Seligman (2006) maintained that our expectations for the future originate from our attributional or explanatory style – our understanding of the *causes* of events that occur in our lives. According to the theory, we develop (during our formative years) an attributional style, which leads us to habitually provide positive or negative causal explanations of life events. This thinking style shapes the ways in which we assign meaning and explain past events, as well as how we envision the future.

Seligman (2006) found that optimists tend to attribute the causes of *adverse* events that occur in their lives to *external, transitory* or *specific* factors. Consequently, they tend to hold positive expectations toward the future, since they believe that undesirable events are not permanent, pervasive or personal. At the same time, they tend to attribute positive events to *internal, stable* and *global* factors, and these beliefs support and maintain their optimistic expectancies. For example, an optimistic student who failed an exam will likely explain that this was as a result of noise that occurred in the exam room (external), that it was a one-off occurrence as she had done well in other exams (transient), and it will not affect other areas of her life, such as degree completion or her job prospects (specific).

In contrast, pessimists explain *negative* events by attributing their causes to *internal, stable* and *global* factors. Their beliefs that the causes of these events are permanent, pervasive or personal may lead to what Seligman termed "learned helplessness" – gloomy expectations toward the future that may trigger depression and discouragement, thus suspending action. Additionally, pessimists tend to explain successful or pleasurable experiences as the upshot of *external, transient* and *specific* factors, and hence, they do not expect these to last. For example, a pessimistic student who failed an exam will likely explain that this happened due to her lack of skill or preparation (internal), that this happens all too often (permanent), and it will affect other areas of her life, such as her capacity to gain an academic degree and later employment (pervasive).

But what is the significance of attributional style? In an extensive review on pessimism Schueller and Seligman (2011) provided evidence that pessimism is strongly correlated with depression. The author's main claim was that optimism can shield people against symptoms of helplessness and depression, thus effectively preventing mental illness.

Optimism interventions

Can pessimists become optimists? Seligman (2006) maintained that optimism is malleable, and that people can alter their attributional style and reduce pessimism. Interventions that are geared to modify explanatory style have been tested and found to improve optimism and reduce depressive symptoms in adults and children (Forgeard & Seligman, 2012).

Drawing on cognitive behavioural therapy methods, which encourage people to become aware of and challenge their own automatic negative thought patterns, Seligman and his colleagues developed and examined an optimism intervention that proved highly successful in increasing optimism, strengthening resilience and preventing depression in children and adults. The intervention can be delivered individually or in a group setting (Gillham, 2000).

Is optimism always beneficial? Peterson (2000) argued that, while it has noteworthy merits, it should not be regarded as a panacea, since it can be hazardous if it leads people to disregard risks or engage in wishful thinking instead of taking action.

Dispositional optimism: optimism as a trait

While Seligman and his colleagues argued that optimism is malleable, Scheier and Carver (1992) described dispositional optimism as a personality trait, and argued that it is fairly stable (though some changes can occur across the life span). According to Carver, Scheier, and Segerstrom (2010), optimism is 25% heritable, and is significantly influenced by childhood environment and socialisation, in particular parental socioeconomic status.

Carver and Scheier (2009) maintained that dispositional optimism is linked to expectancy-value theories and self-regulatory models, which conceptualise human behaviour as goal-directed. According to the model, goals inspire, motivate and direct our behaviours. We take action when we wish to attain a desired goal, or when we attempt to evade adverse outcomes.

There are two core factors that drive people's goal-orientated behaviours (Carver et al., 2010):

- *Expecting* to accomplish desired goals, which provokes the motivation to take action;
- Having the *confidence* that we have the capacity to accomplish our goals, which mainly draws on our past experiences.

If we have no expectation or we are doubtful regarding our capacity to achieve a particular goal, no action is likely to be taken.

Carver and his colleagues (2010) maintained that optimism and pessimism are broad versions of confidence and doubt pertaining to future expectancies. Their argument is that these *broad* expectancies function as a lens through which we perceive varied life situations, and from which *specific* expectations and confidences develop, which influence our behaviours. Their key point pertains to the ways in which optimism and pessimism shape our goal-directed behaviours: optimism promotes motivation and encourages engagement and dynamic pursuit of our goals, while pessimism dampens the motivation to act, resulting in disengagement and stagnation.

The optimism bias: optimism as an inherent human characteristic

While Carver and Scheier (2009) identified optimism as a trait, and Seligman (2006) was able to detect the mechanisms that produce optimism, several researchers argued that optimism is an *inherent human characteristic*, and claimed that the majority of people show a clear optimistic bias in their estimations of the future (Kahneman & Tversky, 1996; Sharot et al., 2011; Taylor & Brown, 1988). These scholars further claimed that positive expectancies are in fact normal, and that the only exceptions are people who are depressed or anxious.

The inclination to hold more optimistic than realistic expectancies was found across different nations, races, age groups, genders, professions and socioeconomic categories. The universality of this phenomenon has led researchers to conclude that optimism is an inborn, natural human characteristic (Sharot, 2011).

Interestingly, researchers who hold this perspective approached the study of optimism from varied disciplines and theoretical stances, and thus hold different views regarding its benefits and risks.

Positive illusions

In a groundbreaking work on positive illusions, Taylor and Brown (1988) argued that normal human thought is distinguished by a robust positive bias about the self, and thus is rarely accurate or realistic. Taylor and Brown (1994) differentiated between three types of positive illusions:

- *Inflated positive self-perceptions;*
- *Exaggerated assessments of personal control;*
- *Unrealistic optimism.*

While the first two types of illusions are often past or present-orientated, they seem to provide the groundwork from which positive future expectancies emerge. Once people believe they can control events, and that they have the necessary skills, they tend to overestimate their chances of success in attaining their goals, while underestimating their chances of failure.

Much of Taylor and Brown's (1994) work was geared towards demonstrating that optimism is common and that it promotes (rather than undermines) mental health. To explain the influence of optimism on people's lives, Taylor (1989) equated the effects of optimism to the power of placebo and self-fulfilling prophecies, suggesting that it is the optimistic expectancies themselves that generate motivation, determination to complete assignments, industrious performance and ultimately, superior achievements. Another important claim that the authors made is that optimism is adaptive in the sense that people modify their expectations when they receive feedback that their estimations are flawed.

Although Taylor (1989) claimed that optimism is normal and natural, she recognised that positive illusions are, after all, an inaccurate view of reality. She therefore warned that illusions can be taken to excess, and urged us to find our "optimal margin of illusion" (p. 238).

Heuristics and biases

A second line of research into the optimism bias emerged from Kahneman and his colleagues' seminal work into heuristics and biases and the psychology of predictions (Kahneman & Tversky, 1996). In a series of studies which focused on decision making, planning, setting goals and assessing future outcomes, particularly in organisational settings, Kahneman and his research associates found an explicit and persistent bias towards overoptimistic inferences among individuals, including directors, entrepreneurs, investors and experts, as well as in work teams and entire organisations (Kahneman, 2011).

These unrealistic expectations, which are often interlinked with an inflated sense of control, extend beyond the self. They are often demonstrated in the underestimation of monetary expenses as well as other resources, such as time, staff, proficiency or knowledge levels that are necessary for achieving organisational goals, or bringing tasks to completion. They also comprise exaggerated evaluations of revenues or achievements, and inaccuracies in assessing the risks involved. Lovallo and Kahneman (2003) therefore listed "delusional optimism" as one of the most prevalent, stubborn and costly cognitive biases that is responsible for the "planning fallacy" – an inclination to underestimate what resources are realistically needed to complete a task.

Kahneman and Tversky (1996) classified optimism as cognitive bias, one of many that they detected in their research on heuristics and biases, and argued that optimism is one of the most harmful biases, particularly when it occurs in economic behaviour. Overoptimistic estimates, they claimed, can result in disastrous outcomes, for people, companies and entire countries. These range from loss of revenue, customers, time, staff, jobs or reputation to liquidations, downfalls of businesses, collapses of stock markets, recessions and even wars and loss of lives.

Despite the grievous consequences of optimism, in later publications Kahneman (2011) concluded that the optimism bias, when kept at a sensible level, can be a positive attribute for companies. It can induce a positive organisational climate, and raise staff morale, motivation and performance, thereby increasing their chances of success. When action is needed, optimism, even if illusory, can be advantageous since it inspires perseverance in the face of challenges. Pessimism, and even realism, he argued, can undermine motivation, and lead to organisational paralysis.

Although the optimism bias is not malleable according to Kahneman (2011), it is responsive to information. However, the ways in which information is communicated can make all the difference: it has to explicitly show the prospects for profit and the associated risk, without undermining people's motivation.

The optimism bias

A third line of work into optimism as an inherent human characteristic was conducted by neuroscientist Sharot (2011), who claimed that most people seem to have optimistic expectancies. Sharot examined the areas in the brain that generate optimism, and argued that optimism is hardwired into the human brain. She reported that the neural mechanisms that engender optimism show irregularities in depressed people. She therefore cautiously concluded that, in the absence of the neural networks that generate optimism, most people might have been mildly depressed. She also found that past thinking is linked to future thinking. When people envisage the future, specific neural networks are activated, and these same areas in the brain are stimulated when people remember occurrences from their past.

Although Sharot et al. (2011) considered that the optimism bias is not malleable, they examined whether it is adaptive by examining people's reactions when they are presented with information that disconfirms their expectations. Remarkably, and in contrast to Kahneman (2011) and Taylor's (1989) findings, they found that unrealistic optimism persisted even in the face of conflicting information.

Similar to Kahneman's (2011) view, Sharot (2011) acknowledged the dangers of overoptimistic estimates, and argued that these can lead to miscalculations, from not applying sunscreen, eating junk food, smoking or not saving for retirement, to ignoring health warning signs, practising unsafe sex or making bad investments. Nevertheless, Sharot claimed that the optimistic bias also protects people from hopelessness, and notably, it keeps people moving forward. Thus, even if a future prediction is unreal, it has distinct advantages in the present.

Measures of optimism

Scheier and Carver (1985) developed the Life Orientation Test (LOT), and its revised version (LOT-R) which includes 10 items (Scheier, Carver, & Bridges, 1994). Both scales measure general optimistic/pessimistic expectancies for the future.

Explanatory style is often assessed by the Optimistic–Pessimistic Explanatory Style questionnaire (Peterson et al., 1982). The scale presents a series of 48 hypothetical future negative events, and respondents are required to consider the likely causes of these events.

Another way of assessing attributional style is through the Content Analysis of Verbal Explanations (CAVE) (Peterson, Schulman, Castellon, & Seligman, 1992). It involves analysing written or spoken material that contains explanations for negative events, and assessing the speaker's or author's explanatory style.

Defensive pessimism

Research on optimism may lead us to conclude that pessimism is maladaptive. However there is a type of pessimism that is considered constructive, and does not show similar correlations to that of pessimism with ill-being. Norem (2001), who developed the concept, labelled it "defensive pessimism".

Defensive pessimism is defined as the *capacity to think of, and plan for the worst-case scenario of a situation* (Norem, 2001). Research suggests that defensive pessimists tend to think ahead of problems that may hinder their capacity to progress with task completion or the attainment of goals, and aim to be prepared for any eventuality. As such, defensive pessimism is often manifested through extensive assessment of a situation, preparation and rehearsal (Norem & Cantor, 2005).

In contrast to optimists, defensive pessimists set unrealistically low expectations for future performance, even when they have experienced successful delivery in similar situations. This type of thinking is used to reduce the impact of potential failure.

While interventions to reduce pessimism have been shown to be successful, interventions to reduce defensive pessimism seem to be counterproductive (Norem & Chang, 2002).

HOPE

Hope is a motivational model that relates to the pursuit of goals. Snyder's (1994) hope theory contends that hope is felt when the *will* to achieve a goal is high and the *way* to achieve it is clear.

Defining hope

Hope is described as *a positive motivational state whereby a person has set a goal, is motivated to pursue it and has a plan in place to achieve it* (Snyder, Rand, & Sigmon, 2005).

Hope therefore entails two components:

- *Agency/will:* A person's motivation to pursue a desired goal;
- *Pathways/ways:* The strategies that a person has set for achieving the goal.

Hope is therefore future-orientated, and goal-focused. Additionally, hope has an element of confidence that underlies both dimensions: the confidence that we can achieve a particular goal, and that the strategies that we plan to use are effective. This element of confidence parallels that of dispositional optimism. However hope differs from optimism due to its strategic thinking, and it is therefore more realistic, concrete and practical than optimism (Snyder et al., 2005).

Hope is particularly significant when the attainability of goals is somewhat in doubt and when the goal is viewed as very important. People who exhibit hope as a trait set more difficult goals, but are also more likely to achieve them. This is not only due to their will, but also to pathways thinking that facilitate achieving goals.

Measuring hope

Snyder, Irving, and Anderson (1991) developed an eight-item Adult Hope Scale. It has four agency items, and four pathways items.

THE UPSHOTS OF OPTIMISM AND HOPE

In a review on the benefits and risks of optimism, Peterson (2000) described optimism as a "Velcro concept" since research has shown significant associations between optimism and numerous concepts including health and longevity, happiness and wellbeing, performance and achievement, coping and resilience, economic behaviours and relationships. In what follows some of this vast literature is summarised.

Health

The association between optimism and a variety of health markers has been extensively studied for nearly 50 years, with research around the globe consistently showing positive associations between optimism (dispositional optimism as well as attributional style) and a variety of health measures. The research has revealed that, compared to pessimists, optimists are generally healthier, report fewer physical complaints, make fewer doctor appointments, experience reduced severity of illness, show better adherence to medical advice, recover faster from injury or acute illness, report better adaptation to chronic medical conditions, experience less stress and show better resilience and self-care, experience fewer relapses and show higher survival rates and longevity even when experiencing life-threatening illnesses such as heart disease, stroke, cancer and AIDS (Rozanski, Bavishi, Kubzansky, & Cohen, 2019; Scheier & Carver, 2018). Similarly, high hope correlates with physical health and effective coping with illness (Snyder et al., 2005).

Research into the association between optimism and cardiovascular disease has been particularly extensive, consistently showing similar, and indeed striking, findings (DuBois et al., 2015). Optimists are less likely than pessimists to develop heart disease, and less likely to die from related causes. Among patients with heart disease, optimism is positively correlated with reduced illness symptoms (including pain), fewer subsequent adverse cardiac events, reduced likelihood of re-hospitalisation, improved health habits, faster recovery pace and better quality of life.

The differences between optimists and pessimists in their health and longevity can be explained by their healthy lifestyles and the preventative health behaviours that they utilise, as well as their coping strategies when facing health problems (Scheier & Carver, 2018). The research also suggests that optimism does not lead people to ignore or minimise threats. Instead, optimists directly tackle their health issues: they seek medical assistance when required, follow medical guidance and keep to their recovery plans. Importantly, they enjoy better social support than pessimists in times of ill-health, which benefits their recovery.

Wellbeing and performance

Researchers have evaluated the association between optimism (dispositional and explanatory style) and depression, and found that pessimism is linked with depression both in adults and in children (Gillham, Shatté, Reivich, & Seligman, 2001). On the positive side, a sizeable body of research has shown that optimism predicts happiness and wellbeing, and is associated with reduced likelihood of depression and stress (Forgeard & Seligman, 2012). Comparable findings were found on hope, which correlates with psychological wellbeing, positive emotions and meaning in life (Feldman & Snyder, 2005).

In addition to experiencing improved wellbeing and being healthier, optimists and hopeful people show better performance and productivity compared to pessimists, and therefore they are more successful in accomplishing their goals. Research has revealed that optimism and hope promote achievements in a variety of life domains, including education, work and career, finance and sports (Forgeard & Seligman, 2012; Snyder et al., 2005).

Carver et al. (2010) found that optimism is associated with healthy self-esteem, self-efficacy and confidence, planning, motivation and goal pursuit persistence. This suggests that optimistic people tend to persevere on tasks until they eventually succeed. Optimism is also linked to effective problem solving and to learning from past mistakes and failures. Similarly, hope is associated with self-esteem, self-efficacy, goal attainment and performance (Feldman & Snyder, 2005).

Does optimism motivate people to persist on goals that are unattainable? Research suggests that optimists know not only when to persevere on a goal, but also when to let go, while pessimists may persevere even when progress is poor (Forgeard & Seligman, 2012).

Optimists and pessimists also vary in how they manage adversity. Research with different populations and life challenges, ranging from everyday hassles to terminal illness, has shown that the differences between optimists and pessimists in their worldview substantially impact their coping and resilience aptitudes. Compared to pessimists, optimists show higher levels of resilience, confidence and persistence, and tend to use adaptive coping strategies that are approach-orientated, problem-focused, preventive or proactive. Optimists and pessimists also vary in their capacity to access and utilise social and economic resources during challenging times. Optimists are therefore more able to maintain higher levels of wellbeing and low levels of stress and distress in difficult times, and when appropriate, they show constructive acceptance and adjustment, while framing the situation in a positive light.

In contrast, pessimists use more maladaptive coping strategies, including avoidance, denial, resignation or escapism. Hope has also been found to be constructive in challenging times, with hopeful people showing effective coping, adjustment following adversity and capacity to sustain change (Forgeard & Seligman, 2012).

Relationships

Optimism and hope seem to be beneficial in the social domain as well. Optimists have larger social networks than pessimists, and are more socially active. They seem to invest more into their relationships, are able to handle conflict constructively, are more liked by others and report better relational satisfaction (while acknowledging that these relationships are not perfect). During challenging times, they are able to draw on their social network for support, and report receiving higher levels of support from their close ties compared to pessimists (Carver et al., 2010; Snyder et al., 2005).

CONCLUSION

This chapter opened with the recognition that optimism is one of the most fundamental concepts in psychology, which has been used to draw the boundaries between normal and abnormal psychological patterns. In an attempt to map nearly 50 years of research into the concept, this chapter centred on the three leading strands of research: learned optimism – optimism as an attributional style (Seligman, 2006), dispositional optimism – optimism as a trait (Carver & Scheier, 2009), and the optimism bias – optimism as an inherent human characteristic (Sharot et al., 2007). The chapter also reviewed the concept of hope.

As can be seen from the review, with few exceptions, much of the scholarly work around optimism and hope highlights their many psychological benefits, though the literature also acknowledges some of their dangers. Despite the usual methodological difficulties in showing causality, and the theoretical complexity of the concepts, the strengths of optimism and hope as self-induced placebos were clearly noted. Their capacity to stimulate, motivate and propel people to take action *in the present* seems to be conducive to our health and wellbeing and therefore much more important than the accuracy or realism of our expectancies. However, as Taylor (1989) noted, balance is crucial, since optimism can be taken to extreme to the point that it becomes delusional and harmful. This suggests that we need to find our own optimal level of optimism. In this sense, perhaps optimism may be equated to red wine: while one glass per day may be healthy and helpful, a whole bottle may not be as productive.

6

GOAL PURSUIT AND CHANGE

GOAL PURSUIT

All of us have goals that we are aiming to achieve: find a job, complete a degree course, lose weight, keep to an exercise routine, complete an assignment by the deadline or improve our relationship with someone. Whether these are high- or low-priority goals, one-off or ongoing, intrinsic or extrinsic, goal pursuit consumes much of our time, effort and energy. They also significantly affect our wellbeing, happiness and performance.

The concept of life-goals and goal setting predates the establishment of positive psychology, and has been studied across several disciplines, including health and sport psychology, education and behavioural economics. It is also a core topic in coaching psychology, and incorporated today in several therapeutic modalities (Milyavskaya & Werner, 2018).

Much of the research on goals attempts to address pertinent eudaimonic questions, particularly relating to optimal functioning. Why are some people more successful than others in making their dreams a reality? Why do we succeed in achieving some goals, but fail to achieve others? How do the goals that we set and pursue affect our performance, wellbeing and happiness? And importantly, how can we set goals in a way that will increase our capacity to achieve what we want, and promote our wellbeing and performance?

This chapter offers a brief review of goals theories, focusing on the association between goals and wellbeing, how goals promote performance and the process of goal pursuit. The chapter closes by exploring the key characteristics of goals that can influence how we pursue them, and the likelihood of attaining them.

Defining goals

"A goal is an object or aim that an individual strives to attain" (Latham, Ganegoda, & Locke, 2011, p. 579). Goals are therefore future-oriented images of a desired state that people wish to pursue.

GOALS AND WELLBEING

According to Self-Determination Theory (Ryan & Deci, 2017), goals are expressions of our primary psychological needs. That is, goal pursuit is a key mechanism through which we can satisfy our fundamental needs. Self-Determination Theory suggests that there are three universal psychological human needs: the need for competence, relatedness and autonomy. All needs are vital for wellbeing and healthy functioning, and therefore when needs are not met, the theory predicts significant psychological costs and psychopathology. Self-Determination Theory therefore contends that goals promote wellbeing by facilitating need satisfaction.

Another way in which goals and wellbeing are associated is through the ways in which people evaluate their lives. Many people evaluate their lives by assessing how successful they are in realising their goals. This evaluation is often expressed in their satisfaction with life (Locke & Latham, 2013). However, Ben-Shahar (2009) argued that the process of working to achieve a goal is as important as attaining the goal for our wellbeing. Goals endow our lives with a sense of purpose and meaning. Hence by working towards a desired goal, our wellbeing and happiness are elevated, since we often engage (as part of our goal pursuit) in activities that we consider meaningful and valuable. Goal pursuit can therefore be seen as a mechanism that elevates wellbeing both by enabling us to embark on a purposeful and meaningful journey to our destination, as well as through the accomplishment of our goals.

The most direct link between goals and wellbeing is manifested in the models of wellbeing (reviewed in Chapter 3), some of which incorporate goal pursuit as a vital component of wellbeing. For example, in Ryff's (2014) Psychological Wellbeing Model, goals and their resulting sense of purpose are among the components of wellbeing, and in the PERMA model of wellbeing (Seligman, 2011) the "achievement" component points to the importance of goal pursuit. This suggests that goals are a key component of wellbeing, one that can facilitate both its hedonic and eudemonic aspects.

GOALS AND ACHIEVEMENTS

Control theory suggests that, once we set a goal and make a commitment to pursue it, a self-regulation process is activated, to enable us to carry out the tasks that are required in order to achieve the goal. For example, when a prospective student sets a goal to embark on a university course, this will likely prompt several actions such as a search for relevant information, which will then be followed by a decision as to which courses and universities to apply to, and then completing the application procedure. Carver and Scheier (2001) viewed this process as a "discrepancy-reducing feedback loop". They argued that, when we compare our current state to the desired state, a gap is often detected. This triggers a motivation to close the gap, which in turn activates goal-promoting behaviours.

Ryan and Deci (2017) argued that goals have the power to inspire persistent action, because they prompt us to assess and address our needs, offering us an opportunity to evaluate our lives and our values. When we set goals, a chain of psychological reactions occurs, such as changes in our sense of direction and purpose, motivation, enthusiasm, creativity, optimism and hope, autonomy and self-efficacy. These psychological reactions empower us to take action and pursue our goals, which can be detected though a rise in our energy, attention and self-regulation, capacity to exert effort and perform, and the ability to persist in the face of obstacles. Importantly, goal pursuit often leads to personal growth. This is because some of the goals that we set may require us to acquire new knowledge or develop new skills, find new resources or explore new options, resulting in self-expansion.

Drawing on nearly 50 years of research into goals, researchers have asserted that setting goals leads to increased performance, directly influencing the chances of success in goal attainment (Locke & Latham, 2013).

On the deficit side, research suggests that in the absence of goals we "would not have any energy to encourage action or sustain motivation" (Milyavskaya & Werner, 2018, p. 167). When people do not set goals, they tend to drift along, taking life as it comes. The result of this mindset is that they may not be able to satisfy their needs, as they may follow goals that other people or organisations set for them, or invest time and effort into tasks or actions that are inconsequential or detrimental in the long run.

Goal-setting interventions

Research on goal-setting interventions spanning nearly five decades has shown that setting goals is one of the most effective wellbeing and happiness-enhancing activities. The exercise usually involves a careful consideration of what we wish to achieve in the near or far future, and is often accompanied by a plan as to how best to pursue the identified goals, and prioritise between them.

The interventions can be conducted periodically, and can pertain to a particular life domain (such as career, health, financial state or relationships), or require us to consider goals in all key life domains simultaneously. They can be conducted individually, with the help of a coach or therapist, or in a group setting.

GOAL PURSUIT

The Rubicon Model of Action Phases (Gollwitzer, 1990) proposes that goal pursuit progresses through four phases (which are not always linear):

- *The pre-decision stage*: This is when we consider options and evaluate our desires.
- *The pre-action phase*: Once we form an intention to pursue a particular goal, we "cross the Rubicon" into the pre-action stage. This is when we make a decision to pursue a goal, and then plan how, when and where we will pursue the goal.
- *The action stage*: This is when we begin to act on our plans, and undertake activities that are geared to achieve our desired objective.

- *The post-action phase*: The action phase leads to an outcome in the form of progress made, realisation of the goal or failure to achieve it or to progress. This prompts a post-action re-evaluation of the goal, or the actions taken, or both, often leading to changes in or abandonment of the goal being pursued, or altering the actions taken.

Scholars have identified several crucial points pertaining to the process of goal pursuit which can shape how we travel to our destinations, and can facilitate or hamper goal attainment. These are briefly detailed below.

- *Making decisions*: We pursue a goal when it has some value for us and therefore is desirable, when we feel that the goal is achievable, and we have a positive expectation to attain it. The varied combination of high/low value and high/low expectancy is defined as "expected utility". Goals that are perceived as having high expected utility are the ones most often pursued (Locke & Latham, 2013).
- *The content of the goal* (what we choose to pursue) is shaped by our needs, upbringing, personality traits (particularly self-esteem, locus of control, emotional stability and self-efficacy), social environment, values, beliefs and culture (Milyavskaya & Werner, 2018).
- *Setting goals for ourselves and for others*: We can set goals for ourselves by ourselves, but at times goals can be set for us by others, or we can set goals for others. For example at work, in education or in sports, goals are often assigned by others (a manager, parent, coach, exam boards). However, researchers suggest that such goals need to be internalised in order for them to be effectively pursued (Ryan & Deci, 2017).
- *Motivation*: What motivates people to pursue particular goals or courses of action? According to self-determination theory there are two types of motivations:
  - *Extrinsic motivation* is often invoked when we are driven to take action by external factors (such as a salary, a prize or people's opinions);
  - *Intrinsic motivation* on the other hand occurs when we are motivated from within, by our own interests, passions, talents and values.

Decades of research into motivation has shown that intrinsic motivation is associated with higher levels of wellbeing, performance and perseverance compared to extrinsic motivation (Ryan & Deci, 2017).

- *Committing to goals*: Latham et al. (2011) argued that commitment is a key to pursuing and attaining goals, and it is particularly important when goals are difficult. Two factors shape our commitment to a goal: the importance of the outcome that we expect, and our self-efficacy – the belief that we can achieve it. One way to increase commitment is to make a public commitment to the goal. Another way is through offering incentives.

Does money increase goal commitment?

In the work domain money is often used as an incentive, but does money increase commitment? Research suggests that it does, but only in some cases. Higher payment can stimulate higher commitment, but mainly in pursuing relatively simple goals. When the goal is difficult or highly complex, skill levels matter, and these cannot be increased through monetary rewards, and hence the increase in effort may not produce the desired results. Additionally, with challenging, long-term goals, rewarding employees only when they reach the goal can undermine their commitment. Alternatively, rewarding employees for performance can increase their commitment to difficult goals. This suggests that matching people's capacities with the level of challenge that their goals present is important for generating commitment, and can determine which type of incentives would be most effective (Aguinis, Joo, & Gottfredson, 2013).

- *Pursuing multiple goals*: Most people pursue several goals at the same time. However, the art of navigating through and acting on several goals simultaneously often requires a delicate balancing act. Researchers considered that short-term goals can be set as a means of facilitating the attainment of larger and more complex goals. Large goals (such as "train to become a medical doctor") can be broken down into smaller sub-goals ("apply to a medical course in a particular university") or steps that are needed to achieve this end goal. These tend to be more concrete than the end goals. Research has shown that focusing on concrete, small goals is highly effective for goal pursuit (Milyavskaya & Werner, 2018).

However, at times, short-term goals can be in conflict with other goals, and can interfere or distract us from pursuing our key goals by competing for our time and other resources. Researchers have found that, when conflict between goals occurs, people are less likely to act on one or both goals, resulting in lower wellbeing.

- *Resisting temptations*: How can we shield ourselves from tempting desires (such as eating a high-calorie snack while dieting) that undermine our goals? A desire is defined as an emotionally charged motivation toward a particular item, activity or person that can bring about short-term pleasure or a relief from pain (Hofmann & Van Dillen, 2012). When a desire clashes with a goal, it is seen as a temptation that can derail our efforts to remain on course. To resist temptations, we often apply conscious and effortful self-control and evaluate the value and cost of indulging. The outcome of this assessment is enacted by either indulging in or resisting temptation.

Gollwitzer and Sheeran (2006) suggested that one way to stay on course in the face of temptations or distractions is to articulate implementation intentions.

- *Implementation intentions*: These are specific if-then plans that can help us consider in advance what might hinder progression, and put a plan in place to circumvent it (for example, for a person following a diet: "If I crave chocolate, I will eat fruit instead"). Once we have in place such pre-determined responses to potential situations, it is easier to act on them. Research has consistently reported that implementation intentions significantly facilitate goal attainment (Gollwitzer & Sheeran, 2006).

- *Assessing progress, completion, modification or abandonment of goals*: An important aspect of goal pursuit is to monitor and assess progress in each of our goals. This in turn generates feedback. When we recognise that we are on course, we are likely to maintain or increase effort, though, at times, this can cause us to reduce effort temporarily. An evaluation that we are not progressing well may lead to increased effort, or to a modification of the goal or the means to pursue it. At times, however, this may lead to "action crisis" – an internal conflict between goal persistence and detachment. If the goal is no longer desirable, viable or achievable, we may abandon it altogether. This is considered an adaptive response, particularly when the goal is unattainable. A continued attempt to pursue it has been linked with depression (Milyavskaya & Werner, 2018).

There are two ways to assess progress: we can evaluate where we are compared to the desired end goal (for example, note the reduction of weight already achieved against the desired weight), or monitor the behaviours that are relevant to the goal (for example, if the goal is to lose weight, avoiding snacks may be monitored as a behaviour that promotes the goal). Research suggests that monitoring progress is more strongly associated with goal attainment than monitoring behaviours (Harkin et al., 2016).

Making satisfactory progress on our goals is associated with improved need satisfaction, wellbeing and happiness, while not making acceptable progress can undermine these and induce anxiety or stress (Milyavskaya & Werner, 2018).

- *Challenges in goal pursuit*: Gollwitzer and Sheeran (2006) found that there are common challenges that hamper people's capacity to achieve their goals. These are:
  - *Failing to start;*
  - *Derailment;*
  - *Overexerting oneself;*
  - *Not disengaging from a goal that is unproductive.*
- *Social support*: Goal pursuit is often perceived as an individual endeavour, yet other people's involvement and support (or lack of) can significantly influence our capacity to act on our goals and achieve them.

Researchers have noted that, while all types of responsive support can benefit goal pursuit, *autonomy support* is particularly beneficial. This is a response that is constructive and reassuring, yet refrains from applying pressure or control. *Directive support*, on the other hand, is less beneficial and can even weaken goal pursuit. This is a response that is encouraging, but also offers direct guidance, advice or solutions (Koestner, Powers, Carbonneau, Milyavskaya, & Chua, 2012). Another line of research makes a distinction between visible and invisible support and found that invisible support is more beneficial than visible support for goal progress (Girme, Overall, & Simpson, 2013).

Measuring goals

The Goal Commitment scale (Hollenbeck, Klein, O'Leary, & Wright, 1989) measures users' commitment to a particular goal that he or she wishes to achieve. The questionnaire has nine items which target a specific goal.

The Achievement Goal Questionnaire – Revised (Elliot & Murayama, 2008) consists of 12 items representing different goal orientation: mastery-approach, mastery-avoidance, performance-approach and performance-avoidance.

GOAL CHARACTERISTICS

Scholars have identified numerous characteristics of goals and noted that goals are not created equal. The contents of goals, how we set them and how we pursue our goals matter. "Wanting and attaining some goals will satisfy basic psychological needs and, in turn, foster wellness and learning, whereas wanting and attaining other goals may leave people devoid of basic needs satisfactions and sometimes even less well" (Ryan & Deci, 2017, p. 272). Below several key characteristics of goals are reviewed, noting some of their known consequences as documented in the extent research.

- *Abstract and concrete goals*: Abstract goals are broad and general (for example, be more assertive). They involve taking action across several contexts, and do not have a distinct criterion or end point that signals that the goal has been achieved. Concrete goals on the other hand are specific (for example, complete a BSc in psychology). The desired outcome and the criteria to assess success are clearly defined, the actions that people need to take are known, and they often have a specific timeframe. Research suggests that concrete goals are more likely to be achieved than abstract goals (Locke & Latham, 2013).
- *The SMART model* (Doran, 1981) is a tool often used in coaching to set goals. It ensures that the goal being set is clearly defined and specified. It offers five specifications that together make a well-defined goal. According to the model, our goals should be:
  - *Specific;*
  - *Measurable;*

- *Attainable;*
- *Realistic;*
- *Timely.*
- *Easy and difficult goals*: Goal-setting theory (Locke & Latham, 2013) posits that goal difficulty can determine performance, since people tend to exert more effort and improve performance when they are pursuing difficult, yet attainable, goals. However, interestingly, setting goals has a stronger and more positive impact on the completion of tasks that are simple rather than complex.
- *Approach and avoidance goals*: An important characteristic of goals is whether we aim to attain a positive, desirable outcome (approach goal), or to avoid a negative, undesirable outcome (avoidance goal). For example, a person can set a goal to avoid unhealthy food or to adopt healthy eating habits. A large body of research has shown that people are more likely to attain approach goals, which in turn increase performance, wellbeing and happiness, compared to avoidance goals which are associated with psychological distress (particularly anxiety) (Elliot, 2006).
- *Autonomous and controlled goals*: Autonomous goals (also termed "self-concordant") are goals that we pursue because we want to: they are aligned with our values and reflect our interests and desires (Sheldon & Elliot, 1999). Controlled goals, on the other hand, are goals that we pursue because we feel that we have to. Often they are not aligned with our values or interests and are driven by an external factor, for example, wanting to please others, to avoid conflict or to keep our job (Milyavskaya & Werner, 2018).

  Although most people set and pursue controlled goals to some degree, because these goals do not reflect what people truly want, people often show lower motivation in pursuing them, which detracts from attaining them. Research that examined this point substantiates the idea that autonomous goals are more likely to be attained and contribute to our wellbeing, meaning in life and happiness. However, the research findings around controlled goals is less clear. Some studies show that controlled motivation can negatively impact goal attainment and wellbeing, while others show no effect (Milyavskaya & Werner, 2018).
- *Intrinsic and extrinsic goals*: Self-determination theory (Ryan & Deci, 2017) defines intrinsic goals as goals that are directly

associated with the pursuit of what is inherently valued, such as close relationships, personal development or contributing to others. Extrinsic goals, in contrast, are those focused on instrumental outcomes, such as attractiveness, fame, money or power. Goals can therefore be placed on an axis from intrinsic to extrinsic. Intrinsic goals are more likely to be autonomous, while extrinsic goals are often controlled.

Research has consistently shown that prioritising, pursuing and attaining intrinsic goals tends to satisfy our basic psychological needs, and is strongly associated with increased wellbeing and happiness, better health and vitality, self-actualisation and spirituality, positive social relationships and social functioning (including care, empathy and respect for others), higher academic success and less greed.

In contrast, focusing and acting on extrinsic goals, and even realising them, often does not satisfy basic needs, and hence does not contribute to our wellbeing and happiness, and can at times undermine wellness. It is also associated with poorer health and lower vitality, psychological distress (depression and anxiety), use of alcohol and drugs, and with high-risk behaviours.

In the relationship domain, extrinsic goals are associated with lower quality of relationships: instrumental relationships, more conflicts, manipulation, prejudice and social dominance, and less trust, caring and empathy. It is also associated with poorer academic outcomes and lower self-actualisation. Researchers have suggested that people whose basic psychological needs are not fully met may turn to extrinsic goals as substitutes.

Finally, people can change their goals over time. People who became more intrinsically motivated have shown an increase in their wellbeing, while those whose goals became more extrinsically motivated over time showed decreased wellbeing (Ryan & Deci, 2017).

Wealth and materialistic goals

Financial goals and materialistic aspirations are associated with extrinsic motivation and research has found that these are linked with poor satisfaction of basic needs, lower wellbeing, negative self-appraisal, loneliness and risky behaviours. Additionally, once basic needs are met, income and possessions seem to have small impact on wellbeing (Ryan & Deci, 2017).

However, Landry et al. (2016) suggested that financial goals are not always extrinsic. If money is used to fund intrinsic goals, it can increase wellbeing. For example, when wealth goals are pursued as a means to support family members, gain stability and security or to contribute to others, they predict wellbeing and needs satisfaction, while setting financial goals for the purpose or gaining power or status predict ill-being and needs frustration.

INITIATING CHANGE

Many goals that we set require us to initiate changes in our lives or in our behaviours. For example, we may wish to marry, become a parent, embark on a professional course, change jobs or careers or relocate to another city or country. These types of goals require us to undergo significant changes in our lifestyle. Other types of goals, such as lose weight, change our exercise regime, quit smoking, reduce financial overspending, learn a new skill, control our temper or be more asser-tive, require us to undertake behavioural changes. However there is mounting literature which suggests that embarking on changes whether in lifestyle or behaviours can be challenging, even when the change is self-initiated (Bridges, 2004).

Why are changes challenging even when self-induced, positive and highly desired? This is because changes interrupt our habits and rou-tines, and at times present challenges to the status quo. This in turn disturbs the peace, order, security and stability that we created in our lives, as we may need to re-think our goals, schedules, routines and habits, and re-prioritise. Additionally, when we embark on a change we often face uncertainty and the unknown, or lack of control, which can be anxiety provoking. Many changes require us to acquire new knowledge and skills. We may lack competence at the start, which can shake our confidence. Steep learning curves are also taxing. They can be time consuming, effortful, cognitively demanding or emotionally draining. Most changes also require us to adapt a new situation or circumstances. The adaptation can be physical, cognitive, behavioural or psychological and hence can be highly demanding. Furthermore, one of the expectations that people have is that a self-initiated change should be controllable. However, this is rarely the case. All changes, whether initiated or forced on us, have parts that are in our control and parts that are out of our control (Bridges, 2004).

The most profound changes we can initiate are those that affect our identities (for example, getting married, becoming a parent, acquiring professional qualifications or relocating internationally). This is because we have an innate need to maintain the integrity of the self over time. Identity is the sense of who we are, while self-integrity is a sense of general efficacy. Events that challenge or threaten our identity and self-integrity can induce stress and self-protective behaviours that hamper the motivation to change and grow (Sherman & Cohen, 2006).

Being aware of these challenges that often occur when we embark on a change and understanding the need to work against internal resistance at times can help us stay on course to achieve our goals.

There are several stage–based models that describe transitions. Two are described below: Bridges' (2004) Transitions Model and Prochaska, Redding, and Evers' (2015) Transtheoretical Model.

THE TRANSITIONS MODEL

Bridges' (2004) model refers to the stages of change that people experience in response to a self-initiated change or to an external change that is forced on them. According to the model, people often experience three distinct stages of change.

- *Phase 1: Ending*: All changes begin with the awareness that a period or a situation is coming to an end. This stage often triggers a strong emotional reaction as people may experience a sense of loss, stress, sadness or anxiety and become emotionally oversensitive. Some people undergo a grief process which involves several stages: denial, anger, bargaining, fear, depression and acceptance (Kubler-Ross & Kessler, 2014).
- *Phase 2: The neutral zone*: This is an in-between (often short) phase between the old and the new. The old life structures have been interrupted by the change, and new structures are not in place yet. During this phase people experience uncertainty, confusion, disorientation, lack of control and anxiety. People may wonder how they fit in and what they need to do.

- *Phase 3: New beginning*: In this phase a learning and adjustment process takes place, where new skills, systems or habits are learned. Most people begin this phase with reduced competence which hampers their performance and can lead to errors, resulting in reduced self-efficacy and confidence. After a while, people will likely master the new skill or system, hence restoring confidence and self-efficacy. Excitement, creativity, innovation and sense of renewal are common, and these are often followed by acceptance, adaptation and realignment.

Bridges' (2004) model suggests that change is a normal part of life, but all changes, even positive changes that are highly desired, can be disruptive, and hence psychologically taxing. Understanding the three phases and being able to anticipate and prepare for them can help us maintain our wellbeing and psychological balance during difficult times.

THE TRANSTHEORETICAL MODEL

Prochaska and DiClemente's (1992) model refers to self-initiated behavioural changes, such as introducing dietary changes, quitting smoking, modifying an exercise routine or study habits. The model describes the typical process that people undergo when initiating such changes. The model emerged from research into health behaviours, particularly around overcoming substance abuse (alcohol, smoking and drug use). According to Prochaska et al. (2015), behavioural changes often unfold through the following stages:

- *Pre-Contemplation*: The first phase of change, importantly acknowledged by the model, is when people are not fully aware of the need to change, and therefore have no intention to initiate a change or to take action. They may have information about their condition but choose to ignore it. For example, a smoker is likely to be aware of the risks of smoking but does not intend to quit at this point.
- *Contemplation*: At this stage people become aware that there is a need to change (often in order to address a problem), and therefore consider taking appropriate action. Hence they may acquire information, consult others and consider different means or

pathways to create the desired behavioural change. A smoker may acquire more information on the risks of smoking and on the means that are available to help him quit at this stage, but does not act on this information. Ambivalence about changing is highly common, since the thought of giving up an enjoyed behaviour is accompanied by a sense of loss, despite the gains that people understand that await down the line. At this stage, no decision or commitment to take action is made, and therefore some people find themselves in a state of "chronic contemplation" and unable to proceed to the next phase.

- *Preparation*: During the preparation stage, people make a decision to initiate a change. They are now aware of the costs and benefits of the change, and make an action plan, as well as prepare to take specific action steps. They may also experiment with small changes as their determination to change increases. A smoker may make a decision to quit, make a detailed plan how to quit, see his doctor for consultation, purchase the necessary aids, join a support group or put implementation intentions in place in case craving occurs.
- *Action*: The fourth stage is where people begin to take action, and modify their behaviour in accordance with their plan. Action may involve one step, or a series of steps. This is when the smoker puts his plan into action: he may throw away unused packs of cigarettes, use the aids as prescribed, attend his support group regularly and apply self-discipline to stay on track.
- *Maintenance*: In this phase, notably the longest, people are actively working to maintain the new behaviour, as well as take action to prevent a relapse to the previous behaviour. A smoker may at this point need to handle temptation or craving.
- *Termination*: At this stage the new behaviour has become habituated and normative, and hence there is less chance of relapse. A smoker now perceives himself as past-smoker, and has no desire to smoke.

Significant evidence indicates that behavioural changes indeed occurs in stages. However the movement through these stages is not linear, but cyclical. The cyclical process entails both progress from one stage to the next, and periodic relapses. The model therefore suggests that, even when the change is successful, people will likely move back and forth between the stages, experiencing one or more periods of regression to the earlier stages, and moving through the stages several times, until they reach the termination stage. Understanding the phases of change and being able to anticipate our progress and prepare for regressions can help us start our journey with more realistic expectations, and persevere to attain our valued goals.

CONCLUSION

Overall, there is vast literature on goal setting and pursuit stemming from nearly 50 years of research. The review offered here focused on personal goals, and explored how goals promote wellbeing and functioning. It also offered key points to consider when setting goals, as to what can facilitate goal accomplishment or the implementation of a change.

The key message is that goals are a crucial means of advancing our achievements and successes in life, and can promote our wellbeing and happiness. However, the choices that we make regarding goal content, and how we choose to set and pursue our goals, matter greatly. Research suggests that intrinsic and autonomous goals are more beneficial to our functioning and wellbeing than extrinsic and controlled goals. It also recommends that we clarify our goals, have a mixture of challenging and easy-to-reach goals, frame our goals as approach-orientated, ensure that our goals align with each other, create implementation intentions and be ready to handle regressions when inducing changes. Finally, research indicates that assessing progress and learning when to disengage are also vital to our wellbeing.

SELF-REGULATION AND GRIT

SELF-REGULATION

Have you ever "lost it" and did something that you regretted? Maybe you lashed out at someone, ate food that does not fit with your dietary requirement, drank too much at a party, overspent when shopping, procrastinated on your studies, overshared information or practised unsafe sex? Unfortunately such events are all too common. According to the Strength Model developed by Baumeister and his colleagues, the main cause of these situations is failure in self-control (Baumeister & Vohs, 2016).

When we apply self-control, it enables us to adjust our behaviours in order to pursue our goals or plans, address our needs, adhere to rules or norms and perform in accordance with our standards. It is therefore considered a crucial component of optimal functioning and an essential key to most of our achievements in life. However, when it fails, many predicaments and indeed misfortunes can occur.

In this chapter, the psychology of self-regulation is reviewed, highlighting the importance of self-regulation for wellbeing and optimal functioning, how it operates, why it fails, the consequences of its failure and how we can strengthen it.

Defining self-control

The term self-control is often used in the literature interchangeably with self-regulation. Self-regulation is a central component of the executive function, which is the part of the self that is responsible for our actions.

Baumeister and Vohs (2016) defined *self-regulation* as the *"processes by which the self intentionally alters its own responses, including thoughts, emotions, impulses, performance, and behaviors, based on standards"* (p. 70).

Self-regulation often occurs through overriding a particular behaviour and substituting it with a preferred behaviour. For example, when a dieter has an urge to consume a high-calorie snack, but instead adheres to her meal plan, she controls her impulses. Self-regulation therefore involves making choices between behavioural options.

Self-regulation can manifest in different forms, including impulse control, the delay of gratification, controlling thoughts and emotions, behavioural control, performance regulation, making decisions and choices, and habit forming or breaking.

THE STRENGTH MODEL

The Strength Model includes several components:

- *Standards*: These are "ideas about how something should or should not be. They include goals, norms, values, morals, laws, expectations, and comparable responses by others or by oneself in the past" (Baumeister & Vohs, 2016, p. 70). In this model they serve as behavioural benchmarks that we wish to meet. The clearer the standards are, the more effective they are in promoting self–regulation.
- *Monitoring*: Self-regulation requires self-monitoring which occurs at different points along the process. Firstly we compare a particular behaviour to the standard that we have in mind. For example, when we bite our tongue to avoid responding angrily to provocation, we self-monitor not only our initial angry reaction but also the tempered response, and we may continue to monitor our responses until the exchange ends.
- *Self-regulatory strength (willpower)*: The act of regulating the self requires the use of psychological or physiological resources which are limited: "Acts of self-control tax one's strength or deplete one's resources, and that afterward there is a period of reduced capacity for further self-regulation. Self-regulation is thus costly in the short run and subject to fluctuations in capacity" (Baumeister & Vohs, 2016, p. 71). The state of reduced resources has been termed

"ego depletion". The model equates willpower to a muscle which becomes tired after use, and hence may fail in performing up to standard in subsequent tasks.

- *Motivation*: The motivation to regulate the self in order pursue a goal or adhere to a standard is central in this model. For example, without the motivation to change our exercise regime, even if all other components are in place, we will likely fail to change our physical activity patterns, since the goal is not important enough.

Measuring self-regulation

The Self-Control Questionnaire (Tangney, Baumeister, & Boone, 2004) includes 36 items and covers five types of functions: control over thoughts, emotional control, impulse control, performance regulation and habit breaking.

SELF-REGULATION FAILURE

Much of the recent research on self-regulation revolved around the attempt to explore the all-too-common declines or failures in willpower in an attempt to examine how, when and why self-regulation fails. Although there is some debate around the reasons for the declines that we experience in our capacity to exert self-control (see Friese, Loschelder, Gieseler, Frankenbach, & Inzlicht, 2019) there is less debate around the fact that self-control fails at times, as we have all experienced it at times.

The key idea behind the Strength Model is that when we engage in a task that requires self-control, some of our willpower reservoir is used, resulting in temporarily reduced capacity to self-regulate in the next task. For example, a dieter who engages in a conflict and exerts self-control to ensure the conflict is handled in a civil manner may find it difficult later on to resist eating food that does not meet her dietary requirements.

This type of decline in self-regulation and performance was evidenced in multiple studies across a variety of domains and functions (Baumeister & Vohs, 2016). In several of these studies participants performed two unrelated tasks, both requiring self-control, one after another. The tasks included physical, emotional or cognitive challenges such as holding one's arm in ice water, inhibiting thoughts or emotions, persevering on boring tasks or typing under various constraints. In other studies participants were asked to make decisions or choose among options.

These studies repeatedly found that decision making, taking action, performing and persisting on the second task were poorer. These outcomes were not only evident in performance tasks. Several studies have shown that depletion is associated with violations of instructions, behavioural norms or ethical guidelines, reduced intellectual reasoning, diminished capacity to make choices and decisions, experiencing more disturbing thoughts and performance anxiety, aggression, prejudice, sexual misbehaviour, unhealthy eating, breaking diets, overconsumption of alcohol, impulsive shopping and laziness (Baumeister & Vohs, 2016).

On cookies and radishes

In one of the most well-known studies that provided evidence on ego depletion Baumeister, Bratslavsky, Muraven, and Tice (1998) tested the effect of resisting temptation on subsequent performance.

The researchers invited 67 students to skip a meal before the experiment, and then invited them into a room where they were baking cookies. The students were sat down around a table that had two plates: one with freshly baked cookies and the other with raw radishes. Half of the students were invited to eat the cookies, while the other students were invited to eat the radishes. The researchers then left the room.

Although the radish group clearly struggled with the temptation, they did not give in. Then all students were taken to another room to work on a geometry puzzle. The purpose of the test was to assess how long the students would persist on the unsolvable puzzle before giving up.

The findings showed that the cookie eaters worked on the puzzle for 20 minutes on average, while the radish eaters gave up after 8 minutes on average. The researchers argued that the radish group experienced ego depletion by resisting the cookies, hence they performed poorly in the puzzle task.

REPLENISHING RESOURCES FOLLOWING DEPLETION

There are several ways to replenish self-regulation strengths following usage. Sleep, rest and meditation seem to be the most effective means to replenish willpower, which can explain why self-control seems to be more effective in the morning (after a good night's sleep), why it weakens later in the day and why sleep deprivation results in reduced self-regulation. Positive emotions and self-affirming one's goals, values or standards have also been found as a means to help restore willpower (Baumeister & Vohs, 2016).

Self-regulation interventions

Ample experimental research has shown that self-regulation capacities can improve with exercises that require consistent applications of self-control, similar to the ways in which a muscle can be strengthened with regular physical activity (Baumeister & Vohs, 2016).

These exercises vary vastly and may include improving body posture, making changes to study habits, practising financial self-restraint, resisting sweets, applying verbal control, using a non-dominant hand, participating in a fitness programme and many others. Most of these require practising for a few weeks.

Research on these interventions has shown significant improvements in self-regulation capacity and reduced depletion (Baumeister, Schmeichel, & Vohs, 2007). There is also evidence to suggest that mindfulness training and practice can improve self-regulation (Hart, Ivtzan, & Hart, 2013).

THE CONSEQUENCES OF SELF-REGULATION

The benefits of self-control to our wellbeing and performance, as well as its upshot when it fails, have been well documented in hundreds of studies, which are briefly reviewed below.

Performance

The capacity for self-regulation is critical to performance since it enables us to behave diligently: progress with tasks and bring them to completion, meet deadlines and remain on track even when distractions occur. Self-regulation therefore directly affects how we perform and the degree to which we succeed in completing a variety of tasks at home and work or in education. Research on self-regulation among students across a variety of age groups and domains has shown that students who show superior self-control completed their assignments and courses with higher marks compared to those with reduced self-regulation capacities. Poor self-regulation was found to be associated with underachievement in education and at work (Tangney et al., 2004).

Another domain that is positively related to self-control is money management. Romal and Kaplan (1995) found that people with high self-control showed better capacity to manage their spending, and showed reduced impulsive purchases, lower debt and more savings (Tangney et al., 2004).

The marshmellow experiment

In a celebrated longitudinal study, Mischel, Shoda, and Rodriguez (1989) and Mischel et al. (2010) explored self-control in children (age 4) with the "marshmallow test". The researchers then followed the participants twice: when they completed secondary school, and when they were in their 40s. The aim of these studies was to assess whether differences in self-control in childhood can predict differences in performance later in life.

In the original study the researchers placed a plate with one marshmallow in front of the participants and explained that the researcher had to leave the room for a few minutes. Then they told the children that if they waited until the researcher returned, they could have two marshmallows, but if they couldn't wait, they could ring a bell and the researcher would return, but then they would only be allowed one marshmallow. As can be expected children varied in their capacity to delay gratification.

About a decade later when the researchers revisited the marshmallow test participants, they found that teenagers who had waited longer in the earlier experiment had higher marks in their final exams. Additionally, their parents rated them as more conscientious, diligent and resilient.

In the last study the participants' willpower was tested again. Remarkably, adults who were less successful in delaying gratification at the age of 4 performed poorly on the self-control task decades later. They also had lower educational achievements, lower self-worth, poorer ability to manage stress and higher levels of substance abuse. This suggests that self-regulation capacities that are formed early in life can linger for decades (Mischel et al., 2010).

Wellbeing

An important aspect of self-regulation that directly impacts our performance and wellbeing is impulse control. Its main function is to constrain the urge to engage with activities that can distract or derail us from pursuing our goals, and prevent us from engaging with maladaptive behaviours. Research into university students has shown that many students find impulse regulation difficult, particularly during the stressful exam periods. Failure in regulating eating behaviours was found to be highly prevalent in female university students with reduced self-control, while alcohol abuse was found to be common in male students with poor self-regulation. Reduced self-regulation also predicted substance abuse in students and adolescents (Tangney et al., 2004).

In the clinical domain, several psychological disorders are considered impulse control disorders and these are diagnosed through the detection of deficiencies in the regulation of thoughts, emotions or behaviours. Among these are pathological gambling, kleptomania, pyromania, trichotillomania, skin picking, intermittent explosive disorder, antisocial personality, drug addictions, obsessive compulsive behaviours, compulsive shopping, certain eating disorders, compulsive sexuality, internet addiction and computer game addiction. These disorders suggest that persistent lack of impulse control can amount to psychological disorders with severe implications for the wellbeing and quality of life of those affected by the disorder, as well as for those around them (Dell'Osso, Altamura, Allen, Marazziti, & Hollander, 2006).

Tangney et al. (2004) also found that higher levels of self-control are linked to lower psychological distress symptoms, including depression and anxiety, hostility and anger, somatisation, obsessive compulsive symptoms, psychoticism and eating disorders. A pioneering study by Gottfredson and Hirschi (1990) suggested that poor self-control is a root cause of criminality and violence, with later studies confirming this assertion. Further evidence has linked self-control to physical health, healthy lifestyle and longevity (Baumeister & Vohs, 2016). In terms of personality, research suggests that high self-regulation is positively associated with self-esteem, emotional stability, conscientiousness and agreeableness (Tangney et al., 2004).

Relationships

Self-regulation can contribute to our relationships in a variety of ways. Self-control promotes harmonious exchanges when people regulate their communication to avoid offence or to avoid damaging the relationships. In the context of romantic partnerships, self-control enables people to resist becoming involved with alternative partners. On the adverse side, low self-control can lead to frequent conflicts, explosive interactions, aggression and antisocial behaviour. Research evidence suggests that adults and children with higher self-regulation capacities form and maintain higher quality of relationships, belong to cohesive social groups, and show high social competencies, including empathy, perspective taking, capacity to manage anger in adaptive ways, reduced prejudice and willingness to forgive others (Tangney et al., 2004).

GRIT

What makes some people achieve extraordinary success? Talent and opportunity are both important, but according to Duckworth (2016) they are not enough: Both self-regulation and grit are key determinants of outstanding achievement.

Grit is defined as *"perseverance and passion for long-term goals"* (Duckworth, Peterson, Matthews, & Kelly, 2007, p. 1087).

Grit requires working persistently to achieve our long-term goals, maintaining engagement and exerting effort consistently over long periods, despite obstacles, plateaus and even in the face of failure. According to Duckworth (2016), grit is the quality that distinguishes between exceptional performers and others. The concept of grit draws on research on experts in a variety of domains which found that, in order to perform at expert level, thousands of hours of effortful and deliberate practice are required, and these can determine success more than talent.

Research on grit has shown that grit is positively associated with lifelong educational attainment, and long-term work or career success, and can predict the completion of demanding, complex goals (such as completing a degree) despite impediments (Duckworth, 2016).

CONCLUSION

Most of the social and personal problems that afflict people in modern Western society have some element of self-regulatory failure at their root. This is not to say that better self-regulation would alone solve all society's problems – but it would probably go a long way toward that end.

(Baumeister et al., 2007, p. 516)

Self-regulation is the process through which we can control our thoughts, emotions and, importantly, our behaviours. It is a key mechanism through which we can pursue our goals and fulfil our needs, and hence it is essential for wellbeing and optimal functioning. It is also essential for exhibiting grit – the quality that enables us to develop expertise. Although much of the extent research is about those times when our self-control fails, the important message that emerges from the research is that self-regulation is a capacity that can be learned through simple exercises, with substantial return on investment.

8

FLOW

Why do people engage with play when it's laborious, challenging or even risky? This was the question that Csikszentmihalyi aspired to answer in his first studies on the merit of play. In his studies he explored the experience of people who regularly engage with varied forms of play, such as rock climbing, chess, dance, basketball, art and music. The conclusion was that across the various tasks people reported that they experienced "flow": an intrinsically rewarding and enjoyable state of complete absorption with the activity, to the point of not noticing the passage of time, their own needs, or the events that are occurring around them. The experience was labelled "flow" because when people described how it felt, they used a metaphor of a wave that carried them along effortlessly (Csikszentmihalyi, 2014).

Flow is considered a core topic in positive psychology, and is incorporated in several wellbeing models (see Chapter 3). This chapter offers a brief review of flow research, by exploring the key conditions and characteristics of flow, and considering both its benefits as well as its dark side.

Flow definition

Flow is defined as an *intense experiential engagement, in the present moment, with an activity which can be physical or mental. Attention is fully invested in performing the activity, and the person performs at his or her highest capacity* (Csikszentmihalyi, 2014).

In sports it is often described as "being in the zone".
The key components of flow are attention, performance and a particular task. Flow is therefore action and performance-orientated and requires a level of skill.

Research suggests that any activity has the potential to become a flow experience, though it was found to be more prevalent in play and at work, and in relatively complex tasks, such as writing, music playing or composing, painting, dancing, playing chess, mountain climbing, video gaming and a variety of sports activities (Csikszentmihalyi, 2014).

THE CONDITIONS OF FLOW

Flow can be experienced in many activities but does not always occur as certain conditions are required for flow to emerge. These are:

- *Clear goals and rules for action*: Flow tends to occur in activities that have a clear set of goals, and an established set of rules for action (such as games, sports or music). Csikszentmihalyi (2014) argued that these goals and rules generate "coherent, non-contradictory demands for action" (p. 10). Accordingly people reported that when they are in flow they have a sense of clarity as to what they are required to do at each stage of the experience.
- *Clear and immediate feedback on progress made*: The activities that promote flow typically contain "ordered rules which make action and the evaluation of action automatic" (Csikszentmihalyi, 2014, p. 144). For example, athletic competitions, games and musical performances have a clear structure, rules and goals against which feedback is continuously provided as to how well the person is performing and progressing with the activity. In response to this feedback, the person may maintain or modify their course of action.
- *Balance between the person's level of skill and the level of challenge that the task presents*: Another condition of the flow experience is the relationship between one's skills and the level of challenge presented by the task being performed. Flow seems to occur only when people engage with tasks that are within their capacity to

perform. It is therefore considered a state of dynamic equilibrium where there is a match between the person's skills and the task being performed. Csikszentmihalyi (2014) noted: "Across all the activities – playing music, bicycling, bowling, or cooking gourmet meals – one prominent common theme was that the activity presented opportunities for action, or challenges, that were just about manageable given the players' level of skills" (p. xx). That is, the challenges presented by the task need to be slightly above the person's existing skills.

However the balance that is achieved in flow between the person's skills and the demands of the task is fragile. If the challenges presented by the task begin to surpass the person's level of skill, one can become vigilant and then anxious. Similarly, if the person's skills are greater than the requirements of the task, one may first relax, and then become bored. If there is no skill and no challenge, apathy may occur.

Importantly, research suggests that flow tends to occur when both skill levels and the challenge are relatively high. The sense of effortless performance can occur when the skills and techniques have been learned, practised and habituated so that they are performed automatically, and there is no need to think about how to perform them.

Entering flow therefore requires a level of mastery in that particular domain. Due to this condition flow is considered a *peak experience*: a state whereby people operate at their full capacity.

It should be noted however that there is some conflicting evidence on this point, suggesting that people can experience flow when the task is not challenging and well below a person's skill level.

The evidence linking "being in the zone" and peak performance is also challenged. Though performers may feel that they are performing at their best, objective measures of their performance do not always confirm this.

Measuring flow

Flow research was initially qualitative and included in-depth interviews with artists, scientists, authors, athletes and others. Later the Flow Questionnaire (Csikszentmihalyi & Csikszentmihalyi, 1988) was developed, which includes three open questions and 12 closed items

which describe features of the flow experience and requires participants to state how often they experience these characteristics and in
what activity.

More recently the Experience Sampling Method (ESM) has been
used to explore flow. This is a research method that can capture what
people do, feel and think during their daily lives, by providing reports
at random times to questions presented on a mobile device. Using this
data researchers have explored how people spend their time, what they
feel when engaged in diverse tasks, how they differ in their psychological states and how frequently they experience flow (Csikszentmihalyi,
2014).

THE FEATURES OF FLOW

There are several defining characteristics of flow:

- *Intense concentration on the task at hand*: Focused concentration of
  attention on the task being performed, in the present moment, is
  considered a defining feature of flow. The engagement with the
  activity is so demanding that no surplus attention is left to monitor other stimuli. Hence the person may not be aware of events
  happening around them or their own needs. The capacity to fully
  concentrate on a task and give it undivided attention is essential
  for entering flow and for maintaining it.
- *Merging of action and awareness*: Within flow, a fusion of action and
  awareness occurs to the point that people report feeling that they
  are completely absorbed in the task, and the actions that they
  are performing moment to moment. "A person in flow does
  not operate with a dualistic perspective: One is very aware of
  one's actions, but not of the awareness itself" (Csikszentmihalyi,
  2014, p. 138). That is, awareness remains focused on the actions
  being conducted for a lengthy period without awareness of any
  thoughts, and hence there is no planning ahead or evaluation of
  what has been completed. Questions such as: "am I doing it well
  enough?" or "is this the right step to take?" do not spring to mind,
  as they create an outside perspective, which breaks the flow.
- *Control of action and the environment*: People in flow often reported
  being fully in control of their actions and of the environment in

which the task takes place. This may be experienced as a sense of mastery and automaticity, whereby people feel that they have the capacity to handle the task, and know what to do and how to do it, without having to think about it or to try and consciously control it. It can also manifest in the absence of concern about one's own level of control of the situation.

- *Loss of ego*: When in flow, attention is taken up entirely by the task that is unfolding automatically. Mind and body are fully engaged in performing the task, and at this point people report experiencing a sense of losing their sense of self or ego, and not being self-conscious for the entire duration of the event. Dancers, musicians, chess players and others may realise after their performance that they are hungry or are experiencing pain which they had not noticed while in flow.
- *Altered sense of time*: Individuals deeply immersed in an activity that generates flow typically report a loss of time-consciousness or a distortion of their sense of time, and they often feel that time passes quickly when they are in flow. Exceptions occur in particular tasks where knowledge of time is required, such as team sports.
- *The autotelic nature of flow*: Flow is an intrinsically rewarding experience and hence Csikszentmihalyi (2014) considered it autotelic – an experience worth having for its own sake.

Most people rarely experience flow

Large-scale polls (Nakamura & Csikszentmihalyi, 2002) reported that more than a third of people (42% in the USA, 35% in Germany) never experienced flow. About half reported it as a rare event, and only a minority (16% in the USA, 23% in Germany) reported experiencing it daily.

Flow is uncommon because it requires a delicate match between the person and the environment. People can experience flow when their abilities fit the opportunities for action presented by the task.

THE OUTCOMES OF FLOW

Flow is autotelic – it's a self-justifying experience, therefore looking into its outcomes is somewhat paradoxical, as it should not be seen as a means to achieve wellbeing or happiness or any other state. However, it was incorporated in wellbeing models (Authentic Happiness and PERMA) because of its link with wellbeing and happiness.

Flow is associated with improved happiness (life satisfaction and positive affect). Flow is found to be correlated with higher motivation and engagement at school and at work. Importantly, studies have reported that flow is associated with various measures of performance, productivity and success in study and at work. In education flow was found to be associated with enjoyment and progression (Csikszentmihalyi, 2014).

Flow leads to skill development

Flow is intrinsically rewarding and therefore leads people to seek more of it. By seeking to experience it repeatedly, flow fosters skill development and growth. This is because flow activities (such as playing music, writing, video gaming and sport games) typically provide "a system of graded challenges, able to accommodate a person's continued and deepening enjoyment as skills grow" (Csikszentmihalyi, 2014, p. 244). That is, there is always a higher level of skill that can be mastered and performed in the context of the task.

When flow occurs, the person's skills match the challenge that they are handling. However, after performing it many times, skill levels are likely to increase with repetition, leading to a higher level of mastery and habituation. Therefore in order to increase flow, the challenge that is embedded in the task must increase as well, otherwise boredom will emerge instead of flow. The distinctiveness of flow activities is that they provide this type of ever-increasing level of challenges that prompts the motivation to develop higher skills in order to keep experiencing flow.

THE DARK SIDE OF FLOW

Flow can emerge in activities that can be self-damaging in the long run, such as gambling, gaming and some that involve high risk. It can also occur in activities that are morally unethical. Csikszentmihalyi (2014) also suggested that flow can have addictive properties. Therefore care is advocated to promote flow in adaptive environments.

Flow interventions

Two types of interventions have been examined over the years which aim to facilitate the occurrence of flow (Csikszentmihalyi, 2014):

- One way to facilitate flow is to shape either the structure of the activities involved or the environments where they take place so that they foster flow and assist the person in maintaining flow when it occurs.
- The second way is to assist individuals in finding activities that are intrinsically motivating for them, identifying skill level that matches the task, upskilling where needed or highlighting areas where optimal experience can be increased.

CONCLUSION

Research on flow has made a significant contribution to our understanding of wellbeing through engagement in activities that are intrinsically rewarding. The concept of flow revolves around the eudaimonic aspect of wellbeing: optimal functioning. Flow enables us to perform and achieve, and in the process to develop and grow, all of which are essential keys to wellbeing. More importantly, it suggests that life without having an intrinsic interest, deep engagement, and without investment of effort and time, and achieving a level of mastery, may not be very fulfilling.

However the research also suggests that the conditions under which flow can be experienced are not easily obtained, and some consideration and planning are required to enter this state and maintain it.

The brief review offered here of the flow model has several implications for human motivation and performance. For example, schools and organisations may find it useful to consider how to assign activities to employees or students in a way that would enable them to experience flow, or how to structure work or study environments in a way that optimises flow.

Today more than ever, when our minds are relentlessly bombarded with multiple and competing demands for our attention, the questions where we place our attention, what we choose to focus on, and how to spend our time are crucial for our wellbeing, and in particular for our functioning. Flow research suggests that more careful consideration is required as to how to make the best use of our attention for achieving a well-balanced and rewarding life (Csikszentmihalyi, 2014).

9

MEANING IN LIFE

Meaning in life is a classic topic that predates positive psychology and has been discussed extensively in religious texts, literature and philosophy. An important distinction to make at the outset pertains to the difference between *meaning of life* and *meaning in life*. The first is a theological question: why are we here? Why are human lives designed in this way? These cannot be answered through the framework of psychology. The second is a psychological and individual question: what makes our lives meaningful? This chapter aims to address the latter question, drawing on research into meaning in life, recently advanced by positive psychology scholars.

Frankl (1963) is widely credited as being a forerunner in the study of meaning. After surviving a Nazi concentration camp in World War II, Frankl recognised that finding meaning and purpose whilst in captivity helped him endure his ordeal. He spent the remainder of his life writing about the importance of meaning in people's lives, and developed Logotherapy (Frankl, 1986), a meaning-centred therapeutic approach. Later work by Steger (2012) and Wong (2012a) and their colleagues further developed the concept theoretically and empirically. Drawing on Frankl's Logotherapy, Wong (2012b) also developed the Meaning-Centred Counselling and Therapy model.

Today, meaning in life is considered a fundamental topic in existential psychology, and is incorporated as a key component in several positive psychology wellbeing models (see Chapter 3).

This chapter opens with a review of the definition and components of the meaning in life concept, and highlights the importance of meaning in life for wellbeing and optimal functioning.

Defining meaning in life

Meaning in life is defined as *the degree to which an individual experiences his or her life as making sense, being guided and driven by worthy goals, and mattering in the world* (King, Heintzelman, & Ward, 2016).

Meaning in life includes three components (Heintzelman & King, 2014):

- *Comprehension* is the cognitive facet of meaning in life. It refers to the degree to which individuals understand their lives and experience a sense of coherence.

  High comprehension is experienced when we feel that our lives make sense, things seem clear, fit well, and feel that they are "as they ought to be". When we experience low comprehension, life seems unclear, incoherent or fragmented.

- *Purpose* is the behavioural component of meaning in life. It represents the extent to which a person experiences life as being directed and motivated by worthy life-goals.

  High purpose is felt when we have a clear sense of direction in our lives, and the goals that we aim to achieve. Low purpose manifests itself in a sense of aimlessness.

- *Mattering* is the emotional component of meaning in life, which refers to the degree to which individuals feel that their existence matters: it is of significance, and has value or impact.

  High mattering is experienced when we feel that our life, goals or actions make a difference. Low mattering occurs when we feel that our existence carries little significance, and non-existence would make no difference in the world.

Meaning in life shapes perception, action and goal striving, which highlights its importance and explains its inclusion in wellbeing models. Wong (2012a) argued that, without a having a sense of meaning and purpose, people would experience life as "being on a ship without a rudder" (p. 6).

THE NEED TO ASSIGN MEANING

Frankl (1986) maintained that we have an innate need to ascribe meaning to events, experiences, people and other aspects of our lives. *Terror Management Theory* (Becker, 1973) suggests that our need to create meaning occurs on the back of our existential understanding that our existence is temporary. According to the theory, assigning meaning to life events is a way of managing death anxiety which enables us to maintain psychological security. Becker (1973) argued that in order to cope with aspects of life such as suffering, inadequacy and death, we need to feel in some ways immortal. Meaning allows us to gain a feeling of value, specialness and usefulness, hence giving us symbolic immortality.

THE QUEST FOR A MEANINGFUL LIFE

Meaning in life is a changing and dynamic experience. The search for meaning in life is often triggered by an existential crisis (Wong, 2010). This could entail facing death, experiencing a tragic event, a misfortune or finding oneself on a major crossroads.

> Since we only go through this life once, we have reasons to wonder how to make the most of it. The worst fear is not death, but the discovery that we have never really lived when the time comes for us to die. We all have the urge to desire to live fully, to do something significant, and to make a difference, so that we don't have to dread the death-bed realisation that we have squandered away our precious life. Therefore, we dread a meaningless life as much as we dread the terror of death.
>
> (Wong, 2010, p. 5)

Yalom (1980) also argued that a judgement that our lives are empty, pointless and lacking meaning can amount to a *crisis of meaning*, which is considered a major cause of psychological distress.

The act of finding our life's meaning is inherently subjective. To identify it, we need to apply introspective exploration. Wong (2010) argued that the quest for meaning requires a *meaning mindset* – the capacity for reflection, self-awareness and self-evaluation. Finding areas of dissatisfaction can trigger a renewed search for meaning, and can prompt significant changes in our life-goals and the associated courses of action.

To facilitate the process of discerning and constructing meaning in life Wong (2012b) developed the sources of meaning model that can be used in counselling or coaching to explore meaning in life.

SOURCES OF MEANING

Sources of meaning in life are basic orientations underlying the quest for meaning. They answer the question: what gives meaning to our lives? Based on studies that explored what people perceive as their key sources of meaning in life, Wong (1998) outlined the following sources of meaning as an "idealised prototype" for meaningful life:

- *Achievement or fulfilment;*
- *Relationship;*
- *Intimacy;*
- *Religion or spirituality;*
- *Self-transcendence or altruism;*
- *Self-acceptance;*
- *Fairness or respect.*

Interestingly, in recent work (Ward & King, 2016) socioeconomic status was found to impinge on meaning in life. Large-scale studies show a positive relationship between meaning in life and educational and financial resources. It seems that income may function in a similar way to social relationships or religion in predicting higher levels of meaning in life.

Meaning in life intervention: the PURE model

Wong (2010) developed the PURE model as a means of assisting people in reflecting on their meaning in life. It contains four domains that Wong urges us to ponder on: purpose, understanding, responsible action and enjoyment or evaluation (see further details in Chapter 13).

SELF-ACTUALISATION AND SELF-TRANSCENDENCE

Deep meaning often occurs from commitment to a higher purpose, and hence meaning in life is linked to self-actualisation and self-transcendence. Maslow (1987) considered meaning in life as the need that drives self-actualisation. Self-transcendence is the cardinal feature in Frankl's (1963) approach to meaning in life. He noted that true meaning in life can only be found when individuals contribute to something bigger than themselves.

> A man who becomes conscious of the responsibility he bears toward a human being who affectionately waits for him, or to an unfinished work, will never be able to throw away his life. He knows the "why" for his existence, and will be able to bear almost any "how".
>
> (Frankl, 1963, p. 127)

A long tradition of Western thought indeed encourages us not to settle for non-transcendent purposes in life.

Measures of meaning in life

Over the years several scales have been developed and tested to measure meaning in life. The Meaning in Life Questionnaire was developed by Steger, Frazier, Oishi, and Kaler (2006). It contains 10 items and two subscales: presence of life meaning subscale, and a search for meaning.

The Personal Meaning Profile (PMP) (MacDonald et al., 2012) has several versions. The brief version includes 21 items intended to measure people's perceptions of personal meaning in their lives. The PMP includes seven subscales: achievement, relationship, religion, self-transcendence, self-acceptance, intimacy and fair treatment.

The Purpose in Life Test (Crumbaugh & Maholick, 1964) contains 20 items which assess the degree to which an individual experiences a sense of meaning or purpose in life.

THE BENEFITS OF MEANING IN LIFE

A substantial body of empirical work has demonstrated that high meaning in life is associated with wellbeing as well as with a range of other positive outcomes. A recent extensive review by Steger (2017) summarised this literature, of which highlights are provided below.

Wellbeing

Meaning in life has been correlated with happiness, wellbeing, vitality and high morale, sense of control, autonomy, environmental mastery, positive perceptions of the world, religious affiliation and spirituality. Meaning and its component purpose are strongly linked to goal pursuit, motivation and engagement with goals, the attainment of valued life-goals, as well as with self-actualisation and self-transcendence.

In populations with chronic and acute health conditions meaning in life has been correlated with quality of life and better adjustment.

On the deficiency side, the lack of meaning in life is correlated with negative affect, rumination, adverse life events, hassles and grief, stress, hostility, sexual frustration and several mental illness conditions (depression, suicidal ideation, anxiety, substance abuse and posttraumatic stress disorder (PTSD)). There is however evidence that therapy can benefit these populations (Steger, 2017).

Personality

Meaning in life has also been linked to several personality traits and characteristics, including extraversion, conscientiousness, openness to experience, agreeableness, self-esteem, self-acceptance, internal locus of control, responsibility, ambition, self-control, psychological adjustment, ego development, future time orientation, hope, optimism, personal growth, adaptive coping skills and resilience.

The lack of meaning in life has been correlated with neuroticism, workaholism, hostility, antisociality, aggression and hopelessness (Steger, 2017).

Health and longevity

Meaning in life has been linked to a host of physical health outcomes, including improved immune function, lower cholesterol, better glucose control, improved cardiovascular health, more conducive health behaviours, reduced use of health services, quicker recovery from illness and better adjustment to chronic conditions (Cross, Hofschneider, Grimm, & Pressman, 2018). A large-scale longitudinal survey in the USA found that those who perceived their lives as purposeful had lower risk of mortality during the 14-year follow-up measurement (Hill & Turiano, 2014).

Relationships

Meaning in life is positively related to various relational aspects: the degree to which the need for relatedness is met, sense of belonging, closeness to others, being supported by family, and social appeal. Additionally, people with high meaning in life seem to function well in their social domains as family members, neighbours and friends. It is noteworthy that social isolation and exclusion reduce meaning in life (Steger, 2017).

CONCLUSION

Research into meaning in life has prospered in the past decades leading to substantial progress in our understanding of the concept and people's experience of meaning in life, and its association with the hedonic and eudaimonic aspects of wellbeing.

The current work into meaning in life suggests that, to discover our meaning in life, some self-reflection and self-awareness are required to make sense of our lives and discover what gives our life meaning, define our purpose through setting life goals and contribute to projects where we can make a difference. Having strong meaning in life enhances our happiness, but more importantly, it promotes deeper levels of flourishing: doing well as well as doing good.

CHARACTER STRENGTHS
AND VIRTUES

Positive psychology has pledged to restore the balance in research and practice in applied psychology: to focus on strength as much as on weakness, to offer the means to make the lives of healthy people more fulfilling, as much as healing the suffering of the distressed, and to facilitate the best things in life, as much as repairing the worst.

True to its pledge, soon after the establishment of positive psychology, Peterson and Seligman (2004) launched a groundbreaking, large-scale, global project to create a classification of positive human traits. The aims of the project were to "reclaim the study of character and virtue as legitimate topics of psychological inquiry" (Peterson & Seligman, 2004, p. 3), to build a solid foundations for a science of human strengths, that will enable people to flourish through the cultivation of positive qualities, and to create a common language for describing and discussing these traits.

The scope of the project was also highly ambitious. The originators aspired to create a "a manual of the sanities" that is similar in breadth, depth, detail and level of usage to the *Diagnostic and Statistical Manual of Mental Disorders* (DSM) which describes each known mental disorder, its diagnostic criteria, its prevalence and recommended treatments, and is frequently used by both researchers and practitioners.

With this intent, Peterson and Seligman (2004) embarked on a 3-year research project, involving 55 scientists from around the globe. The researchers consulted the world's classic religions and philosophical texts, looking for traits and qualities that appeared to have been valued throughout history and across different cultures. The result of this extensive work was the creation of a universal classification of positive character traits, known as the VIA (Values in Action) Character Strengths and Virtues.

Today, the concepts of strengths and virtues are at the heart of positive psychology scientific and applied work, and the project is considered one of the most influential initiatives that the discipline has embarked on.

This chapter briefly summarises the VIA classification as well as reviews the research on the outcomes of strengths use, as revealed through the extensive research conducted on the topic over the years.

Defining virtues and character strengths

- *Virtues* are *"acquired excellences in character traits, the possession of which contributes to a person's completeness"* (Emmons, 2003, p. 121).
- *Character strengths* are defined as *core positive qualities that reflect people's identities and values.* They are personally gratifying, ever present, universally cherished, and contribute to several positive outcomes for oneself and others (Niemiec, 2017).
- *Signature strengths* are a particular type of character strength. They are seen as *"positive traits that a person owns, celebrates and frequently exercises"* (Peterson & Park, 2009, p. 29). Signature strengths are more distinctive than other strengths since they capture and define people's fundamental nature or uniqueness, and are more genuine and natural for people to convey than other strengths.
- *Lower strengths* are character strengths that are underdeveloped or unrealised.

THE VIA CLASSIFICATION

The philosophy that underlies the VIA classification is powerful and aligns with the core tenets of positive psychology. It suggests that we can benefit more from attending to what is right in our lives and cultivating our strengths than from focusing on what is wrong and fixing our weaknesses. The focus on strengths represents a fundamental shift in our thinking, as we are naturally drawn to address our faults and difficulties (Baumeister et al., 2001). In psychology, healthcare, education and business, this shift has been revolutionary (Niemiec, 2017). Importantly, however, the strengths-based approach is not about denying our weakness or ignoring our problems. Instead, it offers a different perspective – one that focuses on personal assets that we already own to tackle problems. It is a different perspective and mindset, a distinctive way of looking at the world.

The VIA classification includes 24 character strengths that are clustered into six virtues (Table 10.1). The main use of the classification is for assessing individuals' strengths profile, hence facilitating strength awareness and an optimal use of strengths. Several measures have been developed to facilitate strengths assessment.

Table 10.1 VIA Character Strengths and Virtues classification

Virtues	Strength	Details
Wisdom and knowledge (cognitive strengths)	**Creativity**	Producing original or novel ideas and showing cognitive flexibility
	Curiosity	Taking an interest in the world and in ongoing experiences
	Judgement/ open-mindedness	Thinking things through and examining them from all sides
	Love of learning	Mastering new skills, topics or knowledge
	Perspective	Being wise and knowledgeable, able to reflect and take stock, and provide counsel to others
Courage (emotional strengths)	**Bravery**	Not shrinking from threat, challenge, difficulty or pain
	Industry/perseverance	Finishing what we start
	Authenticity/honesty	Being open and honest, leading life authentically and with integrity
	Zest	Approaching life with excitement and energy
Humanity (social strengths)	**Kindness**	Doing good deeds for others
	Love	Valuing close relationships with others
	Social intelligence	Adept in understanding our own as well as other people's motives and feelings

Virtues	Strength	Details
Justice (community strengths)	**Fairness**	Treating people equally, with fairness and justice
	Leadership	Influencing and helping others, directing and motivating others towards collective achievements
	Teamwork	Working well as a member of a group or team
Temperance (protective strengths)	**Forgiveness**	Forgiving those who have done wrong
	Modesty	Letting our accomplishments speak for themselves
	Prudence	Being careful about life choices; not saying or doing things that might later be regretted
	Self-regulation	Applying self-control and self-discipline
Transcendence (spiritual strengths)	**Appreciation of beauty and excellence**	Noticing and appreciating beauty, excellence or skilled performance in all domains of life
	Gratitude	Being aware of and thankful for the good things that happen
	Hope	Expecting the best in the future and working to achieve it
	Humour	Enjoying laughing and teasing, bringing happiness to other people
	Spirituality	Having coherent beliefs about the higher purpose and meaning of life

(Peterson & Park, 2009.)

VIA measures

The VIA measures are geared to offer users an assessment of their own strengths profile: their signature strengths (top strengths), lower strengths, as well as a rank order of all other strengths. The original adult VIA measure included 240 items. Over the years several shorter scales were developed, with the shortest containing 24 items. There are also different versions for adults and children.

The scales were translated into 37 languages, and over the years nearly 5 million people have used these scales.

All scales are freely available on the VIA Institute on Character website (www.viacharacter.org) (Niemiec, 2017).

Niemiec (2017) highlighted the following key points about strengths:

- Character strengths are the building blocks of goodness in people, and enable us to enact our best selves.
- Everyone has strengths.
- All strengths have equal value.
- Character strengths are pathways to the expression of virtues.
- VIA strengths differ from skills, talents, expertise, resources or values, as they are traits that reflect our identities and core values.
- Character strengths contain both "being" and "doing". They express our "being" since they represent our identities and our authentic selves. They consist of "doing" since character strengths are enacted through our interaction with our environment.
- Strengths need to be identified, celebrated and used habitually. However, many people are blind to their own strengths and hence unable to utilise them.
- People own and use many strengths. These strengths are often expressed in combination, hence creating a personal profile unique to each person.
- Strengths usage is context-dependent: a person may use a particular strength at work and at home.
- Character strengths can be overused and underused. Optimal use is essential to gaining the benefit of their usage.
- Strengths are fairly stable traits, but there is evidence to suggest that they can change over time and that they can be developed.
- The VIA classification is not considered comprehensive or exhaustive, since other strengths and virtues not included in the classification may be useful in particular contexts.

Strength interventions

A large body of research reveals that identifying, using, optimising and developing our strengths can improve our wellbeing as well as promote other positive outcomes, such as increased performance and relationships. Since the launch of the VIA classification several interventions have been developed. The majority of strengths interventions involve facilitating strengths identification and optimal usage. The interventions can be offered in a group setting or individually with the help of a coach or trainer. Some are fairly brief and include one session while others include several sessions (Niemiec, 2017).

THE IMPORTANCE OF STRENGTHS

Why do character strengths matter? Research has explored the association between strengths usage in key life domains, such as wellbeing, personality and resilience. Below are some of the outcomes as summarised in a recent review by Niemiec (2017).

Several studies have shown a strong link between the awareness of one's strengths and the frequency of strengths use, and wellbeing, with several studies also reporting on positive correlations between strength usage and increased happiness or satisfaction with life. Strengths spotting and deployment have also been associated with self-reflection, sense of purpose and meaning, optimism, insight, confidence, vitality, resilience, positive relationships and lower levels of depression. In a clinical population strength interventions are often used as a foundation for therapy.

At work, character strengths usage is associated with engagement, and with higher levels of productivity and achievements, constructive work relationships, citizenship behaviours and low tendency to exhibit counterproductive behaviours. It is also linked with self-esteem, problem solving, creativity, job satisfaction, reduced stress and low turnover intention, high work meaningfulness and viewing one's work as a calling.

In education, character strengths use has been identified as a key source of wellbeing. Strengths have also been associated with students' engagement and enjoyment, academic performance and achievement, improved physical and mental health, and social skills.

CONCLUSION

Character strengths and virtues have significant value and consequences for individuals, organisations and societies. The unique work on character strengths conducted by positive psychology scholars encourages us to look beyond our weaknesses, problems and deficiencies to explore assets that all of us already have: character strengths and virtues. It urges us to identify our unique strengths and to use them regularly as an expression of our individuality as well as a pathway to wellbeing.

The VIA project represents the promise of positive psychology to shift the balance in psychology, and devote attention to good character as an essential key to a full life.

11

POSITIVE RELATIONSHIPS

Relationships are tremendously important for a life well lived, and as we have seen in earlier chapters, scholars consider social relations a vital component of wellbeing, an essential key to happiness and productive functioning, and a primary source of support in difficult times. Accordingly, relationships were incorporated into most wellbeing, coping and resilience models, underscoring their prominence. Moreover, research has consistently shown the benefits of flourishing relationships for health and vitality, recovery from illness, and even longevity (Warren, Donaldson, & Lee, 2017).

However, on the negative side, dysfunctional relationships are known as the most common source of stress, and a prime cause of psychological anguish and disorder, including trauma. Abusive or toxic relationships can have a devastating effect on our quality of life, physical health and illness, and are associated with a high risk of mortality. Equally, however, loneliness, social isolation or exclusion can cause comparable damage to our psychological and physical wellbeing. Researchers have therefore argued that both social privation and distressed relationships can yield colossal human costs that can gravely impair individuals, organisations and communities (Reis, 2012).

Given the extent of the destruction that social deficiency or adverse relationship can inflict, it is perhaps unsurprising that, prior to the emergence of positive psychology, most early studies focused on troubled relationships, with the aim of informing therapeutic practice (Berscheid, 1999). However, even after the establishment of positive psychology, and despite the strong scientific evidence that the quality of relationship matters, research has been fairly silent about what positive relationships entail. Presently, there is scarce work and theorising around the defining qualities of positive relationships, what can predict their emergence, and how they can be developed and maintained. Much of the existing research focuses on the *outcomes* of thriving relationships, particularly how they can impact physical and psychological wellbeing, though there is still limited theoretical work that can explain the mechanisms that bring about this impact.

With this critique in mind, and drawing on the vast relationship science literature, this chapter endeavours to address a crucial question: *What makes a positive relationship?*

It is worth noting here that satisfying and beneficial relationships are not the opposite of distressing and harmful relationships and that the absence of negative relationships does not guarantee good outcomes (Reis & Gable, 2003).

In exploring the ingredients that make up high-quality relationships, this chapter reviews relevant theories and empirical research on the factors that shape the quality of relationships. The chapter concludes with a brief review on the impact of relationships on wellbeing, health and other aspects of life.

THE VARIETY OF SOCIAL RELATIONSHIPS

Social interactions are an integral aspect of human life. Even in this technological age, where a significant portion of our social exchanges occur through email, phone applications and other technologies, and less time is spent in the (physical) presence of family, friends, colleagues and acquaintances, in reality, most of us spend a significant amount of time in a social context, interacting with individuals or groups, face to face or through technology.

Conceptualising relationships

According to Hinde (1979), *"a relationship involves a series of interactions between two individuals known to each other. Relationships involve behavioural, cognitive, and affective aspects"* (p. 2).

There are several key features that make up a relationship (Hinde, 1997):

- A relationship is more than the sum of its interactions.
- Relationships do not reside in the individuals involved. In time, they generate distinctive rhythms that are displayed though the patterns of the interactions.
- Relationships are temporal and require a degree of continuity.
- Mutual influence is a key aspect of relationships.
- "A relationship itself is invisible; its existence can be discerned only by observing its effects" (Berscheid, 1999, p. 261).

While social interactions are indeed necessary for a relationship to exist, they are not sufficient, and many interactions that we have today, particularly on social media sites, demonstrate this point, as they do not amount to a relationship.

One way to classify relationships is along an axis that extends between "close relationships", most likely entailing romantic relationships, family ties and friendships, and "weak ties" on the other side, which include a large range of relationships, from service providers to acquaintances, and some of our social media "friends" or "followers". Along this axis we may place people with whom we have relations that vary in closeness, such as work colleagues, managers, neighbours, teachers, clients, medical professionals and many others.

While all types of relationships and interactions have the potential to be meaningful and consequential, much of scholars' attention has been devoted in the past 50 years to close relationships, though in recent years there has been some work around weak ties.

THE NEED TO BELONG

Why do we need relationships? The first and perhaps the most intuitive answer to this question is that through our social ties we can satisfy our basic social needs. The idea that we are social creatures, motivated by an innate need to interact, bond and belong, was noted by Aristotle who made the following observation:

> Man is by nature a social animal.... anyone who either cannot lead the
> common life or is so self-sufficient as not to need to, and therefore does
> not partake of society, is either a beast or a god.
>
> (Barker, 1946, pp. 7–8)

Several prominent classic scholars and clinicians followed this line of thought, including Maslow (1987), who argued that having regular, positive social contact is one of the most fundamental human needs, and Bowlby (1969), who claimed that satisfying social needs is crucial for survival, healthy development and mental health.

In an extensive review of the large body of evidence that supports these assertions, Baumeister and Leary (1995) concluded that we have a "pervasive drive to form and maintain at least a minimum quantity of lasting, positive, and significant interpersonal relationships" (p. 497). The authors further argued that, in order to satisfy our need to belong, several conditions should be met: some stability, continuity and mutuality is necessary in the relationship, the interactions should be fairly frequent, convey care, and ideally be "positive or pleasant" and relatively "free from conflict and negative affect" (p. 500).

The authors emphasised that we only require a few close relationships to satisfy the need to belong, and once the need is fulfilled, the motivation to establish additional relationships is reduced.

Social needs

Drigotas and Rusbult (1992) classified social needs into five categories:

- *Intimacy needs*: The need to confide in another, share thoughts and feelings;
- *Companionship needs*: The need to spend time and engage in shared activities;
- *Physical needs*: From hand-holding to sexual intercourse;
- *Security needs*: The need for stability and capacity to rely on others for safety and support;
- *Emotional involvement needs*: Emotional semblance and capacity to influence each other's emotional experiences.

Some of the support for relational needs theories comes from the naturalness with which we establish relationships with others, the constant effort that we put into developing and preserving our relationships, and from the distress that we experience when our relationships are in trouble or facing dissolution. Accordingly, there is mounting evidence that demonstrates the shattering impact of unmet social needs. Research on separation, loss and relational deprivation suggests that these can cause long-term impairment to development, functioning, physical and mental health, and ultimately pose serious risks to survival.

CLOSE RELATIONSHIPS

Much of the extent literature in the scientific study of relationships, as well as within positive psychology, examines close relationships. This is because these are the relationships that matter most. They can dramatically impact our happiness, wellbeing and health, both positively and negatively, and hence the question posed earlier – what makes a positive relationship? – is of major importance in the context of these relationships.

Defining close relationships

Considerable scholarly work has attempted to define what is a "close" relationship and debated how to measure it, but the concept remains ambiguous.

A close relationships is one in which *"two people interact with each other frequently, across a variety of settings and tasks, and exert considerable influence on each other's thoughts and actions"* (Collins & Madsen, 2006, p. 194).

It is also characterised by *"strong, frequent, and diverse interdependence that lasts over a considerable period of time"* (Kelley, 1983, p. 38).

According to these definitions, close relationships have a "soft" aspect and a more "concrete" aspect:

- *The soft aspect* of intimate relationships includes features such as the level of mutual knowledge and sharing that is conveyed, the level of interdependence or trust in the relationship, or the influence that people exert on each other.

- *The concrete aspect* of close relationships refers to facets such as how often the parties meet or communicate, where meetings take place, how the communication occurs, the longevity of the relationships, the social context or the roles that people hold in the relationship.

The definitions cited above suggest that interactions in close relationships should be frequent, occur across varied settings, and that the relationship should last for a fairly long period in order for it to meet the criteria for close relations. They also suggest that interdependence and mutual influence are the key factors that make close relationships distinct from other types of relationships. Intimacy is a key aspect of closeness in relationships, and often used as a means to assess the quality of close relationships.

Intimacy

Researchers often distinguish between different levels of closeness in a relationship by assessing their degree of intimacy. An intimate relationship is defined as *"individuals who share an intimate relationship have necessarily conjointly experienced multiple interactions in which both partners have engaged in self-revealing behaviours, experienced positive involvement with the other, and achieved shared understandings"* (Prager & Roberts, 2004, p. 45).

Intimacy is assessed through the presence of seven components (Miller, 2015):

- *Knowledge*: Intimate relationships involve having personal, often confidential, knowledge about each other. The information that is shared can include life histories, attitudes and feelings, life preferences, strengths and weaknesses, triumphs and losses. This knowledge is accumulated through mutual self-disclosure.
- *Trust*: To trust another person means that we expect that they will treat us fairly and honourably, and will do us no harm. Trust is an essential component in intimate relationships, partly because it is a necessary precondition for self-disclosure to occur.
- *Interdependence*: This component represents the extent to which the lives of intimate partners are intertwined, and the degree to which they influence each other. They can influence actions,

thoughts and emotions. The influence is likely to be meaningful, encompassing several domains, long-lasting, and fairly frequent. The mutual influence can be intentional when people consult each other, but can be unintentional resulting from a person's actions, attitudes or behaviours.

- *Mutuality* refers to the feeling of overlap between two lives: the extent that people feel a part of a system, whether a couple, family or group. This means that they recognise that their close connections have expanded their identities, and they have developed an identity that signifies "us". The use of words such as "we" or "us" often reveals the shift in the relationship that reflects this component.

- *Responsiveness*: Intimacy in close relationships tends to increase when people believe that their companions

> understand, respect, and appreciate them, being attentively and effectively responsive to their needs and concerned for their welfare ... Responsiveness is powerfully rewarding, and the perception that our partners recognise, understand, and support our needs and wishes is a core ingredient of our very best relationships.
>
> (Miller, 2015, p. 5)

- *Caring*: Having a concern for and attending to the other person's needs and feelings. When care is present, it tends to bring about mutual appreciation and affection. Caring also involves an investment of time, energy and other resources to offer small gestures of good will that express appreciation and care for the other person. These are particularly impactful during times of hardship.

- *Commitment*: The final component of an intimate relationship is commitment to the relationship. This embodies the expectation that the partnership will continue into the future, and the willingness to take the necessary steps to maintain the relationship during good times and bad. This necessitates spending time and energy in preserving the openness and closeness achieved, working through disagreements, conflicts or other challenges, and being willing to compromise, and at times make sacrifices for the good of the relationship.

Measuring intimacy

The Miller Social Intimacy Scale (MSIS) (Miller & Lefcourt, 1982) is a 17-item instrument that measures intimacy in any interpersonal relations (not necessarily in marriage).

Self-disclosure

One of the markers of healthy, satisfying intimate relationship is self-disclosure (Laurenceau, Rivera, Schaffer, & Pietromonaco, 2004). It involves sharing personal information with another person. It tends to develop over time, as partners expand the breadth and depth of the topics that they discuss. Self-disclosure necessitates reciprocity, as partners tend to match each other's level of openness. It also requires responsiveness in order to build trust in the relationship, which enables self-disclosure and intimacy to deepen.

There are some differences between men and women in their self-disclosure: women tend to be more self-disclosing than men, and can also elicit self-disclosure from others. Men tend to experience higher levels of self-disclosure with women than with men. Women, on the other hand, experience equal levels of self-disclosure with men and women (Reis, 1998).

Using intimacy as a criterion for evaluating quality in relationships offers is a solid starting point for conceptualising positive relationships. However, when assessing relational intimacy, it is important to consider the capacity of the parties involved to participate and meet the criteria of intimacy. Attachment theory suggests that our relationships are heavily affected by the way we were brought up, and our past relationships. These shape how we participate in our current adult relationships, and can either promote or hinder our efforts to create flourishing, intimate relationships.

Attachment theory

Attachment theory was originated by Bowlby (1969), who observed infants' attachment patterns to their main caregivers (usually their mothers). Bowlby noticed that when the toddlers were hungry, wet or scared, they turned to their caregivers for support. Depending on the typical response that they received, they developed different attachment styles:

- *Secure attachment style*: Some children received stable, nurturing and kind attention, and hence they internalised an understanding that other people are reliable, safe and kind. Consequently they developed a secure attachment style: they willingly bonded with others, turned to them for support when needed and trusted them.
- *Anxious-ambivalent attachment style*: For some infants, nurturing attention was inconsistent. There were times when their caregivers were sympathetic and caring, but at other times they were emotionally unavailable. These children developed an insecure attachment style. Being unable to trust their caregiver, these children became tense and needy in their relationships with others.
- *Avoidant attachment style*: A third group of children received attention and care that was provided by unreceptive, reluctant and at times rejecting carers. These children formed an observation that they cannot rely on others for support, and developed an avoidant attachment style. They were often suspicious or angry, attempted to withdraw from others and found it difficult to form close relationships.

Nearly two decades later, Hazan and Shaver (1987) found that adults exhibited similar attachment styles in their close relationships, and demonstrated the association between people's adult and childhood attachment styles. Originally the model included three attachment styles, but this was later modified by Bartholomew (1990), who proposed four categories of adult attachment:

- *Secure attachment style*: This style corresponds to the secure style found in children. People in this category find it easy to form intimate relationships with others. They are trusting and comfortable depending on others, and equally, they are at ease when others rely on them.
- *Preoccupied attachment style*: Bartholomew renamed the anxious–ambivalent category to reflect people's preoccupation with

the status of their relationships. People who exhibit this style have a strong desire to form intimate relationships, and when lacking close relationships they become anxious. However, when they are in a close relationship, they are often concerned that the other party does not appreciate them as much as they do.

The third and fourth attachment categories differentiate between two patterns of *avoidant* styles:

- *Fearful attachment style*: People who display this attachment type avoid intimacy with others, since they fear rejection. Although they desire to be liked by others, they find it difficult to trust others, and worry about being hurt. They are therefore uncomfortable becoming close to others.
- *Dismissing attachment style*: People who exhibit this style are content without intimate relationships, and prefer not to rely on others, nor to have others depend on them. They consider intimacy to be overrated, and not worth the effort. People in this category tend to avoid interdependency, and wish to remain independent and self-sufficient.

According to Shaver and Mikulincer (2013), there are two factors that distinguish between these four attachment styles:

- *Intimacy avoidance*: People differ in their capacity to engage with intimate relationships. Some people are at ease in close relationships, and are therefore considered as low in avoidance of intimacy. Others feel distrust towards others, and distance themselves from others, and are considered high in intimacy avoidance.
  Those with secure and preoccupied attachment styles tend to show low intimacy avoidance, while adults with fearful or dismissing attachment styles are more likely to experience high intimacy avoidance.
- *Abandonment anxiety*: People also vary in their fear that others will find them undeserving and abandon them. Those with a secure or dismissing attachment style are not concerned that others might desert them. Conversely, people who have a fearful or preoccupied attachment style tend to show high abandonment anxiety, and hence they are uncomfortable in their close relationships.

An important, and indeed optimistic, point to make is that attachment styles are learned from our early experiences, and since they are learned, they can be unlearned through new experiences. Researchers noted that people can change attachment styles over time. A painful relationship dissolution can trigger a change in a securely attached person, who might adopt other attachment styles, and vice versa, a positive, solid relationship can make a fearfully attached person more secure (Arriaga, Kumashiro, Finkel, VanderDrift, & Luchies, 2014). Nevertheless, for many people, their original attachment styles can endure, since at the outset people tend to search for new relationships that validate their existing styles.

Measuring attachment styles

A 12-item attachment scale was created by Brennan, Clark, and Shaver (1998). Users are asked to rate their agreement or disagreement on each item.

Love and the search for happily ever after

The longing and search for intimate, loving relationships is a significant driving force in the lives of most people. Many of us spend years, and devote substantial efforts and resources, in an attempt to find our soulmates, and create our own Hollywood version of "happily ever after". But what is love?

Conceptualising love

Fredrickson (2013a) defined love as a supreme emotion: a *"micro-moment of warmth and connection that you share with another living being"* (p. 10).

She claimed that love is an "essential nutrient that your cells crave" (p. 4). Hence, love is vital for our psychological and physical wellbeing, and its absence is sensed as a yearning that is both psychological and physical.

According to Fredrickson, "love is a connection", which "blossoms virtually any time two or more people – even strangers – connect over a shared positive emotion" (p. 17). It is most distinctly felt when three events occur:

- Positive emotions are shared between people.
- There is synchrony between people's behaviours and their biochemistry.
- There is an underlying motivation to care for each other.

When the three elements are present, moments of positive resonance occur between parties, in which positive energy is exchanged. These reverberations are transient and sooner or later fade away.

Two conditions are necessary for love to occur: face-to-face interaction where the sensory connection can take place, and safety – an assessment that we are safe within the union that we have with others.

Types of love: the triangular theory of love

While Fredrickson conceptualised love as an emotional outcome that emerges from or in a close relationship, Sternberg (2006) viewed love as a type of relationship, and argued that there are three components that make up all types of love:

- *Intimacy*: Feelings of closeness, which manifests itself through shared knowledge and understanding, warmth, mutual trust and support. Intimacy is the emotional component of relationships.
- *Passion*: Physical and psychological arousal, exhilaration or desire, including sexual lust. Passion is the motivational factor in relationships.
- *Commitment*: Sense of durability, longevity or stability in a relationship, which is often a result of a conscious decision to commit to it, and work to preserve it. Commitment is the cognitive component of relationships.

According to the model, each of these elements is a descriptor of the love that any two people may share. They can vary in their intensity (from low to high), therefore creating countless possible combinations. The key prototypes are described below.

- *Non-love*: When intimacy, passion and commitment are all lacking, love does not occur. We are likely to perceive people with whom we have such relationships as "acquaintances", and fittingly, the relationship will likely be superficial, casual and uncommitted.
- *Liking*: When intimacy is high but passion and commitment are low, liking occurs. These ties may be seen as friendships, where there is a genuine sense of warmth and closeness, but no arousal, nor an expectation for longevity in the relationship.
- *Infatuation*: This type of relationship occurs when there is intense passion, but no intimacy or commitment. This is often experienced when people who barely know each other feel aroused.
- *Empty love*: Commitment to a relationship that lacks both intimacy and passion is considered empty love. It is most likely to occur in "depleted" relationships in which over time both the amicability and passion have dwindled, and the decision to stay together keeps the relationship going. Notably, in cultures where arranged marriages are common, empty love may be the starting point of a relationship.
- *Romantic love*: When passion and high intimacy are both present, but there is no long-term commitment, people feel romantic love. While many of us expect that commitment will follow, Sternberg argued that it is not a defining feature of romantic love.
- *Companionate love*: In this type of relationship, intimacy and commitment are both high, but passion is low. Closeness, care and investment are the key features of these deep, long-term friendships. This type of love can at times be found in long-term, happily married couples, where the passion has gradually faded away.
- *Fatuous love*: When passion and commitment are present but intimacy is absent, a superficial type of love emerges. It can occur when two people who do not know each other well marry hastily, on the basis of irresistible passion;
- *Consummate love*: When passion, intimacy and commitment are all present in a relationship, people experience consummate (complete) love. This is the ideal "happily ever after" type that many people dream about. However, Sternberg (1987) equated it to losing weight: it is easy to keep on track for a while, but difficult to sustain over time.

Another type of love that is not included in Sternberg's triangular theory is compassionate love (Fehr & Sprecher, 2013).

- *Compassionate love*: This is a type of love defined by its altruistic nature and involves care and concern for another person. It combines intimacy with compassion and caring. The key features of this type of love are empathy, concern and generosity, and some level of self-sacrifice.

It is noteworthy that one of the key ingredients of love is passion – a fleeting state that tends to diminish over time, and is difficult to control. Accordingly, Sternberg noted that people often change the type of love that they experience within an existing relationship. Romantic love decreases over time due to the loss of passion, leading to high rates of divorces occurring in the fourth year of marriage. However, as happily married couples age, the intimacy, care and friendship that they developed typically increase, hence showing higher levels of companionate love.

Measuring love

The Passionate Love Scale (Hatfield & Sprecher, 1986) includes 15 items and is designed to measure romantic love.

Love styles

Hendrick and Hendrick (1992) distinguished between different types of love-seeking styles:

- *Eros*: The erotic lover is driven by attraction and seeks an intense, passionate relationship.
- *Ludus*: The ludic lover treats love as a casual game, and likes to "play the field".
- *Storge*: The storgic lover seeks sincere friendships that will eventually lead to long-term commitment.
- *Mania*: The manic lover is demanding, possessive and obsessed.
- *Agape*: The agapic lover is giving, altruistic and treats love as their obligation.

- *Pragma*: The pragmatic lover is practical, careful and logical when searching for a companion.

What do people want in a partner?

During the search and dating phase, people assess potential partners for long-term relationships in accordance with criteria that seem to be similar cross-culturally (Tran, Simpson, & Fletcher, 2008):

- *Cordiality and fidelity*: We tend to look for partners who are kind, supportive, understanding and trustworthy.
- *Attractiveness and vivacity*: We are attracted to those who are good-looking, sexy, sociable and cheerful.
- *Social standing and resources*: Socioeconomic status and financial resources indeed count.

For women, good character, warmth, loyalty and status are more important than looks. However, men have different priorities. Although they place significant value on friendliness and faithfulness, beauty and liveliness are more important to them than status and resources (Fletcher, Tither, O'Loughlin, Friesen, & Overall, 2004).

Interestingly, men seem to hold more romantic attitudes than women. They believe in love at first sight, are less discriminating in their mating choices, fall in love faster than women, think that if you truly love someone nothing else matters, and are often the first to say "I love you". Women seem to be more cautious and selective than men, and feel passion more slowly (Miller, 2015).

Attraction

What attracts us to particular people?

Berscheid and Walster (1974) argued that attraction involves two elements:

- Physiological arousal;
- The belief that a particular person is the cause of our arousal.

Accordingly, romantic love can be formed, or increased, when arousal is linked with the presence of an alluring person. Intriguingly, the researchers found that *any* form of arousal that causes faster heartbeat (from funny film to running) influences our emotional reaction, making us feel attracted to others.

Miller (2015) argued that there are certain conditions that can ignite the fervour of attraction:

- *Rewards*: We are attracted to people whose presence in our lives promises particular rewards, such as attention, validation or instrumental rewards.
- *Proximity*: Access to people increases the probability that two people will meet and interact, and therefore we are more likely to select our lovers from people who are already around us. Physical proximity is positively linked with attraction: the closer we are, the higher the attraction. Proximity is convenient, while distance is effortful, and can be costly.
- *Familiarity*: Repeated exposure and contact generate familiarity, which in turn breeds attraction.
- *Beauty*: Standards of beauty vary significantly across cultures, but looks certainly count when it comes to attraction. We tend to assign other positive characteristics to beautiful people, which makes us desire them even more. Interestingly, physical attractiveness is more important for men than women. And here is a tip for a date: wearing red increases our attractiveness.
- *Matching*: People tend to match with others who they think have the same age, levels of beauty, health, wealth, talent and fame as they do.
- *Similarity*: We are attracted to those who are similar to us in some ways, including background, culture, values and attitudes, and personal qualities. This suggests that *opposites do not attract*.
- *Reciprocity*: We seem to be attracted to people who signal that they like us, and avoid situations where we are likely to be rejected.

Is love really blind?

The short answer is that indeed it is! Flooded with passion and sex drive, lovers tend to idealise their partners, and overlook information that does not fit with their rosy depiction. The problem is that, in time, passion and illusion wane, and familiarity, routine and reality interrupt the fantasy, leading to a more levelheaded perception of our partners (Goodwin, Fiske, Rosen, & Rosenthal, 2002).

Marriage

Many changes have occurred in marriage patterns in the past 50 years, particularly in the West, and these ultimately affect the quality of marriages as well as the expectations that we bring with us into this union. Firstly, fewer people are marrying today than ever before, and many prefer to cohabit instead. There are also more people today who are not in a relationship. In the UK marriage rates have been steadily declining since 1970. Back then, 90% of people were married by the age of 30, and the average age of first marriage was 24. By 2019, marriage rates had dropped to less than 30%, and the age of marriage has risen by 8 years. Cohabitation was rare in the 1970s, but today about two-thirds of young adults live with their partner (ONS, 2016). About half of all marriages end in divorce, but there is also evidence to suggest that even higher rates of separation occur among those who cohabit (Wolfinger, 2005). These grim statistics urged scholars to search for the keys to happy, stable marriages.

Happily ever after?

Lucas, Clark, Georgellis, and Diener (2003) examined the occurrence of hedonic adaptation in the context of marital life by following 24,000 German residents for 15 years. Their findings revealed that most people experienced an upsurge in their happiness when they got married (they were happiest about a year before their wedding day); however, on average after about 2 years most participants returned to their baseline – their pre-marriage happiness levels.

Interdependence Theory: exchanging rewards and costs

Interdependence Theory (Van Lange & Rusbult, 2012) views relationships as transactions between people, in which people exchange rewards and costs. Metaphorically, a relationship can be viewed as a shared bank account. If there are more positive than negative transactions in the shared account, people are likely to be satisfied in their relationship, and preserve it. But if the account has more negative than positive transactions or is overdrawn, people are likely to be unhappy with the relationship, and if this persists, they may bring the partnership to its end. According to Miller (2015), "people seek rewards and want to avoid costs but … only when both motivations are fulfilled simultaneously are people wholly content" (p. 189).

Miller (2015) combined the two motivations to derive four relational patterns:

- *Flourishing relationships* are those that offer ample rewards and few costs and hence are enriching and stimulating.
- *Boring relationships* are low in terms of costs, but also low on rewards, and therefore they are dull but safe.
- *Precarious relationships* are rich in rewards, but also have significant costs, and consequently these relationships are insecure.
- *Distressed relationships* are low on rewards but bear high costs and as such they are unstable and unsafe.

Research and soaring divorce rates provide ample evidence that marital satisfaction declines during the first years of marriage. Interdependence Theory suggests that this is due to people encountering unexpected costs, and fewer rewards than anticipated.

One problem with rewards and costs in a relationship is that partners do not always notice the rewards − the caring and affectionate behaviours their partners display towards them − though they are likely to notice the costs. Additionally, they may disagree as to the value or meaning of the rewards that they exchange. Also husbands and wives desire different rewards.

How relationships promote self-development

- *The self-expansion model*
  According to Aron, Lewandowski, Mashek, and Aron (2013), people have a primary desire to develop and expand their sense of self. Being in a loving relationship provides an opportunity for self-expansion, since partners engage in new, stimulating and arousing experiences that prompt personal growth and heighten self-awareness, particularly in the early stages of the relationship. A typical symbol of the self-expansion is the frequent use of "we" or "us".

> • *The Michelangelo phenomenon*
> Another way in which relationships can help people grow is when partners encourage and support each other to pursue and fulfil their best possible selves: the people that they wish to become (Drigotas, 2002). When partners endorse and promote each other's self-actualisation, this strengthens the union, and enhances their well-being. This is known as the Michelangelo phenomenon. It describes how "close relationship partners are often active participants in each other's personal development and goal pursuit" (Gable & Gosnell, 2011, p. 271). It is named after the celebrated sculptor who fashioned inspiring works of art from ordinary materials.

Common tensions in marriages

There are several common tensions, often described as "dialectics", that recurrently occur in romantic relationships (Erbert, 2000):

- *Autonomy and connection*: On one hand, partners want to have the freedom to do as they please, but on the other, they also desire to establish close connections with each other, which will make them more dependent on each other.
- *Stability and change*: Happily married couples seek to maintain and protect their relationship by minimising change. However, couples seek novelty and excitement in their relationship. Too much stability can lead to stagnation or boredom, while too much change increases stress and can lead to friction.
- *Integration and separation*: This tension relates to the associations that a couple has with their social network: family and friends. The need (and at times obligation) to interact with other people can come at the expense of time that people would have liked to be able to devote to their partnership.

According to Erbert (2000), across the life span, people's preferences swing between autonomy and connection, stability and change, integration and separation. These dialectics seem to account for more than a third of conflicts that married couples have, and tend to linger.

Communication

Communication is a vital aspect of intimate relationships, and one that can significantly shape the quality of a relationship. Gottman (1994) argued that communication styles, and in particular conflict styles, can distinguish between happy and unhappy marriages, and can predict the continuity or dissolution of a relationship with nearly 90% accuracy. Gottman (2014) conducted extensive research lasting nearly 40 years into the communication patterns of hundreds of married couples. His analyses produced a set of distinctive features that enabled scholars to differentiate between "masters and disasters" of relationships, and predict their fate.

The studies found that happily married couples communicate messages that convey support, affection, care and humour more often than unhappily married couples. They also tend to use accommodation (withhold negative comments even in the face of provocation) and agree on a variety of topics. In contrast, unhappily married couples seem to display more disagreement, criticism and negative emotions, convey fewer supportive comments and humour in their communication, and display less self-restraint. Gottman and Levenson (1992) claimed that, in order to remain satisfied within our marriages, we need to have more positive than negative exchanges (a ratio of 5-to-1 at least).

Conflict

Gottman (1999) argued that conflict is unavoidable in close relationships, and that most relational conflict is perpetual and not solvable. Some of these become gridlocked conflicts, that gradually move from minor negative exchanges, to the *Four Horsemen of the Apocalypse* which contain:

- *Criticism;*
- *Defensiveness;*
- *Contempt;*
- *Stonewalling.*

Conflict transpires whenever a person's motivations, objectives, principles, attitudes or behaviours are discordant with those of another, or obstruct the other partner from achieving his or her goals.

Peterson (2002) classified the actions that prompt conflicts into four categories:

- *Criticism*: Verbal or non-verbal communication that displays dissatisfaction with the partner's behaviour, attitudes or character;
- *Illegitimate demands*: These are requests that seem unfair or excessive;
- *Rebuffs*: When "one person appeals to another for a desired reaction, and the other person fails to respond as expected" (Peterson, 2002, p. 371);
- *Cumulative annoyances*: Trivial incidents that become annoying with repetition, and may take the form of "social allergies", whereby a person develops a disproportionate reaction to these episodes.

What are couples fighting over when in conflict?

Papp et al. (2009) found the following conflict themes to be the most common (frequency of topic raised noted in brackets).

- *Children*: How to care for and discipline children (38%);
- *Chores*: How to distribute chores, and what standards of performance are expected (25%);
- *Communication*: How we pay attention, listen, convey disagreements and handle misunderstandings (22%);
- *Leisure*: What we do for recreation, with whom, and how much time and resources we spend (20%);
- *Work*: How much time we devote to work or to colleagues (19%);
- *Money*: Income, bills, what we purchase and how much we spend (19%);
- *Habits*: Irritating activities or behaviours (17%);
- *Relatives*: Issues around engaging with in-laws, extended family, ex-spouses and stepchildren (11%);
- *Commitment*: The significance of commitment, and the consequences of adultery (9%);
- *Intimacy*: How much we display affection, frequency of sex (8%);
- *Friends*: How much time we spend, how frequently and what activities we do with friends (8%);
- *Personality*: The partner's talents, skills or traits (7%).

Engagement and escalaction of conflicts

There are several typical patterns of conflict engagement and intensification according to Peterson (2002):

- *Avoidance* occurs when both partners attempt to dodge a sensitive issue. This occurs either when a topic is not seen as important enough to clash over, or when the matter seems unsolvable, and conflict seems futile.
- *Negotiation* occurs when a couple attempts to arrive at a resolution through problem solving, and in a sensible manner. Being responsive to each other and mutual validation can help lower the heat (Canary & Lakey, 2013):
  - *Direct tactics* involve openly discussing issues, showing willingness to address problems, taking responsibility, compromising, supporting the other's perspective, engaging in self-disclosure and showing approval and warmth.
  - *Indirect tactics* involve by-passing issues, but at the same time soothing each other through friendly touch or humour (Gottman, Coan, Carrere, & Swanson, 1998).
- *Escalation* occurs when a conflict becomes heated. It often involves dysfunctional communication, whereby other topics may be dragged into the exchange, when partners show disrespect, and when confrontational demands or threats are made. Fiery warfare may follow, where partners exchange nasty roars at each other:
  - *Direct tactics* involve allegations or criticism, aggressive or threatening commands, hostile interrogation or sarcastic disapproving remarks.
  - *Indirect tactics* involve implied or hints of disapproval or hostility, negative affect in the form of gloom or complaints, evasive remarks or efforts to change the topic.
- *Negative affect reciprocity* occurs when partners develop a *pattern* in which they exchange ever-increasing provocations.
- *The demand–withdraw pattern* is a pattern of behaviour that tends to exacerbate conflict, in which "one partner engages in demanding forms of behaviour, such as complaints, criticisms, and pressures for changes, while the other partner engages in withdrawing forms of behaviour, such as halfhearted involvement, changing

the topic, avoiding discussion, or even walking away" (Eldridge & Baucom, 2012, p. 144). This pattern causes escalation since the demander has to "increase the heat" in order to be heard, and for issues to addressed, which often makes the withdrawer more resistant. Interestingly, women are often the demanders and men are often withdrawers.

Well-adjusted married partners rarely reach escalation point or use dysfunctional conflict tactics, and research suggests that couples who regularly have fiery battles are much more likely to divorce than others with more productive conflict management tactics (Gottman et al., 1998).

Ending conflicts

Conflicts can end in several ways (Peterson, 2002):

- *Separation* occurs when one or both companions withdraw from the argument without reaching a resolution. It can be used to protect the relationship when it brings to an end a battle that can inflict irreversible damage, giving them time to cool off. However it leaves the problem with no resolution.
- *Domination* occurs when one partner is more powerful than the other, and forces the other to accept their way.
- *Compromise* is displayed when both partners agree to a mutually acceptable solution. In this case neither partner gets everything they wanted, but both get something.
- *Integrative agreements* occur when both partners work together to help achieve their aspirations. They may need to refine their desires, and seek new ways to attain their goals without imposing on the other person.
- *Structural improvement* is a fairly rare pattern that occurs when conflict leads the couple to rethink their lifestyle and habits and change them.

Conflict styles

Gottman (2014) offered a typology of married couples that reflects their communication and conflict management styles:

- *Stable couples*:
  - *Conflict avoiders*: Couples in this group attempt to reduce arguments, and instead highlight their common grounds. They are marginally expressive and therefore tend to sidestep conflict, and likely to avoid articulating their needs. They are generally content with their relationship. A common feature of these couples is that in their balancing act between independence and interdependence, they see themselves as autonomous individuals with discrete interests, though they are engaged and considerate in their joint areas.
  - *Volatile couples*: These couples are highly expressive. When they discuss an area of conflict, they often start with persuasion tactics, which they continue to use throughout. They seem to enjoy their squabbles, but keep them respectful, and often use humour alongside expressions of negative affect. They are highly interdependent, and while they may debate their roles, they prioritise their connection and value honesty in their communication.
  - *Validating couples*: The interaction between these couples can be described as calm and comfortable. They are expressive but use mostly neutral language. They put significant effort into supporting and understanding each other's perspectives, and show empathy and concern. They tend to handle some of their difficulties or areas of difference, but not all. During conflict, they are slightly expressive.
- *Unstable couples*:
  - *Hostile couples*: Hostile couples tend to display high levels of defensiveness in their interactions. Their communication style includes significant amount of criticism in the form of "you always" and "you never" statements, and complaining. When locked in conflict, each partner tends to restate their own point of view, and there is little understanding, interest or respect conveyed for the other person's standpoint. They also tend to show negative emotions and at times all "Four Horsemen" are present: criticism, defensiveness, contempt and stonewalling.
  - *Hostile-detached couples*: According to Gottman, these couples resemble two fighters involved in a mutually exasperating deadlock, with no winners. They may criticise and pester

one another during conflict, and convey emotional aloofness and resignation. The studies revealed an escalation in their conflict over time, though one of them tends to withdraw eventually.

Research provides abundant evidence to suggest that communication and conflict management styles can make or break a partnership. Therefore the answer to the question of what makes a positive and resilient partnership lies in *constructive dialogues.*

Lauer, Lauer, and Kerr (1990) asked 100 happily married couples (who were married for 45 years on average) to explain what made their marriage a success. The couples made the following points:

* They valued their marriage and saw it as a long-term commitment.
* They sincerely valued their spouses and wanted to spend time with them.
* The similarities between them helped, as they agreed about most things.
* Their sense of humour helped in maintaining good relationships.

The models and research findings presented here offer us a sound ground for optimism, that with consistent maintenance work, and with the help of scientific knowledge, perhaps we can have our "happily ever after".

Positive relationship interventions

Several relational interventions have been tested by researchers and have shown promising results in improving partnerships, family relationships, friendships and collegial relations.

The interventions include empathy, compassion, forgiveness, acts of kindness, gratitude (that is other-oriented) and capitalisation (Warren et al., 2017).

In the context of partnerships, Gottman and Silver (1999) developed the Sound Relationship House Theory: a therapeutic approach containing a seven-step programme that aims to lay a foundation for couples in building healthy, intimate and durable relationships. The programme is also designed to improve the quality of communication, and therefore places equal emphasis on managing conflicts in a constructive manner, and building a positivity habit into the relationship (see details in Chapter 13).

FLOURISHING FAMILIES

Adler (2013) was one of the first scholars who considered the question: What makes a healthy, thriving family? According to the Adlerian approach, a healthy family displays the following four vital qualities:

- There is warmth and respect among family members.
- The parents' or carers' decision-making style is democratic rather than authoritative.
- There are household rules and practices in place that promote children's emotional growth and foster autonomy and maturity.
- The family has pleasant and productive relationships with others.

Since then, the structures and functions of families changed dramatically around the globe, making it more difficult for researchers and practitioners to define a healthy or functional family. Nevertheless, the importance of the family unit and its long-term impact on our psychological wellbeing and the health of its members remains indisputable (Walsh, 2012).

Changes in the family structure

Among the many changes that occurred in the family structure, researchers highlighted the following key points (Walsh, 2012):

- *Declining marriage and birth rates*: Marriage and birth rates have sharply decreased in many countries, and accordingly childbirths are delayed.
- *Increasing cohabitation*: Cohabitation is widespread today, and child-drearing by cohabiting couples has also become fairly common.

- *Same-sex couples*: The past decades have seen a dramatic increase in same-sex couples, particularly with the legalisation of gay marriages.
- *Single living*: A growing number of people live on their own.
- *Dual-earner families*: Most couple-based families in the West are dual earners.
- *Together but living apart*: A relatively new trend is to be in a steady, intimate couple relationship, yet live separately.
- *Single-parent households*: Unmarried or divorced parents who run their households are now commonplace.
- *Divorce and remarriage*: Rising divorce rates and remarriages have made stepfamilies an increasingly common phenomenon.
- *Adoptive families*: Adoptions have also been on the increase for both couples and single parents.
- *Kinship care*: In many families grandparents live far away and cannot provide kinship care. On the other hand, there is a growing trend whereby extended family provide regular care for children.
- *Gender variance*: Concepts around gender identity and sexual orientation have become more fluid.
- *The decline of traditional gender roles.*
- *Interracial and interfaith unions* are increasingly common.

Clinical psychologists often assess a healthy family through the use of a negative measure: the absence of psychopathology. This deficit-based approach has been challenged by positive psychology scholars, who have argued that a flourishing family environment involves more than the absence of problems. More importantly, "no families are problem-free; all families face ordinary problems in living. Thus, the presence of distress is not necessarily an indication of family pathology" (Walsh, 2012, p. 3). Accordingly, Walsh (2012) defined a "functional family" as a workable system that enables "achieving family goals, including instrumental tasks and the socioemotional wellbeing of family members" (p. 8).

Families face tremendous challenges today, more than ever before, and there is often scarce social support available to families, and fewer state-provided safety nets. Hence, it is perhaps unsurprising that researchers have been exploring resilience in families. Black and Lobo

(2008) generated a list of family qualities that have been found by researchers in healthy and resilient families:

- An assured and affectionate marital relationship;
- Children's basic needs are met;
- Dedication of family members to each other;
- Constructive communication;
- Clear domestic rules and limitations;
- A decision-making style that is founded on open discussion and negotiation;
- A democratic parenting style which combines parental responsiveness with appropriate levels of demand;
- Promotion of individual autonomy and accountability, and positive self-image;
- A religious affiliation;
- Having shared leisure and recreational activities;
- Adaptive and effective stress management strategies;
- Sense of belonging and intimacy among family members;
- Humour and laughter.

Social support

Support is a central aspect of most close relationships, which can play out most intensely during times of trouble. There are four types of social support that often overlap (Barry, Bunde, Brock, & Lawrence, 2009):

- *Emotional support*: This includes having someone to talk to, consult with or share news with, a shoulder to cry on, and getting a warm, caring, approving or comforting response from others;
- *Physical comfort*: Includes touch, hugs or cuddling;
- *Advice*: Provision of information, advice and guidance;
- *Instrumental support*: These are the tangible types of assistance that people can offer each other, from babysitting to money lending.

Offering and receiving support can significantly enhance our relationship, though how we provide support matters. Attentive and empathic support that fits our wishes and preferences is constructive, but some forms of support are not beneficial. Too much support, help that is intrusive, or that comes with expectation of payback, or one that diminishes our self-esteem, often has high emotional costs (Brock & Lawrence, 2009). Additionally, studies into social support suggest that how we perceive support is more important than what people actually do for us (Lakey, 2013).

FRIENDSHIPS

Fehr (1996, p. 7) defined friendship as *"a voluntary, personal relationship, typically providing intimacy and assistance, in which the two parties like one another and seek each other's company."*

There are several qualities that make up a good friendship (Hall, 2012):

- *Affection*: Close friends feel affection towards each other. They are fond of each other, and convey mutual trust, respect and genuineness.
- *Communion*: Good friendship involves self-disclosure, mutual support and feeling equal, where both partners' preferences are taken into account.
- *Companionship*: Friends share interests and take part in recreational activities.

Friendship norms

Rules for relationships are often embedded in cultural values, norms and beliefs systems and hence they vary across cultures. In a pivotal study, researchers created a set of friendship rules and asked participants in the UK, Italy, Hong Kong and Japan which rules apply in their cultures (Argyle & Henderson, 1984). The study was able to produce a list of friendship norms that seem to be universal:

- Don't nag.
- Keep information confidential.

- Provide emotional support.
- Provide assistance when needed.
- Confide in your partner.
- Share good news.
- Avoid jealousy.
- Stand up for your partner.
- Repay debts, favours and compliments.
- Keep the other happy when spending time together.

Friendships change as we mature, and there are also significant gender differences. Women's friendships involve self-disclosure, emotional sharing and affection, whereas men's friendships revolve around mutual interests and activities, camaraderie and entertainment (Fehr, 1996). Wright (1982) noted that women's friendships occur "face-to-face", whereas men's are "side-by-side".

WEAK TIES

Nearly 50 years ago, Granovetter (1973) recognised "the strength of weak ties". Although he noted that we rely on our close relationships more often for support, he argued that our weak ties (colleagues, acquaintances, friends of friends) are sometimes more effective than close ties because they "are more likely to move in circles different from our own and will thus have access to information different from that which we receive" (p. 1371). Granovetter argued that weak ties are particularly useful for acquiring instrumental support. In his study, he found that many people found a job by networking with people with whom they had weak ties.

However, today, with easy access to information, and a vast number of weak ties, researchers have been questioning the effectiveness of these ties. Recent studies suggest that we are less likely to acquire new information through weak ties in a variety of domains, and that groups with weak ties may not endure for long. However Gee, Jones, and Burke (2017a) argued that weak ties are still helpful in obtaining jobs, in linking to people outside our network and in sparking new ideas. In a large-scale analysis of 17 million social ties from 55 countries on Facebook, Gee, Jones, Fariss, Burke, and Fowler (2017b) found that: "Most jobs come from a weak rather than a strong tie in all 55 countries" (p. 371).

Much of our communication with people with whom we have weak ties occurs through technology – whether email, text, tweets or "likes". Are these as effective as face-to-face communication? Researchers argued that communicating through technology indeed differs in many ways from face-to-face interaction. Firstly, the pace of exchanges through technology is slower, and hence we can consider what we want to say and how to communicate it. Also, without the non-verbal cues, less unintended information is conveyed. Hence we have more control over our transmissions. This makes the communication safer, more manageable and more comfortable (Van Zalk, Branje, Denissen, Van Aken, & Meeus, 2011). Research suggests that we make an effort to make our communication clearer, though despite this, miscommunications still occur frequently. Privacy can be an issue online, and people manage it less attentively online than they do in face-to-face exchanges. Social media and technology-based exchanges are helpful in finding romantic partners, and texting can help us preserve our relationship even when we are away, and to show others that we care (Valkenburg & Peter, 2009).

Are your Facebook "friends" really your friends?

Clearly some are, as most of us will likely have our closest friends included in our Facebook page. However, many of us will also likely have in our Facebook list of "friends" people whom we regard as acquaintances, as well as strangers that we have never met. Therefore our lists may include hundreds of "friends", but only a small fraction of them are in fact real friends.

On the negative side, social media sites can also bring some disappointment and harm. We may be upset when others overlook or reject a friend request, remove our messages or photo tags or don't "like" our posts (Tokunaga, 2011). We may also feel excluded when we learn of events that we weren't invited to. Seeing lots of photos of other people having more fun triggers social comparison, making us feel bad. Because we have easy access to so many people, we no longer value these relationships. Posting our relationship status to the world is often a source of annoyance between new couples, particularly when one partner feels that they are "in a relationship" and the other doesn't (Papp, Danielewicz, & Cayemberg, 2012).

The bottom line regarding social networks is that extensive online networks of weak ties cannot replace the depth, richness and support of close ties. We can't depend on our Facebook "friends" for support, and research suggests that scrolling through newsfeeds does not make us happy, nor improve our wellbeing, but time spent with family and close friends does (Satici & Uysal, 2015).

Dating sites

Does digital proximity work? Today a growing number of people meet online on dating websites and social media sites, or through phone applications that can help seekers find people who reside in their area.

Recent studies show that online exchanges are now a common way for couples to become acquainted. While these sites and applications can give us access to others and supply a significant amount of information about potential partners, the outcomes can be disappointing. For one, there is seemingly an abundance of choices, but research is showing that this isn't conducive, as users are overwhelmed and distracted by the hundreds of profiles, and become less selective. Consequently, they may seek attractive people with whom they have little in common, date several people simultaneously, and be less able to commit. Nevertheless, today about 30% of marriages in the USA started online (Sprecher & Metts, 2013).

THE POWER OF RELATIONSHIPS

There is ample research evidence that demonstrates the potency of relationships, in particular close ties. The following sections offer a brief summary of the mounting scholarly work on this topic.

Mental health, wellbeing and happiness

In the past 50 years scholars around the globe have made a consistent observation: close relationships are vital to our mental health, and are a primary predictor of psychological wellbeing and happiness. People who have a close circle of family and friends with whom they have nurturing, trusting and supportive relationships report higher levels of happiness, wellbeing, purpose and meaning in life and resilience. They also report lower levels of stress and mental illness, particularly depression. These findings were consistently found across different genders and age groups, and among healthy populations as well as those with acute or chronic illnesses (Warren et al., 2017).

Accordingly, happily married people show higher subjective wellbeing than divorced, single people, and unhappily married people. A more refined analysis has shown that relational quality, intimacy, self-disclosure and relational satisfaction are associated with happiness (Warren et al., 2017). Among married people, a warm, attentive and supportive relationship with one's partner matters more than money: income has less impact on happiness than social support does (North, Holahan, Moos, & Cronkite, 2008).

On the negative side, the absence or loss of social bonds, and dysfunctional relations, are known as primary risk factors for mental illness. In 1897 Durkheim (1963) discovered an association between widowhood and suicide. Further research confirmed that the death of a spouse is a highly traumatic event, associated with depression, stress, low wellbeing, loss of meaning in life and dissatisfaction with life. Some differences were found between men and women: widowed men were found to be more isolated and depressed compared to widowed women, and researchers argued that this is due to having fewer close relationships that they could rely on for support. With the passage of time most people eventually adapt, though according to the research, bereavement can take about 7 years to recover from, and some people never recover (Miller, 2015). Similar findings were found in bereaved parents (particularly fathers) who reported poorer wellbeing 20 years after the event (Ryff, 2018).

Research on newly divorced couples found that they experience loneliness, depression and self-harm tendencies, and were more likely to attempt suicide compared to couples who remained together. Longitudinal studies have shown that, for the vast majority of divorcees, wellbeing returns to pre-divorce levels after 3 years on average, though some may never fully recuperate. Notably, 9% of divorcees experience increases in their wellbeing immediately following the divorce. About two-thirds of those who get divorced remarry, and see an upsurge in their wellbeing. Unfortunately, remaining in an unhappy marriage seems to have similar maleffects to separation: couples in dysfunctional marriages are more likely to experience major depression (Miller, 2015).

Research has shown that divorce has a negative effect on children's mental health, which manifests most commonly in depression, anxiety, substance abuse, challenging behaviours, social isolation and poor academic performance. Additionally, they are more likely to experience divorce themselves in adulthood. Researchers seem to agree that the primary cause of children's distress following divorce is parental incessant conflict, which often begins long before the divorce (Barber, 2003). Once parents establish more stable, amicable interaction patterns and routines, children's wellbeing improves, particularly if they continue to see both parents regularly. Researchers seem to agree that children's wellbeing is harmed to a lesser degree by divorce than by living in a conflict-ridden household (Miller, 2015).

Research has also shown that the lack of parental support in childhood is associated with long-term lower wellbeing in adulthood, including depression and anxiety. Physical and psychological abuse in the hands of family members can leave people psychologically scarred for life (Miller, 2015).

Another known source of stress is caring for spouses with chronic illnesses, disabled children or elderly parents. These can negatively affect the carer, and can lead to long-term lower wellbeing and depression (Miller, 2015).

Lonliness and social isolation

Loneliness is defined as *"a distressing feeling that accompanies the perception that one's social needs are not being met by the quantity or especially the quality of one's social relationships"* (Hawkley & Cacioppo, 2010, p. 219).

Loneliness is distinct from social isolation, which is an objective condition, whereby a person lacks social relationships and contact.

Loneliness is a subjective experience. People can lead relatively self-contained lives, but not feel lonely, and equally, they can lead busy social lives, yet feel lonely nonetheless. It therefore depicts people's evaluation of the quantity and quality of their relationships against a desired standard.

Loneliness is a common experience, with nearly 80% of youth and 40% of adults over 65 years old reporting being lonely sometimes. While loneliness seems to lessen between the ages of 20 and 65, research suggests that for 15–30% of people in the West, loneliness is a lingering condition. Research also suggests that men and women differ in their tendency to experience loneliness, with women reporting higher levels of loneliness than men (Hawkley & Cacioppo, 2010).

Counterintuitively, loneliness is higher in collectivistic cultures where sensitivity to exclusion is stronger than in individualistic cultures (de Jong Gierveld, van Tilburg, & Dykstra, 2006).

Loneliness is also considered partially hereditary and linked with particular traits, such as poor social skills, social anxiety, low self-esteem, neuroticism, low assertiveness and shyness, and strongly associated with a range of mental disorders including stress, anxiety, depression, personality disorders, psychosis and suicidal ideation. It is also linked with reduced cognitive performance, self-regulation and executive control, low self-esteem, anger and pessimism (Hawkley & Cacioppo, 2010).

In the health domain, social isolation and loneliness are associated with poorer health markers: weaker immune responses, higher blood pressure, higher levels of cholesterol and cortisol, sleep disturbances, accelerated ageing, reduced cognitive performance, memory loss and poor executive control, slower recovery from illness, higher risk of heart disease and Alzheimer's disease and higher mortality rates.

Loneliness is also linked to poor self-care, unhealthy behaviours and non-adherence to medical advice in patients with a variety of illnesses, leading to re-hospitalisation and lower survival rates.

Researchers have argued that loneliness generates "wear and tear" in the body that reduces resistance to illness and the capacity to recover (Hawkley & Cacioppo, 2013). Scholars therefore consider social isolation as a high-risk factor that is comparable to the risk presented by smoking, lack of exercise or poor diet. The impact of social isolation on mortality was comparable to that of regular smoking (Holt-Lunstad, Smith, Baker, Harris, & Stephenson, 2015).

Hawkley and Cacioppo (2010) argued that "loneliness is the social equivalent of physical pain, hunger, and thirst" (p. 219). When left untreated, it can have severe psychological and health consequences. Fortunately, however, loneliness is often a transitory state that can be managed by re-engaging, and establishing new ties with individuals or groups.

Measuring loneliness

The UCLA Loneliness Scale (Russell, 1996) contains 20 items that measure isolation from others, lack of close connection, meaning of relationships and lack of social connection in general.

Health and longevity

In medicine scholarly work has been vast, and has produced some of the strongest and most consistent evidence on the impact of relationships on health and longevity. Research evidence that spans across 50 years in different cultures and age groups has shown that morbidity and mortality rates are lower among those who have networks of close, positive and supportive social ties around them (Holt-Lunstad, Smith, & Layton, 2010). The studies have shown that positive relationships are associated with improved physiological measures (including immune system functioning, cardiovascular health, cortisol, neuroendocrine function and blood pressure), which can predict onset and recovery from illness (Holt-Lunstad & Uchino, 2015).

By far the most convincing evidence regarding the impact of relationship quality on health outcomes emerged from research into social support. In a study on the association between stress and colds, researchers found that high levels of stress are linked to vulnerability to colds; however, people with stronger social support were less likely to develop a cold, even when highly stressed (Cohen, Doyle, Skoner, Rabin, & Gwaltney, 1997). Scholars have therefore argued that social support can buffer the effects of stress on the body. Social support has also been associated with resistance to illness, better compliance with medical treatment, reduction in medication, increased self-care and adoption of health-promoting behaviours, faster recovery from illness, injury and surgery, enhanced quality of life and better survival rates in patients with heart disease and cancer (Holt-Lunstad & Uchino, 2015).

Research into the effects of touch demonstrate its healing properties: kissing and affectionate touch among couples can reduce cholesterol and stress hormones, ease pain and even improve healing of wounds (Gouin et al., 2010).

Social control

Researchers claim that one of the mechanisms through which relationships can produce the impressive outcomes reported in a variety of patient groups is social control. This occurs when people around the patient provide instrumental care (such as shopping or cooking for them) and motivate them to adhere to advice, medication and healthy lifestyle. An important aspect of social control, however, is how it is perceived by the patient. When social control is viewed positively, it can lead to better compliance with medical advice, but when social control is seen as judgemental or unnecessary, it can hinder the adoption of constructive health behaviours (Holt-Lunstad & Uchino, 2015).

In studies that compared married people to non-married individuals, divorcees and widowers, sickness and death rates were significantly lower among married people, though men seem to benefit from marriage more than women. A supportive marriage can influence how quickly people recover from illness or injury, while a hostile marriage can slow down recovery time. Interestingly, self-disclosure, a marker of intimate relationships, was found to be linked with improved health (Miller, 2015). Similarly, the importance of parent–child bonds in reducing loneliness and providing social support in both childhood and in adulthood is undisputed. Siblings are considered a special type of bond that can alleviate the loneliness of those who lack intimate partnership or children (de Jong Gierveld et al., 2006).

The importance of friendship in reducing loneliness and providing support and social control is also well documented. Close friends can replace the function of kinship when lacking. Communal organisations can also offer a means to counter social isolation. Participation in religious or communal activities and volunteer work can bring people together and enable the formation of new ties which are more easily maintained through routine social activity. Indeed, closeness with one's ethnic or racial group and positive group identity can reduce loneliness with its associated health risks, while exclusion and discrimination can negatively impact health (Lewis, 2002).

Although research shows that larger social networks with both strong and weak ties offer better social support and stronger protection against loneliness, there is evidence to suggest that most people rely on four key ties to provide the majority of social support. Men seem to be content when they can turn to their partners for support, while women require a larger and more complex social network to meet their affective needs (de Jong Gierveld et al., 2006).

The impact of distressed and conflictual relationships on our physical health can also be extensive. Dysfunctional marriages take a toll on the couple's health, and researchers found that their immune systems were significantly disrupted during conflict. Conversely, positive behaviours did not have an effect on immune functioning. Similar to those who have recently divorced, unhappily married couples report more health problems and require more medical appointments compared to happily married couples. It is noteworthy though that women experience more impairment to their health compared to men (Pietromonaco & Collins, 2017).

Conflict and health

Conflict is a risk factor for health. People who endure relentless conflicts with family, colleagues or friends are more likely to experience stress. Similarly, people who had difficult relationships with their parents in childhood have high allostatic load, which is the wear and tear in the body that occurs as a result of chronic social stress. If they continue to encounter negative interactions with their close relationships in adulthood, this can amount to allostatic overload, which presents serious risks to their mental and physical health.

Repeated conflicts that involve harsh elements, such as contempt, defensiveness, stonewalling or hostility, tend to elicit chronic stress, that weakens the immune system. As a result partners in conflict become susceptible to illness, particularly to heart disease (Pietromonaco & Collins, 2017).

Research has demonstrated that "dying of a broken heart" is not merely a poetic metaphor. Bereavement significantly increases the risk of mortality, particularly for men, in the first months following the loss of a loved one. Cardiovascular problems are the prime cause of death among bereaved spouses (Elwert & Christakis, 2008).

Similarly, data from a large-scale longitudinal study found that those who were separated or divorced at the start of the study were more likely to die earlier (Sbarra & Nietert, 2009). Likewise, disruption of a close relationship that occurs early in life can make people more susceptible to chronic health problems (Fletcher, Simpson, Campbell, & Overall, 2013).

CONCLUSION

Researchers consistently found that close relationships are a vital source of longevity, health, wellbeing and resilience. While their mere existence can make a difference to our wellbeing, the research provides strong evidence to suggest that their quality significantly matters. When our relationships are of high quality, people typically experience positive outcomes in the form of higher levels of physical and psychological health and happiness. But when the quality of the relationship is poor, or when the relationship is terminated, a wide range of negative outcomes can arise, including death. It is therefore unsurprising that people seek professional help to help save their relationships, and that relationship problems are the most common topic discussed in therapy.

Relationships can be equated to a brick-and-mortar house. If we give it the regular attention and pre-emptive maintenance that it requires, it will last for longer, keeping us safe and content. The knowledge shared in this chapter, underlined by relationship science, aimed to help us establish and manage positive, fulfilling, loving partnerships, friendships and family relationships that stay fresh, and demonstrate resilience and endurance. Holding reasonable expectations, continuously investing in our relationships and communicating in a constructive manner seem to be the central keys to a thriving "happily ever after".

12

STRESS, COPING, RESILIENCE AND POSTTRAUMATIC GROWTH

The winters of life entailing challenge and hardship are common to all of us, and can occur in many forms, and at any time. How we journey through them matters greatly to our wellbeing, quality of life, relationships, resources and development. There are times when we can cope by standing strong. At times we may succumb to tragedy or pain, and at others, we find ways to heal and recover. And there are times when these winters of hardship can become an opportunity to develop and grow. Stormy winter-times can bring about stress, harm, loss, pain and trauma, as we face the true nature of the human condition: its fragility and impermanence, and also the remarkable power of the human spirit.

Although the terms adversity, hardship, suffering and trauma may not be naturally associated with positive psychology scholarship, how we face and manage these events through strategies involving coping, resilience and posttraumatic growth has become a core topic in positive psychology. We may not be able to avoid the trials of life, nor change them, but we can indeed learn how to handle them to lessen impairment to our wellbeing.

This chapter reviews four interrelated topics: stress, coping, resilience and posttraumatic growth. The chapter defines each concept, unpacks their key components and briefly reviews the empirical research around them.

STRESS

Stressful situations are all too common in our lives. Day-to-day hassles, worries about family, health, work and money, and distressing news can all become sources of stress. Unfortunately today work has also become a key source of stress for many of us.

Stress is an inevitable part of life. It is a natural and instinctive response to danger and can protect us in life-threatening situations. Many of us can probably recall situations when our swift stress response protected us from peril. Nevertheless, in the research literature stress is often vilified, and presented as a detrimental experience that can put our physical and mental health at risk. It is therefore important to make the following distinction at the outset: occasional stress is not harmful, and at times can be crucial to our survival. Stress becomes harmful when it is high, chronic and out of proportion. Coping, resilience and posttraumatic growth are types of strategies that are designed to manage stress or the sources that triggered it in order to restore our psychological and physical equilibrium.

> ## What is stress?
>
> The Transactional Model of Stress and Coping (Lazarus & Folkman, 1984) describes stress as a *psychological, physiological and behavioural reaction that occurs when individuals perceive that they cannot adequately handle the demands being made on them.*

Stress emerges in situations where there is an interaction between a person and his or her environment "that is appraised by the person as taxing or exceeding his or her resources and as endangering wellbeing" (Lazarus & Folkman, 1984, p. 19). The Transactional Model therefore conceptualises stress as an outcome of the transaction between the demands that people face and their capacities to meet these demands. Stress emerges when there is imbalance: when the demands cannot be met by the available resources. Crucially, the model suggests that how people *perceive* and *evaluate* the situation and their capacity to meet the demands can determine whether stress will emerge or not (Figure 12.1).

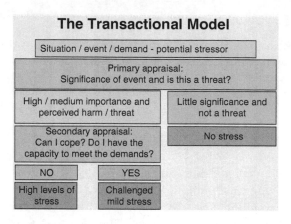

Figure 12.1 The Transactional Model of Stress and Coping (Lazarus & Folkman, 1984).

Demands and stressors

Demands can range between everyday hassles to traumatic events. They can be an illness, a relationship situation, a deadline, a test, financial circumstances, wars, accidents, and many other life occasions. They can be real or imagined, anticipated or unforeseen, single events, intermittent or ongoing situations. They can originate from external sources or be self-imposed, and counter-intuitively, they can be both negative and positive life events. They also vary in their intensity, severity and impact. Importantly, every day we meet numerous demands at home and at work without becoming stressed. Demands become *stressors* when we appraise that we cannot meet these demands.

Appraisals

According to the Transactional Model, two appraisals occur when we face demands. These appraisals are key moments because they affect whether stress will emerge, and how we cope (Lazarus & Folkman, 1984).

- *Primary appraisal*: Firstly the demand of the situation is appraised: how significant is the demand or situation? Is it causing harm or loss, or is it a future threat? If we consider that the situation is not important and causes no significant detriment, then no stress will be experienced. If on the other hand we evaluate that the situation carries great weight and can cause damage, then stress will transpire, and the secondary appraisal will take place.

• *Secondary appraisal*: In this appraisal we deliberate whether we have the appropriate resources or capacities to handle the situation. It therefore places the demands of the situation against our abilities or assets. If we arrive at the conclusion that we have sufficient resources to handle the situation mild stress will emerge, and we will likely feel challenged. If on the other hand we estimate that we do not have the necessary capacities to address the demands, then high levels of stress will be experienced.

These appraisals are highly individual. What one person may perceive as a stressor may not appear as a stressor to another person. Appraisals are affected by personality traits, such as neuroticism and pessimism. They are also influenced by vulnerabilities: past pain or trauma which can make individuals more sensitive to particular types of challenges. Appraisals are also context-dependent: a demand seen as a stressor today may not be seen as a stressor tomorrow. Mood, fatigue and even hunger or thirst can affect how we appraise demands. Research also suggests that people are often unable to accurately assess the demands, and at times miscvaluate their resources and capacities.

Resources and capacities

There are several types of stress-relevant resources and capacities:

• *Coping and resilience skills* (see sections below);
• *Relevant life or professional knowledge and skills;*
• *Resources* that we have access to (for example, time, money, power);
• *Personality traits* that can buffer against stress (such as optimism, self-efficacy and humour);
• *Social support* (emotional and instrumental).

TYPES OF STRESS

Selye (1993) distinguished between several types of stress:

- *Eustress – positive stress*: This is a mild stress response that has been found to have a positive effect on performance. It prompts psychological and physiological alertness and high energy. These in turn generate motivation, which can enhance people's capacity to persevere on tasks. It is usually short-term, and recovery is essential to maintain its benefits. In sports, coaches often induce eustress in their trainees to increase performance.
- *Distress – negative stress*: There are two types of distress that invoke strong, negative physiological, psychological and behavioural stress responses. Both tend to undermine performance:
  - *Acute stress*: This is an immediate, instinctive response to an event. It is a short-term, infrequent stress response, followed by recovery. As noted earlier, it is a natural response, crucial for facing danger. It can generate high energy, vigilance, activation and drive. It has no harmful long-term consequences *provided that it is followed by appropriate recovery*. Acute stress can become chronic stress if it becomes frequent and there is little recovery.
  - *Chronic stress*: This is a recurrent or continuous stress response, with little or no recovery, often labelled as "being stressed out". It tends to drain physical and psychological resources and has harmful long-term consequences. With chronic stress two issues emerge. In addition to managing the demands of the initial stressor, chronic stress becomes yet another problem that needs to be addressed. Additionally, it creates a vicious cycle, whereby the chronic stress leads to reduced capacity to manage the demands. As a result, the demands that are not being met gradually accumulate. The person then experiences increased stress levels that further impede their capacities, leading to further build-up of unmet demands.

The stress response

The stress response is often described as a sequence of internal events that occur once a demand is present and noted (Lovallo, 2015). The process can be instant and rapid and can conclude in seconds. The typical sequence involves:

1.   A demand is noticed.
2.   Cognitive appraisals take place. If the appraisal concludes that the demand is potentially detrimental and exceeds one's resources, the next stage occurs.
3.   Emotional arousal is prompted.
4.   The emotional response stimulates areas in the brain, which in turn activate several physiological mechanisms.
5.   The physiological reactions generate psychological and behavioural manifestations in the form of fight, flight or freeze.
6.   Coping behaviours are then enlisted to restore wellbeing.

Stress is a state of physiological and psychological imbalance. The brain reacts to stress by activating a range of physiological responses, including the secretion of stress hormones. These in turn stimulate other physiological responses such as muscle contraction, and increased blood pressure, heart rate and respiratory rate. Importantly, several essential functions are suppressed during episodes of stress, including immune response, digestion, growth and the reproductive system.

In acute stress, these reactions are temporary, and in the recovery stage the body resumes its normal functioning. But when people experience chronic stress, these reactions relentlessly occur, flooding the body with harmful levels of stress hormones, and causing physiological erosion of these organs or functions, which is why chronic stress is considered a health hazard (Lovallo, 2015).

Measuring stress

The Perceived Stress Scale (PSS-10) is a 10-item questionnaire which assesses how often certain stressful experiences occurred in the past month (Cohen, 1988). The scale is available in 26 languages.

THE UPSHOTS OF STRESS

Stress, and in particular chronic stress, is strongly associated with a variety of health and psychiatric disorders, and can exacerbate existing conditions.

Health outcomes

On the health front, chronic stress poses a high risk for the onset or deterioration of cardiovascular disorders and stroke, which can result in sudden death. Stress is linked to the onset or worsening of several chronic illnesses such as AIDS, multiple sclerosis, fibromyalgia, rheumatoid arthritis, chronic fatigue syndrome, diabetes, irritable bowel syndrome, hypothyroidism, asthma, osteoporosis, and a variety of skin disorders and allergies. It can also induce a long list of minor to major health problems, including pain, breathing difficulties, sleeping problems and fatigue, indigestion, diarrhoea or constipation, bloating and nausea, appetite change, weight loss or gain, ear ringing and hair loss. Stress has also been linked to reduced sex drive, irregular menstrual cycles, low sperm production and impotence. Over long periods, chronic stress can contribute to the development of a weakened immune system and accelerated ageing, resulting in frequent illness, and slower recovery from illness and injury (Lovallo, 2015).

Allostatic load

Allostasis theory suggests that when people are exposed to chronic stressors and need to repeatedly engage coping strategies to maintain equilibrium, they are at high risk of developing allostatic overload: a wear and tear in the body that results in impaired capacity to respond to stress. It can manifest itself in cognitive and physical dysfunction, and cardiovascular disease, and is associated with high mortality risk (McEwen, 2005).

Psychological effects

The psychological upshots of stress are also substantial. Stressful life events can cause the onset of depression, suicidal ideation, posttraumatic stress disorder, anxiety, panic attacks, personality disorder, eating disorders and obsessive compulsive disorder. People who are stressed are more prone to experience difficulties in concentration, memory and performance, resulting in more errors and accidents.

Stress is also associated with difficulties in making decisions, applying judgement, and feeling confused and disorientated. At work, stress is linked to burnout, feeling overloaded, low self-esteem and sense of inadequacy or powerlessness.

Compulsive behaviours and nervous habits, frequent worrying or obsessing, crying spells, rumination, agitation, frustration and anger, and reduced self-control are also common among those who are chronically stressed. Chronic stress is also linked to loneliness (Everly & Lating, 2019).

Behavioural manifestations

The renowned fight–flight–freeze stress reactions can manifest in a variety of behaviours, including isolation, excessive TV watching or video games, abuse of alcohol, cigarettes or drugs, over-eating or under-eating, lying, tardiness and procrastination, recklessness, hyperactivity, and at times apathy. Stress is also associated with lack of self-control and inhibition, combative or explosive responses, agitation, frustration and anger (Everly & Lating, 2019).

COPING

Defining coping

"Coping refers to the person's cognitive and behavioural efforts to manage (reduce, minimise, master, or tolerate) the internal and external demands of the person–environment transaction that is appraised as taxing or exceeding the person's resources" (Folkman, Lazarus, Gruen, & DeLongis, 1986, p. 572).

Lazarus and Folkman (1984) conceptualised coping as an attempt to re-establish balance and wellbeing when facing a stressor and experiencing stress.

Coping strategies serve two key functions:

* *To moderate the stress that is experienced*, reduce its physiological and psychological impact and restore wellbeing.
* *To handle or manage the stressor* – the situation or problem that provoked the stress. This requires the person to directly engage with and modify aspects of the stressful event.

Coping is a dynamic process. It consists of phases of dealing with one or more stressors, and engaging with different aspects of these stressors. Within a coping episode, a person may adopt several strategies, and alter them if ineffective. At times, appraisals may be revisited and reconsidered, and resources may be sought or replenished when depleted. Coping is therefore a flexible and effortful activity which aims to rebalance demands against resources, recover from losses or setbacks, or prepare for impending trials (Skinner & Zimmer-Gembeck, 2007).

Stress management and coping interventions

There are numerous interventions that have been tested by researchers and shown to be effective in managing stressors and reducing stress. These are routinely offered today in high-risk workplaces, and often presented in a variety of formats: brief workshops, group-based courses, individual therapy sessions and self-guided online courses or phone applications.

Stress management interventions often include psycho-educational content on stress, as well as practising a variety of coping strategies (see examples below). Examples of stress management interventions include the Mindfulness Based Stress Reduction (MBSR) programme, cognitive behavioural therapy (CBT), solution-focused therapy, physical exercise classes, biofeedback and relaxation techniques (Romas & Sharma, 2017) (see further details in Chapter 13).

COPING STRATEGIES

There are more than 400 ways of coping with stressors and stress (Skinner & Zimmer-Gembeck, 2007). Research suggests that people who are aware of and capable of applying a larger repertoire of coping behaviours, are able to cope more effectively with stress than those who have a more limited repertoire of coping strategies. The common strategies can be classified into several clusters (though some overlap):

- *Appraisal-focused strategies* prompt individuals to revisit their initial appraisal and reconsider if the stressor is indeed a threat, loss or harm, and whether they have the resources that would enable them to meet the demands presented by the situation. A modification of a person's initial appraisal can often lead to diminished stress.

- *Proactive coping* is the process of foreseeing potential stressors and acting in advance to prevent them or to limit their impact.
- *Primary vs. secondary control strategies* consider whether one attempts to change the situation or change oneself:
  - *Primary (assimilative) control* involves changing the situation, the environment or the demands that one faces.
  - *Secondary (accommodative) control* strategies involve adapting, developing or changing oneself to be able to address the stress or meet the demand.
- *Problem vs. emotion-focused strategies*:
  - *Problem-focused strategies* directly influence the stressor. They are likely to involve attempts to address problems, change the situation or reduce the demands in practical ways. They may involve strategies such as: information gathering, exploring possibilities, planning, making decisions, assessing risk, reprioritising or rescheduling, resource reallocation, seeking new resources, renegotiating demands and upskilling.
  - *Emotion-focused strategies* aim to address the stress that is experienced, and in particular, to lessen the distressing emotions that are felt. These are well suited for stressors that are uncontrollable and hence cannot be resolved through problem-focused strategies. Emotion-focused strategies may involve acceptance, perspective taking, accepting responsibility, willingness to compromise, avoiding overthinking, using humour, applying self-compassion, adopting a positive outlook, positive reframing, challenging unhelpful interpretations, distracting oneself, avoiding social comparison, boosting positive emotions, engaging in nurturing activities, savouring little joys, celebrating success, writing a diary – and smiling.
- *Engagement vs. disengagement*:
  - *Engagement strategies* involve direct and active engagement with the stressor or with the stress.
  - *Disengagement strategies* are those that involve disengaging or distancing from the situation or the stressor, or distracting oneself from the stress that is felt. Denial is also a disengagement strategy. These are often useful for short-term relief, but considered maladaptive if used long-term. They are particularly appropriate for chronic stress, to allow the person some periods of respite.

- *Relational and social support strategies*: Relational strategies are intended to enlist emotional or instrumental support when needed from one's social circle. They are useful for tackling the demand of a situation as well as the stress symptoms. Examples include seeking emotional and instrumental support, seeking advice, guidance or perspective, collaborating with others, delegating tasks to others, nurturing relationships, asserting boundaries in relationships, managing conflicts, reducing deception and inauthenticity, initiating physical touch, showing forgiveness, kindness or empathy, and contributing to others.
- *Meaning-focused coping*: In stressful times often central beliefs, values and mindsets are challenged and questioned. Meaning-focused strategies can help people face these questions. When using meaning-focused strategies, people draw on their beliefs, values, purpose and meaning in life to motivate and sustain coping during difficult times. Examples include contemplating the meaning and purpose of one's life, a positive reappraisal of the situation or benefit finding, revision of goals or life priorities, turning to spiritual beliefs, values clarification, reconnecting with one's authentic self and engaging with a faith or spiritual community or activities.
- *Self-care*: In challenging times taking care of our health and wellbeing is essential. Self-care strategies may include relaxation techniques, breathing exercises, physical exercise, practising mindfulness or other types of meditation, taking "downtimes" or "me" time, taking time to reflect, connecting with nature, engaging with a recreational activity, adopting a healthy diet, taking care of one's appearance and sleep hygiene.
- *Approach vs. avoidance strategies*:
  - *Approach strategies* aspire to achieve a positive desired outcome or solution. They have been found to be more effective than avoidance strategies in reducing stress and mitigating stressors.
  - *Avoidance strategies* aim to prevent a negative situation or reduce its impact.
- *Adaptive vs. maladaptive coping strategies*: Coping strategies are considered to be adaptive − effective and productive in tackling the demands or the stress or both, or maladaptive − ineffective, unhelpful or even damaging in the long run.

- *Adaptive coping strategies* are those that handle the stressor and reduce stress effectively while at the same time promoting wellbeing and adjustment. The following strategies are considered adaptive: solution- or emotion-focused strategies, situational control, seeking instrumental or emotional support and meaning-focused coping. The following stand out as highly effective strategies: planning, acceptance, humour and positive reframing. These are associated with psychological wellbeing, fewer depression symptoms, resilience, posttraumatic growth and lower physical stress symptoms.

- *Maladaptive coping strategies*, on the other hand, can reduce stress in the short term, but often undermine wellbeing in the long term. Researchers consider the following strategies maladaptive: avoidance, disengagement, withdrawal, resignation, giving up, denial or wishful thinking, rumination, aggression, self-distraction, substance abuse, self-blame and venting. These are associated with depression, anxiety and addictions.

Measures of coping

The Ways of Coping Questionnaire (Folkman & Lazarus, 1988) measures coping processes in several stressful contexts. It includes 66 statements that refer to eight coping strategies: confrontative, distancing, self-controlling, social support, accepting responsibility, escape avoidance, planful problem solving and positive reappraisal.

The COPE scale (Carver, Scheier, & Weintraub, 1989) includes 60 items, which cover 15 coping strategies: positive reinterpretation and growth, mental disengagement, focus on and venting of emotions, instrumental social support, active coping, denial, religious coping, humour, behavioural disengagement, restraint, emotional social support, substance use, acceptance, suppression of competing activities and planning.

RESILIENCE

Facing life stressors is common to all. However people respond and adapt differently to adverse events, whether facing the conventional hassles of life or harrowing, life-changing events. Resilience is one of the capacities and processes that defines and shapes the upshot of these encounters.

The study of resilience emerged from well-documented observations that many people are able to maintain healthy functioning despite experiencing severe adversity. Resilience research aims to explain why some people develop stress-related mental disorders while others do not when facing similar conditions.

Research into resilience spanning five decades emerged initially from developmental psychology. In a large volume of studies, researchers explored the experiences of people who endured substantial, and often recurring, adversity in their childhood. The studies reported that, despite these scarring experiences, the majority of individuals developed into well-functioning, adept adults. The term resilience is used in this context to portray a range of capacities and protective factors that enabled these adults to flourish in spite of the risks to their mental health presented by their developmental circumstances (Masten, 2015).

A second strand of research into resilience revolves around the consequences of trauma for mental health in adults. In this context, researchers have been exploring acute adversities – single, isolated incidents involving life-changing, distressing events that occurred in normative environments, or chronic adversities – facing repeated and enduring, highly taxing life stressors (Long & Bonanno, 2018). The literature on adult resilience facing both types of adversities has shown similar findings to that of developmental resilience: most people seem to be resilient.

The main message that emerges from this body of research is that resilience is ordinary, not extraordinary. People commonly demonstrate resilience when facing life stressors. Even when grappling with traumatic events, most people show healthy functioning and wellbeing (Long & Bonanno, 2018).

Defining resilience

Resilience is defined as *"patterns of positive adaptation in the context of past and present adversity"* (Riley & Masten, 2005, p. 13).

What is resilience?

- *Resilience transpires when protective factors outweigh risks*
  Some scholars described resilience as a collection of capacities, traits or resources that enables people to respond to stressors in productive ways. These are often described as protective factors that can buffer individuals against the risks presented to their well-being by the adversities that they are contending with. From this perspective resilience is described as an equation: a state where the person's protective factors outweigh the risks (Masten, 2015).
- *Resilience is an indication of an effective adaptation process and positive outcomes*
  Other scholars described resilience as a dynamic process of adaptation, involving an interaction between the person's skills, traits and resources, the characteristics of the adversity they are facing, and their coping actions and reactions. This suggests that resilience can be witnessed and evaluated only after the process has ended, and when the outcomes become evident (Long & Bonanno, 2018).

Measures of resilience

The Connor–Davidson resilience scale (CD-RISC) (Connor & Davidson, 2003) is a 25-item scale that measures resilience and can be used both in clinical and non-clinical populations.

The Resilience Scale for Adults (RSA) (Friborg, Hjemdal, Rosenvinge, & Martinussen, 2003) is a 37-item scale that examines intrapersonal and interpersonal protective factors which help to facilitate healthy adaptation.

Adversity characteristics

Adversities vary in their severity, duration and impact. Researchers often make a distinction between acute and chronic adversity (Long & Bonanno, 2018):

- *Acute adversity* involves a single event that is typically isolated. Examples include a natural disaster, terrorist attack or a car accident. While the primary impact of the incident can be relatively short in duration, its upshots may linger for months or years depending on the harm that it has inflicted.

• *Chronic adversity* refers to an intermittent or chronic occurrence of adversity, which exerts a cumulative impact on the person, and drains one's capacities and resources. Examples include prolonged neglect or abuse, living with a debilitating chronic condition or living in a war zone.

ADAPTATION FOLLOWING ADVERSITY

Scholars have made a distinction between several types of resilience (Lepore & Revenson, 2006):

• *Resistance – standing strong*: This form of resilience occurs when people show marginal or no sign of disturbance when facing hardship. That is, they maintain normal functioning, and experience low psychological distress. This pattern is more commonly found in people who face ordinary life challenges, but rarely observed in people experiencing severe trauma.

• *Recovery – bouncing back*: This mode of resilience is manifested in people who experience some disruption in the short term when facing adversity, but after a period of recovery are able to resume their regular, pre-stressor, level of functioning. This pattern is commonly found in people experiencing everyday difficulties as well as in those who encounter acute, and even traumatic events.

• *Reconfiguration – transforming*: This type of resilience emerges when people make adjustments to their lives and craft a new normal way of functioning after facing adversity. Hence, after a remedial period, they do not return to their pre-stressor state. Instead, they redefine and recreate an altered life formation that enables them to achieve equilibrium. This pattern is more commonly found in people experiencing grave chronic adversity. This resilience pattern bears some similarities with the concept of posttraumatic growth, described later.

When people exhibit low resilience this may result in reduced adaptation:

* *Succumbing – giving in:* When people succumb to an adversity or trauma they may experience long-term psychological (or other) impairment which often manifests in the form of a mental disorder. They may be unable to restore wellbeing and normal functioning, and are therefore at risk of developing a prolonged state of dysfunction. Fortunately, there is ample evidence that psychological interventions can support people in this state and promote recovery.

Resilience in development

In a classic study on resilience in development, Werner (1993) observed the life course of a multiracial cohort of children who grew up in chronic adverse conditions and stress, including poverty, familial conflict and break-up, and parental illness. Werner followed the children for more than 30 years.

The study revealed that the majority of children showed positive adaptation despite their harsh childhood circumstances. Those who demonstrated resilience were competent, caring and motivated in their teens, and were successful in several life domains, including school work and social functioning. In adulthood, the resilient individuals continued to show healthy psychological functioning and professional achievements that were comparable to those of their low-risk peers.

KEY PREDICTORS OF RESILIENCE

What are the factors that promote resilience? Researchers have found that there is a set of factors that across studies and populations has been consistently associated with increased resilience. Among these, however, no single factor was found to have a dominant influence on the emergence of resilience (Bonanno, Westphal, & Mancini, 2011).

Resilience in development

Several factors have been found to promote resilience in development and therefore often considered as protective factors (Masten, 2015):

- *Home and social environment*: Nurturing and supportive carer–child dynamic, constructive carer disciplinary style, stable living conditions and positive ties with peers have been shown to promote resilience in the context of chronic childhood adversity.
- *Personal qualities and skills*: Self-esteem and positive self-image, intelligence, problem-solving abilities, easy temperament and flexibility, positive outlook, faith and emotion regulation have been found to predict resilience in development.

Adult resilience

A number of characteristics and resources have been noted in the literature as key predictors of adult resilience (Long & Bonanno, 2018):

- *Personality*: Positive emotions, emotional intelligence, optimism, positive reframing, low rumination, humour, flexibility, self-regulation, self-efficacy, goal commitment, perceived control, problem-solving skills, spirituality and meaning in life seem to predict better psychological adjustment following adversity.
- *Relationships*: Ample research has reported that access to social support (both instrumental and emotional), the quality of the support that is available, community involvement and contribution to others are associated with resilience.
- *Resources*: Education and physical fitness have been associated with positive adaptation. Economic resources also seem to predict increased resilience. Earlier encounters with sporadic adverse life events can have a positive impact on later adaptation, a process which is described as inoculation.
- *Appraisals*: The appraisal of an adversity as a threat or harm, or as an opportunity for development (see coping section above) influences people's stress levels and coping behaviours, and ultimately their resilience trajectory, with gloomy and exaggerated appraisals noted as factors that can undermine resilience.

Resilience interventions

Resilience skills can be learned and developed, and there are several resilience-building interventions that are evidence-based for both adults and children. Leppin et al. (2014) defined *resiliency* as the process of *building resilience*, and described *resiliency programmes* as *"interventions that systematically seek to enhance resilience in individuals or groups"* (p. 2).

Resilience programmes for children are usually offered in schools and weaved into the curricula, or offered to vulnerable groups separately. Some offer parallel programmes to the parents. The programmes aim to reduce developmental risks, while fortifying environmental resources and strengthening relevant personal skills (Masten, 2015).

Numerous adult resilience-building programmes are offered today in workplaces, in military academies and in healthcare. They can be offered in the context of individual therapy or coaching, brief or lengthy group-based programmes or self-guided online courses.

Both adult and children's resilience interventions typically provide psycho-education, and engage the participants in exercises that explore one or more of the following topics: adaptive coping strategies, exercises for boosting positive emotions, development of optimism or hope, goal setting, facilitating reframing, mindfulness practice, building self-efficacy and strengthening self-regulation.

The Penn Resilience Programme is a notable example of resilience programmes implemented widely in education as well as for military staff (Gillham et al., 2013; Reivich et al., 2011) (see further details in Chapter 13).

THE OUTCOMES OF RESILIENCE

By definition the key benefits of being resilient include positive adaptation in the face of adversity and stressors: being able to stand strong in the face of adversity, bouncing back following challenging times, or growing from difficult experiences. But there are additional benefits according to the research. Resilience is linked to improved health, energy, cardiovascular health and recovery from illness. It is also correlated with improved mental health: lower stress, exhaustion, depression, anxiety and negative emotions. On the positive side resilience is associated with improved psychological wellbeing, happiness, quality of life, mastery, growth, hope, optimism, self-efficacy, positive outlook, calm, satisfaction with life and acceptance. In the work domain, resilience is associated with increased motivation, self-regulation, grit, performance, goal attainment and productivity (Zautra, Hall, & Murray, 2010).

POSTTRAUMATIC GROWTH

Traumas are gruelling life occasions when people face mortal stakes. Posttraumatic growth research focuses on people who had journeyed through tragic events, endured harrowing upheavals and anguish, and have emerged from these experiences stronger than before.

The concept of personal development that follows from hardship and suffering is not new, and can be found in several religious and spiritual philosophies. From a psychological perspective, posttraumatic growth portrays people's exceptional capacity to adapt. The research around posttraumatic growth explores people's path to adaptation, its facilitators and outcomes.

Defining posttraumatic growth

Posttraumatic growth is described as *the experience of positive change that a person may experience as a result of the struggle with a major life crisis* (Tedeschi, Shakespeare-Finch, Taku, & Calhoun, 2018).

The term posttraumatic growth is often used interchangeably with stress-related growth, adversarial growth, perceived benefits, thriving and positive adaptation.

Models of posttraumatic growth

The Shattered Assumptions Theory (Janoff-Bulman, 1992) argues that at the heart of our inner world are fundamental assumptions about life and the world:

At the most fundamental level of our inner world, we believe that who we are and how we act determine what happens to us: if we are good people (justice) and we engage in appropriately precautionary behaviours (control) bad things will not happen to us.

(Janoff-Bulman, 2004, p. 33)

Traumatic events shock and shatter these core assumptions, inflicting a "seismic impact on individuals' assumptive world" (Calhoun & Tedeschi, 2013, p. 29), that rupture the person's life narrative, and create a sense of "before and after". Posttraumatic growth can be seen as a by-product of the struggle to cope with the harmful event, and primarily from the effort to make sense of the new reality, and rebuild one's core assumptions.

Posttraumatic growth has been witnessed in various contexts, including bereavement, acquired physical disability, war, fire, sexual assault, life-threatening illness and many others. The research suggests that 40–70% of people report some positive outcomes in the aftermath of trauma, and 30–90% describe some elements of posttraumatic growth (Tedeschi & Calhoun, 2004).

Importantly, posttraumatic growth scholarship does not advocate suffering as a facilitator of growth. Rather, it aims to examine it, and facilitate its occurrence in clinical settings (Tedeschi et al., 2018).

There are two leading models of posttraumatic growth. The models differ in their perceptions of the processes that lead to the emergence of posttraumatic growth, and where their focus lies, though both document similar upshots of posttraumatic growth.

- The *Transformational Model* (Tedeschi et al., 2018) is a clinical approach to posttraumatic growth which explores the process and its outcomes, and its key facilitators. The model suggests that, once a person faces a traumatic event, it fragments core elements of the person's worldview, higher-order beliefs and values, and often disrupts key life goals. It also taxes their ability to manage the psychological pain. The resulting distress burden triggers a process of rumination, and coping behaviours that are designed to reduce the distress. At the outset, rumination tends to be an uncontrollable, persistent, invasive and unwanted "brooding". After the first coping strategies are engaged, leading to some reduction of the distress, rumination becomes more deliberate and focused, and can be described as deep cognitive processing. At this stage, the person attempts to comprehend, analyse, reappraise and assign meaning to the event that occurred and its impact, and consider a way forward. According to the model, this is the key process from which posttraumatic growth emerges. It can lead to profound changes in people's core beliefs, identities, life narratives, life goals and behaviours, and to the development of wisdom. Social support is immensely important at this point to promote the growth process (see details below).

- The *Organismic Valuing Theory* (Joseph & Linley, 2006) is a person-centred approach which contends that humans are naturally orientated towards growth. The model focuses mainly on how people rebuild their core assumptions once these have been shattered by a traumatic, life-altering event. According to the model, there are two approaches that people tend to adopt when undergoing this process: either construct new assumptions (accommodation), or modify their old worldviews (assimilation). These can influence whether the person will experience posttraumatic growth.

  - *Assimilation*: This strategy is described as a person's attempt to return to their previous state, by modifying their old worldviews in order to incorporate the traumatic event in their core assumptions. The theory suggests that, similar to a shattered vase that has been glued back together, this strategy will likely leave the person more fragile than before, and hence more susceptible to mental illness, and more vulnerable to future stressors.

  - *Accommodation*: This pattern portrays a person's effort to adapt by rebuilding new core assumptions that enable them to include the traumatic event within their new worldview. Using the shattered vase metaphor, the model suggests that, instead of gluing back the fragmented vase, one can use the pieces to create something new, such as a collage artwork. This strategy is more likely to engender the experience of posttraumatic growth, leading to increases in eudaimonic wellbeing and personal development. It also strengthens people's psychological capacities, making them less susceptible to mental illness, and more adept in addressing future adversities.

Measuring posttraumatic growth

The Posttraumatic Growth Inventory (PTGI: Tedeschi & Calhoun, 1996) is the most widely used scale to measure posttraumatic growth. The has 21 items and has been translated into several languages.

A shorter scale (PTGI-SF) (Cann et al., 2010) with 10 items is also available, and recently a 25-item expanded version of the PTGI (PTGI–X) has been developed (Tedeschi, Cann, Taku, Senol-Durak, & Calhoun, 2017), which is useful in a broader range of cultural settings.

OUTCOMES OF POSTTRAUMATIC GROWTH: AREAS OF GROWTH

Researchers have classified the domains of growth that people typically experience into five categories (Tedeschi et al., 2018).

- *Personal strength*: Following the experience of facing trauma and experiencing posttraumatic growth, people often report on an "increased sense of self-reliance, a sense of strength and confidence, and a perception of self as survivor or victor rather than 'victim'" (Tedeschi et al., 2018, p. 27). This may also manifest through a stronger sense of self-efficacy or mastery; a notion that having survived this level of turmoil, there is nothing that the person cannot handle. This can at times lead to changes in people's focus: they may wish to engage in a novel venture, or to learn a new domain or skill.
- *Relating to others*: This area of growth captures the experience of positive changes in one's relationships in the aftermath of trauma. This may include changes in the quality of relationships such as becoming more empathetic or compassionate, or connecting more deeply with others. It can also involve experiencing changes in one's relational attitudes or behaviours in positive ways, such as increased disclosure, willingness to accept help from others, making a conscious effort to spend more time with family and friends, and expressing gratitude, appreciation or love more frequently. Changes in relationships may at times consist of decisions to establish new ties, or terminate a relationship. It may involve becoming closer to some people or groups, or distancing oneself

from negative, conflictual or destructive relationships. It may also manifest in learning to place stronger boundaries in uneasy or prickly relationships.

- *New possibilities*: This domain often occurs when people identify new goals or possibilities for their lives, following their existential struggle with adversity. This often manifests through relevant actions: taking a new or different path in their professional, voluntary or other aspects of life. A person may change their career or work, move to another place, develop new interests, join an organisation or group, or try out new activities. The changes often include an altruistic element.

- *Appreciation of life*: In the aftermath of trauma and distress, people often report feeling a greater appreciation for life. They may notice things that they have taken for granted before, value small pleasures and have a more intense awareness of positive aspects of life that survived the event. Some people report seeing life in a different way: grasping its vulnerability, seeing it as a precious gift, and cherishing the second chance that they have been given. People report that having dealt with a major upheaval has made them realise the importance of their support network, the need to have more downtime, or to take life more lightly.

- *Spiritual and existential changes*: Lastly, this area of growth reflects the experience of religious as well as non-religious people, who have experienced religious or spiritual growth after grappling with trauma. This may include engagement with religious or spiritual beliefs, practices or communities. Often this is done as a means to garner meaning, connect with a sacred higher power, find peace, belong or contribute to a meaningful venture. It is also likely to involve reflecting on existential or philosophical questions such as belief, mortality and morality.

Posttraumatic growth entails a positive transformation following trauma resulting in new insights, and several areas of growth. These have been associated with other benefits, including higher levels of psychological wellbeing, quality of life, life satisfaction, meaning in life, self-esteem, positive affect, hope, optimism and wisdom. Posttraumatic growth is also associated with lower levels of mental illness (depression and anxiety) and reduced substance abuse (Hefferon, Grealy, & Mutrie, 2009; Tedeschi et al., 2018).

FACILITATORS OF POSTTRAUMATIC GROWTH

Researchers have reported on several key facilitators of posttraumatic growth (Tedeschi et al., 2018).

- *Demographic features and the person's characteristics pre-trauma:* Female gender, older age, higher socio-economic status, higher education, religiosity and secure attachment style seem to facilitate the occurrence of posttraumatic growth, while poor mental health and earlier exposure to severe or chronic stressors may impede its occurrence.
- *Personality traits:* Optimism, hope, extraversion, openness to experience, creativity and positive emotions, as well as deliberate rumination capacity seem to facilitate posttraumatic growth.
- *Social support:* Social networks and the support they can offer can facilitate posttraumatic growth in several ways. The awareness of social network availability, having a support group or role models, establishing new ties and the provision of emotional and instrumental support have been consistently reported as factors contributing to the emergence of posttraumatic growth. Self-disclosure is considered a key facilitator of posttraumatic growth. It can alleviate distress, promote cognitive processing, bring unconscious thoughts and feelings to awareness and encourage problem solving.

Posttraumatic growth interventions

There are few posttraumatic growth interventions. Tedeschi et al. (2018) suggested that this is because the facilitation of growth following trauma tends to occur in the context of clinical trauma therapy which often involves the use of cognitive behavioural therapy or exposure therapy. Narrative and expressive therapies can be effectively used to foster posttraumatic growth by promoting meaning reconstruction, cognitive and emotion processing, and insight generation. Other interventions that can facilitate the process of growth include expressive writing, mindfulness and physical activity.

Calhoun and Tedeschi (2013) reported on an evidence-based group programme that was developed and implemented with combat veterans. The programme included psycho-education on trauma response, distress management strategies, self-disclosure, the development of a new life narrative and the expression of revised life principles.

It is worth noting that some people experience posttraumatic growth as a naturally occurring response to trauma. Joseph's (2013) THRIVE model is useful in this context as it offers several signposts along this journey:

- Taking stock;
- Harvesting hope;
- Re-authoring;
- Identifying change;
- Valuing change;
- Expressing change in action.

CONCLUSION

Stress is a highly common process that has significant implications for health and psychological wellbeing. It impacts multiple physiological systems, and triggers a number of psychological and behavioural reactions, and can contribute to both constructive and harmful outcomes. The Transactional Model suggests that stress emerges from an interaction between a person and their environment, whereby the person assesses that they cannot meet the demands presented to them with the available resources. However, crucially, events and demands generate stress indirectly: it is in fact the person's interpretation of the events and their appraisal of their capacity to meet the demands that flare up the stress response.

Coping and stress are bound by definition. When people cope with a stressful event, they may choose to manage the stressor, or the stress reaction, or both. Conceptualisations of coping have contributed to our knowledge of how people deal with adversity to restore life balance and wellbeing. Coping strategies are therefore essential, mostly self-induced wellbeing interventions.

Resilience is considered a vital coping resource. Research on resilience consistently reports that, even in the most testing and distressing circumstances, most people are able to function well. Resilience research provides some insights into the processes and factors that enable people to display this level of potency. Resilience involves a range of protective factors in the form of capacities, traits and resources. These are enlisted to facilitate effective processes of negotiation and adaptation in challenging circumstances. Resilience is therefore highly beneficial to our wellbeing: it enables us to stand strong in the face of stressors, bounce back following challenging times and develop and grow from difficult experiences. Importantly, resilience skills can be learned and developed.

Finally, the phenomenon of growth following from a battle with a traumatic event is now well documented, and research around it has offered a detailed and nuanced analysis of the process of adaptation that can facilitate growth and the development of wisdom following from a major life crisis. The process of posttraumatic growth can be best conceptualised as an iterative, longitudinal process of self-reflection on one's own life experience and journey. It may commence with rumination, and later transform into a growth-oriented reflection, and autobiographical reasoning. The outcome is a deeper self-awareness, emotional relief, cognitive clarity and a capacity to integrate the traumatic event and the insights gained from it into one's life story. The growth occurs as a result of battling with the fundamental, existential aspects of human existence, and from the process of reconstructing one's higher-order schemas.

The concepts described in this chapter communicate a powerful message. We may not be able to avoid or change the winters of life with the darkness and storms that they bring, nor can we remove them from our biography, but we can indeed learn and grow from them, and transform our lives for the better.

POSITIVE PSYCHOLOGY INTERVENTIONS

Positive psychology scholarship involving theoretical work and empirical research offers a strong indication that we can increase happiness, wellbeing, performance, resilience and other positive states through deliberate positive activities, such as conveying gratitude, engaging in acts of kindness, using character strengths, setting goals and practising mindfulness. Experimental research on positive psychology interventions has prospered since the launch of positive psychology and has become one of the cornerstones of the discipline, rendering the applied side of positive psychology a strong empirical foundation.

In the earlier chapters of this book, positive activities that are relevant to each topic were briefly presented. This chapter offers an overview of the research and theory on positive psychology interventions. The chapter opens with a definition of positive psychology interventions, and then describes several types of activities. The chapter then proceeds to discuss the optimal conditions that can facilitate their delivery and impact. Lastly, the chapter considers some of the key findings around their upshots.

Defining positive psychology interventions

Sin and Lyubomirsky (2009) defined a *positive intervention* (also termed "positive activities") as "*treatment methods or intentional activities that aim to cultivate positive feelings, behaviours, or cognitions*" (p. 468).

Parks and Biswas-Diener (2013) suggested that positive activities should meet the following criteria:

- The key purpose of the intervention should be to promote a positive outcome (for example, happiness, wellbeing, meaning in life, hope).
- The interventions should operate a positive mechanism (for example, using strengths, practising mindfulness, conveying gratitude).
- The interventions should be evidence-based.
- Positive interventions should be applied optimally, responsibly and ethically to fit the needs of the target population, and do no harm.
- The activities should focus on cultivating positive processes or outcomes, rather than repairing flaws, addressing deficiencies or healing pathologies.

TYPES OF POSITIVE INTERVENTIONS

There are two types of positive psychology interventions:

- *Composite programmes* containing several topics, modules or sessions and a number of relevant activities or exercises. Examples include Wellbeing Therapy (Fava, 2016), Quality of Life Therapy (Frisch, 2006), the Mindfulness Based Stress Reduction (MBSR) programme (Kabat-Zinn, 2003), Positive Psychotherapy (Rashid & Seligman, 2018) and the Penn Resilience Programme (PRP: Gillham et al., 2013). The programmes are protocolled, and usually delivered by a trained facilitator or therapist. Some are delivered in a group setting, while others are delivered individually, and there are programmes for adults and children. A few of these are delivered online.
- *Discrete activities* that are designed to promote particular positive states or outcomes, such as happiness, wellbeing, performance, engagement, optimism, awareness, relationships and other positive states. It is worth emphasising that not all activities are intended to increase happiness. The exercises are typically brief, mostly simple to apply, and the majority do not require a special setting or equipment. Examples include setting goals, writing a

gratitude diary, strengths identification, reframing, acts of kindness and savouring. Some can be done once, while others require some repetition to optimise their delivery and outcomes. The majority of these are now available in books, cards, websites or phone applications and can be self-induced, and few require a therapist or a coach to deliver them.

COMPOSITE PROGRAMMES

A sample of composite evidence-based programmes containing positive psychology interventions for adults are detailed below.

The Fundamentals for Happiness Programme

The Fundamentals for Happiness Programme (Fordyce, 1983) was the first happiness programme entailing positive psychology principles to be developed and implemented. The programme revolves around 14 fundamental happiness principles that are designed to induce or maintain happiness. The principles are taught and practised over a 10–20-week period, and participants are expected to implement and habituate these principles in their everyday lives. Since its launch in the late 1970s it has been implemented mainly in a group setting or incorporated into individual therapy, and has been shown to have a significant impact on participants' happiness and wellbeing. The 14 principles are based on characteristics that have been observed in naturally happy people and include:

1. Be more active and keep busy;
2. Spend more time socialising;
3. Be productive at meaningful work;
4. Make plans and organise;
5. Don't worry needlessly;
6. Lower your expectations and aspirations;
7. Develop positive, optimistic thinking;
8. Focus on today;
9. Work on a healthy personality;
10. Be outgoing;
11. Be yourself;

12. Don't bottle things up;
13. Nurture close relationships;
14. Value your happiness.

The Happy Life: Voyages to Wellbeing

The Voyages to Wellbeing programme (Cloninger, 2006) is a psycho-educational programme. It targets people who are recovering from mental illness, and supports them in regaining normative functioning, wellbeing and happiness. It incorporates cognitive behavioural therapy principles and mindfulness practice. Its core mechanism is the elevation of self-awareness. The programme is delivered in a group setting or individually, facilitated by a therapist, and requires participants to engage with the ideas and practise the exercises learned in their everyday lives. The research on this programme suggests that it can indeed induce happiness, improve wellbeing and reduce mental illness.

The programme includes 15 sessions:

1. What makes you happy? – recognising what brings joy;
2. What makes you unhappy? – understanding traps in thinking;
3. Experiencing well-being – quieting the mind's turmoil;
4. Union in nature – awakening your physical senses;
5. Finding meaning – awakening your spiritual senses;
6. Beyond mindfulness – cultivating soulfulness;
7. Observing and elevating your thoughts;
8. Observing and elevating your human relationships;
9. Charting your maturity and integration;
10. Contemplation of being;
11. Can you learn to reduce stress?
12. Calming your fears;
13. Observing the power-seekers in your life;
14. Contemplation of mysteries;
15. Constant awareness.

Wellbeing Therapy

Fava (2016) developed Wellbeing Therapy as a relapse prevention method for individuals recovering from clinical depression and anxiety. Drawing on cognitive behavioural therapy and on Ryff's (1989) model of psychological wellbeing (see Chapter 3) it aims to enhance each component of the model (purpose, autonomy, growth, mastery, relationships and self-acceptance) to achieve better overall wellbeing. The programme can be delivered individually or in groups, and necessitates home practice. A robust body of research on this programme revealed that it can elevate all aspects of psychological wellbeing and alleviate anxiety and depression.

Wellbeing Therapy includes eight sessions and three phases:

1. Awareness of trigger events – keeping a diary of wellbeing and experiences that impact wellbeing and may generate distress.
2. Developing skills for identifying negative automatic thoughts. These draw on cognitive behavioural therapy techniques and aim to consciously promote wellbeing through deliberate activities.
3. Becoming aware of how negative automatic thoughts impact wellbeing, learning to challenge maladaptive thought patterns and moving towards optimal functioning in each area.

Quality of Life Therapy

Quality of Life Therapy (Frisch, 2006) defines quality of life as the "subjective evaluation of the degree to which our most important needs, goals, and wishes have been fulfilled" (p. 22). The programme combines cognitive behavioural therapy techniques with positive psychology interventions. It was initially developed for clinical populations, but today it is applied in non-clinical populations. It can be delivered in a group setting requiring 15–18 meetings, or individually with the guidance of a therapist. Research that tested the efficacy of the programme revealed that it can promote quality of life and improve symptoms of mental illness.

The programme covers 16 life domains: health, self-esteem, learning, values, money, work, play, love, helping, children, relatives, neighbours, creativity, friends, home, and community.

It also applies the CASIO model of life satisfaction as an outline for the therapy, involving:

- *Circumstances*: The situations that the person is facing;
- *Attitudes*: The person's interpretation of these circumstances;
- *Standards* that the person has set for fulfilment or achievement;

- *Importance*: How important the situation is for the person's happiness or wellbeing;
- *Overall satisfaction* with life.

Positive Psychotherapy

Positive Psychotherapy (Seligman, 2018) is designed to increase wellbeing and alleviate psychopathology, through building people's strengths and increasing positive emotions and meaning. It is mainly aimed at people who are unwell, and offered in the context of individual or group therapy.

Positive Psychotherapy is founded on Seligman's PERMA model of wellbeing (see Chapter 3) which includes five components: positive emotions, engagement, relationships, meaning and accomplishment. The programme typically offers 14 sessions with each containing a core topic for discussion and one or more positive exercises, though this can be adapted to fit the client's needs. Research on the programme revealed positive outcomes both in increasing wellbeing and reducing mental illness.

An overview of Positive Psychotherapy sessions with its key wellbeing component is offered below:

1. Orientation;
2. Gratitude (positive emotions);
3. Character strengths (engagement);
4. Signature strengths action plan (accomplishment);
5. Open vs. closed memories (meaning);
6. Forgiveness (relationship);
7. Gratitude (positive emotions and relationships) and therapeutic progress (accomplishment);
8. Satisficing vs. maximising (positive emotions and meaning);
9. Hope and optimism (positive emotions);
10. Posttraumatic growth (meaning);
11. Slowness and savouring (positive emotions and engagement);
12. Positive relationships (relationships);
13. Altruism (meaning);
14. Positive legacy (meaning and accomplishment).

The Mindfulness Based Stress Reduction programme

The MBSR programme was developed in the late 1970s by Kabat-Zinn (2003) and was initially offered to people who suffered from chronic pain. Later it was tested with numerous other physical and psychological conditions, including stress. Since its launch, thousands of people have taken the MBSR course all over the globe.

Mindfulness means paying attention in the present moment, on purpose and non-judgementally. It nurtures self-awareness, clarity and acceptance of present-moment reality. Mindfulness is a way of engaging with life intently, and turning off the automatic pilot. It enables us to observe our own mind, but at the same time be less emotionally attached to our perceptions and emotions. This level of cognitive engagement and emotional detachment can help us remain calm and in control under duress.

The MBSR programme is commonly delivered in a group setting, and consists of 8–10 weekly group meetings, and a day or two of silent retreat. Some programmes are delivered online or through books and are self-guided.

The programme offers psycho-education content on mindfulness and stress, as well as training in varied mindfulness skills, including formal meditation practices, informal mindfulness exercises in everyday life, yoga exercises and group discussions. Participants are required to apply several mindfulness practices daily.

Nearly 50 years of research on MBSR indicates that the training is effective in decreasing pain, stress, depression, anxiety, sleeping problems, fatigue and several other psychological disorders, and also improves physical and cognitive functioning, including immune function, concentration, self-control, creativity, problem solving and wellbeing, happiness, energy and self-esteem.

Following these impressive reports, numerous other mindfulness programmes have been tailored for particular patient groups, following a similar structure. One of these is the Mindfulness Based Cognitive Therapy (MBCT) programme which was endorsed by the NHS as a treatment for depression (Segal & Teasdale, 2018). The programme combines mindfulness with cognitive behavioural therapy techniques.

The Penn Resilience Programme (PRP)

The PRP is a prevention programme offered to adults and children. Its key aims are to promote resilience, and prevent the onset of mental illness (Gillham et al., 2013). The adult programme is typically delivered in a group setting with a trained facilitator.

The programme contains cognitive behavioural principles and covers several topics, including emotional intelligence, self-control, problem solving, decision making, flexibility, social awareness, relational skills, self-efficacy and optimism. It offers both psychoeducational content and relevant exercises. The cognitive component trains participants to become aware of maladaptive interpretations of taxing situations, to challenge these thoughts, and replace them with more adaptive thoughts. The participants are also trained in applying a variety of problem-solving and coping strategies. The programme underlines the importance of social support, and embeds in the training a variety of social skills. The programme was successfully delivered in the US army as well as in many other businesses and considered one of the widest educational programmes implemented worldwide.

Reviews of the research conducted to assess the effect of the programme revealed that it develops resilience, improves mental health, increases performance and reduces stress. Similar results were found in school-based resilience programmes (Gillham et al., 2013).

Meaning in life intervention: the PURE model

The PURE model (Wong, 2010) assists people in reflecting on their meaning in life. It is usually delivered in an individualised therapeutic context under the guidance of a qualified therapist. It contains four domains:

- *Purpose* is the motivational component of meaning in life. Purpose includes goals, directions, incentives, values and aspirations, and can be prompted by working through questions such as: What should I do with my life? What really matters in life?
- *Understanding* is the cognitive component of meaning. It includes making sense of situations, and understanding one's own drivers, values and identity. It can be triggered by questions such as: What happened? What does it mean? How do I make sense of this event? Who am I?

- *Responsible action* is the behavioural component of meaning in life. It includes appropriate actions, doing what is morally right, finding the right solutions and making amends when needed. Questions that trigger responsible action may include: What is my responsibility in this situation? What is the right thing to do? What options do I have? What choices should I make?

- *Enjoyment/evaluation* is the emotional and evaluative component in Wong's model. It involves assessing satisfaction with life generally or in a given domain. It is concerned with the questions such as: Am I content with how I lead my life? Have I achieved what I set out to do?

Positive relationship intervention: the Sound Relationship House Model

The Sound Relationship House Model, developed by Gottman and Silver (1999), is a seven-step programme that is designed to assist couples in building healthy, intimate and durable relationships. The seven steps are best followed in the order shown below.

1. *Build love maps*: A love map is a way of getting to know your spouse intimately: knowing their habits, values and history. It allows us to chart a map of our partner's inner world, by asking open-ended questions.

2. *Nurture fondness and admiration*: Expressing our affection and respect in small, everyday moments can mitigate negativity and escalation.

3. *Turning toward each other* instead of away or against each other. Connecting with each other in small talk, responding positively to bids for connection, finding points of agreement and communicating them are essential for healthy relationships.

4. *Allowing our partners to influence us*: The authors encourage couples to fully listen to their partner's ideas and suggestions, acknowledging the merit of their views, and reacting with respect and a positive sentiment, even if not in agreement.

5. *Addressing resolvable issues*: Using a gentle approach to start a difficult conversation or to voice complaints can differentiate between masters and disasters. Learning to make or accept restoration attempts when disagreements escalate is also an important skill.

6. *Overcome gridlocks*: Couples are encouraged to keep working on unsolvable problems. Having a dialogue about our dreams and desires can open up the way to possible solutions. Physiological soothing can predict growth versus worsening over time in relationships.
7. *Create shared meanings*: This can be done by establishing small rituals of connection and support, and through discussing and moving towards shared goals and values.

POSITIVE ACTIVITIES

Boniwell's (2017) ACTIONS model organises the main discrete evidence-based activities into seven categories according to their aim and core mechanisms:

- *Active interventions*: These activities involve mainly physical activities, such as yoga, aerobic exercise, dance, tai-chi and group walking.
- *Calming activities*: This category consists of self-soothing exercises mainly drawing on mindfulness and other meditative practices, for example, present-moment awareness, mindfulness meditation, prayer, practising non-judgemental acceptance and breathing exercises.
- *Thinking exercises*: The activities in this category are designed to induce reflection and assign meaning, and require writing about or discussing life experiences. Examples include benefit finding, expressive writing, developing a growth mindset, creativity exercises, replaying positive experiences, cognitive reframing and writing a gratitude diary.
- *Identity interventions*: The activities in this category include mainly mental exercises that are designed to elevate self-awareness, support identity clarification and encourage self-development. Examples include character strength identification and usage, the best possible self exercise, values clarification, job crafting and wisdom.
- *Optimising exercises*: This category includes exercises that are geared to enable the optimisation of behaviours and actions, such as setting and pursuing goals, promoting hope, practising

optimistic thinking, developing resilience, exercising one's psychological capital, the life journey exercise, satisficing, flow and showing courage and patience.

- *Nourishing interventions*: These activities encourage self-care, respite and pleasure and include activities such as taking "me" time to engage in enjoyable activities, savouring little pleasures, using humour, engaging with nature and practising self-compassion.
- *Social activities*: This category revolves around relationships and social life. It includes exercises such as socialising, the gratitude letter, acts of kindness, practising forgiveness, capitalisation, active listening and practising empathy and compassion.

An extensive research review of positive psychology interventions is offered in *The Wiley Blackwell Handbook of Positive Psychological Interventions* (Parks & Schueller, 2014), while *The How of Happiness* (Lyubomirsky, 2011) provides guidance on how to practise these activities. Details of a sample of interventions is offered below; all the interventions are evidence-based.

Gratitude interventions

Emmons and Shelton (2002) defined gratitude as "a felt sense of wonder, thankfulness, and appreciation for life. It can be expressed toward others, as well as toward impersonal (nature) or nonhuman sources (God, animals)". Gratitude interventions are happiness and wellbeing-inducing exercises that require participants to convey gratitude in different ways.

There are several versions of gratitude interventions that were explored in empirical research and shown to be effective (Lomas, Froh, Emmons, Mishra, & Bono, 2014b):

- *The gratitude diary/counting blessings*: In this exercise participants are invited to ponder on three good things that exist in their lives for which they are currently feeling grateful, and write them in their diary. These could be people in their lives, events that occurred or achievements. These need not be life-changing events: participants are encouraged to bring to awareness small everyday occurrences such as the garden in bloom, the kindness of a colleague, a tender moment shared with a loved one. The exercise is best repeated weekly for a few weeks, with new good things highlighted in each entry.

* *Three good things*: In this gratitude activity participants are asked to write down each day for one week three good things that had happened to them in the course of that week and consider the causes of these positive events.

* *The gratitude letter/visit*: This activity requires participants to write a gratitude letter to a person in their lives to express their appreciation for something that they have done for them. The letter should detail what the person has done and how it affected their lives. The letter can be delivered personally or mailed, though research suggests that it does not need to be delivered to produce a positive effect.

Acts of kindness

In this happiness-boosting intervention participants are asked to perform five acts of kindness towards other people in one day (Lyubomirsky et al., 2005a). The acts can be small or large, and the person on the receiving end may or may not be aware of the act. Research that tested the efficacy of this exercise found that the acts varied vastly and included buying small gifts, assisting someone with home tasks, donating blood, visiting a friend in need and providing guidance to a colleague. They also found that performing all five acts in one day was highly effective, and that it was not effective to spread the five acts of kindness over the course of a week.

Best possible self

This brief yet powerful evidence-based activity is designed to promote optimism and induce happiness. In this exercise participants are given the following instructions:

> Think about your life in the future. Imagine that everything has gone as well as it possibly could. You have worked hard and succeeded at accomplishing all of your life goals. Think of this as the realisation of all of your life dreams. Now, write about what you imagined.
>
> (King, 2001, p. 801)

Capitalisation

When we share good news or events with our family or friends, how do they react? Gable, Gonzaga, and Strachman (2006) suggested that people's reactions matter, and can enhance or diminish our own joy. Some people may react with an enthusiastic, congratulating response when we share good news. However at times, we may get a fairly bland response from others, and sometimes people may communicate a "not interested" response. Capitalisation (also termed active-constructive response) occurs when we receive excited, gratifying responses to our positive news. These seem to increase our pleasure, and this in turn boosts our relationships, as we feel closer to those who respond well to our happiness (Reis et al., 2010).

Empathy: perspective taking

Empathy is described as a capacity to understand or share the emotional state of another person. An intervention that is commonly applied to increase empathy is perspective taking (Davis & Begovic, 2014). It can be delivered in two ways:

- *Direct perspective taking* occurs through role playing, whereby one person assumes the role of another person and is placed in a similar situation. Role playing can occur in many settings and can take many forms. For example, it can be used when attempting to enhance medical students' understanding of their patients' experience.
- *Indirect perspective taking* is applied by encouraging the participant to *imagine* the experiences, thoughts and emotions of a person who is facing a particular situation, for example, belonging to a group that is stigmatised.

Research on perspective taking has revealed that it increases empathy, sympathy, relevant helping behaviour and willingness to forgive.

Forgiveness

Forgiveness is often considered a relational activity and linked to reconciliation. However, as an intervention, forgiveness is seen primarily as an internal process whereby a person who has experienced a transgression can accept and let go of the negative emotions associated with the event and the perpetrator (Worthington, Wade, & Hoyt, 2014). This can at times result in changes in the relationship with the transgressor, but does not always manifest in this way. The emphasis in the literature is on emotional forgiveness, as holding on to the blame and the associated pain seems to negatively affect health.

The REACH model is an evidence-based approach to forgiveness (Worthington et al., 2014). It requires the person to undergo the following stages and is typically offered in the context of therapy:

- *Recall* the event.
- *Empathise*: Develop empathy for the offender.
- *Altruistic* act: Frame empathy and forgiveness as a noble act.
- *Commit* to forgive.
- *Hold* on to that forgiveness.

It is worthwhile noting that forgiveness is not always appropriate and in certain cases (for example, forgiving a spouse who is regularly violent) could likely lead to escalation of the abuse (Sinclair, Hart, & Lomas, 2020).

Savouring

Savouring is the capacity to notice and appreciate positive experiences (Bryant & Veroff, 2017). Savouring activities are considered happiness-inducing exercises. They require the person to intentionally attend to and engage with past, present or future events, and replay the experiences, thoughts or emotions associated with the event. The intention is to regenerate, intensify or prolong the enjoyment derived from the positive event. Savouring can be a thinking exercise, it can be done in writing or by sharing the details of the event with others and can be facilitated through taking photographs.

Expressive writing

The early studies of expressive writing began in the late 1980s. In these experimental studies which explored the benefits of self-disclosure, people were asked to write about an emotional upheaval that they experienced for a period of 3–4 days for up to 30 minutes per day.

The research around these interventions has consistently shown that participants benefited from writing and saw significant improvements in their physical health. Following from these impressive findings, expressive writing has been introduced into the psychological treatment of several health conditions, including AIDS, cancer and diabetes (Pennebaker & Chung, 2011).

Later on researchers queried whether writing about positive experiences can lead to equally beneficial results. The research on writing about one's best possible self, life goals, positive experience and positive outcomes deriving from negative experience have shown that indeed these exercises can uplift mood and overall wellbeing (Burton & King, 2009).

OPTIMISING THE PRACTICE OF POSITIVE ACTIVITIES

In recent years researchers have recorded several optimal conditions under which positive activities can be best applied to maximise their effects (Layous & Lyubomirsky, 2014). These are briefly summarised below.

- *Characteristics of the activities: timing, dosage, variety and means of delivery*

  Researchers have asserted that *how* positive activities are enacted matters, and can enhance or undermine their impact. Several characteristics of the interventions, including their timing, dosage and variety, seem to impinge on their effectiveness. For example, a study reported that participants who counted their blessings once a week for six weeks showed more benefits to their wellbeing compared to those who conducted the exercise three times a week for the same duration (Lyubomirsky et al., 2005a). The authors also noted that those who performed it more frequently found it tedious, which detracted from its benefits.

  The duration of an activity can also affect its outcomes. Layous and Lyubomirsky (2014) suggested that there is a curvilinear relationship between the length of the activity and its impact: activities that are too short may not have a lasting effect. However, if the same activity is performed without variation for a long period, people may become bored with it, and its impact may diminish. The authors therefore suggested that applying several activities and varying between them could be more effective than engaging with one activity. This method also helps to overcome the effects of hedonic adaptation.

Activities can be delivered in different ways: they can be offered as part of an individual or family therapy or coaching, or as part of group therapy or training. They can also be self-induced from a book, an internet site or a phone application. While delivering positive activities through books, the internet or phones expands the reach of positive psychology interventions, "self-help interventions were typically associated with small effect sizes as opposed to the medium to large effects produced by more intensive face-to-face interventions" (Bolier & Abello, 2014).

- *Characteristics of the person: motivation, beliefs and effort*
Over the years positive psychology interventions have been applied with varied populations: healthy people and those who are physically or psychologically unwell, adults and children, and in varied cultural contexts. Several important factors influence the successful application and outcomes of positive activities: the person's motivation to engage with the activity, the belief that the exercise can be useful in achieving a desired result and the amount of effort that they exert. Individuals who manifest these orientations are more likely to find the activities more effective. Another factor that is of particular importance for experimental research is to enable the participants to voluntarily opt to conduct these activities as well as to educate them as to what it entails and its purpose.

The pursuit of happiness: a caveat

One caveat that emerged however in happiness-inducing activities is that being highly motivated to become happier can in fact diminish the impact of the exercises. Hence it is recommended to direct the focus of participants to the experience itself and to its instructions.

Other considerations regarding the person's characteristics that can influence the delivery of positive activities are culture, age and their initial level of wellbeing. Activities need to be culturally appropriate to be effective. In terms of participants' age, researchers have reported that older participants seem to gain higher benefits from positive interventions compared to young participants. As for the participants' wellbeing, most activities are designed for healthy individuals. Hence the presence of mental illness or low levels of wellbeing can make some activities too emotionally challenging for people to execute. It is therefore recommended to offer activities to individuals showing lower levels of wellbeing by a trained clinician. In view of these findings, Layous and Lyubomirsky (2014) concluded that it takes both a "will" and a "proper way" to apply or deliver positive activities in order for them to be effective.

- *Social support*
Social support or its absence can impinge on the successful application of positive interventions and on their outcomes. Group work conducted by organisations such as Alcoholics Anonymous and Weight Watchers provides ample evidence on the potency of social groups and their capacity to encourage behavioural changes.

How the support is offered and perceived also matters, and researchers have noted that support that comes across as condescending, nagging or intrusive can undermine the activity.

Person–activity fit

People have distinct preferences for particular positive activities, and no one activity is likely to fit all, or work for all. The Positive Activity Model (reviewed in Chapter 2) considers that people will likely see greater benefits from interventions if these fit well with their preferences and lifestyle (Layous & Lyubomirsky, 2014). Research around the question of person–activity fit has indicated that people who showed a preference for particular activities were more likely to adhere to these interventions, engage with them more intently, perform them for longer and consequently they saw greater increases in wellbeing, happiness or other desired outcomes. A preference for an activity can manifest in several ways: participants may enjoy them more than other activities, feel that they value them and gain more from them and find them natural or easy to perform.

The person–activity fit diagnostic

The fit questionnaire (Lyubomirsky, 2011) is designed to aid participants in choosing activities that best fit their preferences. It contains 12 activities: gratitude, optimism, avoiding overthinking and social comparison, acts of kindness, positive relationships, coping strategies, forgiveness, engagement and flow, savouring, goal pursuit, religious and spiritual practices and physical activities.

Participants are required to state the degree to which each activity feels natural, enjoyable, valued or conducted out of guilt or because the situation necessitates it. The score given by the questionnaire enables participants to discern the activities that are most fitting.

THE BENEFITS OF POSITIVE INTERVENTIONS

In the earlier sections we have seen that some positive psychology interventions are delivered as part of composite training programmes that are facilitated by a trainer and contain several topics, practices and home exercises. These programmes engage the participants in a deliberate process of behavioural change and habituation that occurs over the duration of the programme. It is therefore perhaps unsurprising that the research on these programmes consistently shows a moderate to strong impact of the intervention on participants' wellbeing, happiness, resilience, relationships and other states that the programmes are geared to promote.

But what impact can be realistically expected from positive interventions when they are delivered as standalone exercises, without the psycho-educational content, the skill building or habituation process, and often without expert facilitation that a composite programme can offer? As we have seen earlier, some of these activities are indeed simple. They are fairly brief, often require little effort and usually do not require more than a few applications for a short duration. Surely such interventions should not be expected to generate dramatic or eternal impact on wellbeing, happiness, relationships, health, coping or other desired outcomes? However, surprisingly, most of these interventions consistently show moderate impact, a few show low impact, several show strong impact and some show long-term benefits.

Research on these interventions which attempted to consolidate the findings across different interventions and outcome measures to offer a "bottom line" figure that would represent their average impact came under intense scrutiny recently. In an early review (Sin & Lyubomirsky, 2009) of 51 studies which tested the outcomes of positive interventions, the authors concluded that these interventions can indeed significantly enhance wellbeing and alleviate depression. The effect of the interventions was considered mostly moderate, with few revealing low or high impact.

Later studies, some with a different focus or a narrower scope (Bolier et al., 2013; Donaldson, Lee, & Donaldson, 2019; Meyers, van Woerkom, & Bakker, 2013; Weiss, Westerhof, & Bohlmeijer, 2016), reported similar findings and fairly similar effect sizes (though with some variations). However, recently two reviews reported contradictory findings: while White, Uttl, and Holder (2019) reported on much weaker (though statistically significant) effects of the interventions on wellbeing and depression compared to earlier publications, Koydemir, Sökmez, and Schütz's (2020) report seems to be more consistent with the earlier findings and reported a mainly moderate impact of the interventions on wellbeing, with few showing weaker or stronger impact, in the 68 studies reviewed.

An important point to bear in mind with regard to the question of impact is how experimental research is conducted. Sheldon and Lyubomirsky (2019) pointed out that experimental studies may not be an efficient means to assess the impact of intentional activities. This is because they are often conducted in laboratory settings where the researchers may offer a happiness-boosting intervention to an audience who may not be aware what they are being offered, and may not be motivated or willing to exert the effort or commitment that is required to induce short- or long-term benefits. Because of the unnatural setting in which they are offered, they differ from real-life situations where people choose to embark on a behavioural change by applying positive interventions, and hence show much higher levels of motivation and commitment in conducting these activities. However, unfortunately, real-life settings do not easily lend themselves to the conditions that are required for conducting experimental research.

Layous and Lyubomirsky (2014) considered that the key impact of positive interventions is in the learning that is gained when people apply them. That is, by applying positive exercises people gain knowledge and experience in techniques that they can later use when needed to improve their levels of wellbeing or other states. Similar to stress-relieving techniques that induce relaxation, one may not need to use them if not experiencing stress, but knowing how to apply them when feeling stressed can make all the difference to their capacity to cope.

CONCLUSION

The scientific exploration of positive activities and their outcomes reviewed in this chapter conveys a powerful message: we have some control over our happiness, wellbeing, success and performance in many domains, including health, relationships, employment and finances. Though there are other factors at play that can indeed impinge on these aspects of our lives (such as genetic factors and circumstances), the important point is that we are self-determined, autonomous and potent, and that what we choose to think and do matters to our wellbeing (Lyubomirsky et al., 2005a).

The second message conveyed through the myriad of positive interventions reported by researchers is that these activities vary vastly in terms of the time, motivation and effort required to implement them. Some activities, such as the gratitude journal or savouring practices, may require a few minutes, with modest effort. People often convey surprise when they witness the difference that such small activities can make. Other activities, such as mindfulness practice or developing resilience, require undertaking an initial course, followed by consistent daily practice requiring time, effort and resolve. All activities however require intention, drive and motivation, and should not be forced on others.

The third message emerging from the recent research on positive activities is that no intervention fits all. The interventions reviewed in this chapter need to be carefully considered in terms of their good fit to our personality and lifestyle preferences.

REFERENCES

Adler, A. (2013). *The science of living*. Psychology Revivals Routledge.

Aguinis, H., Joo, H., & Gottfredson, R. K. (2013). What monetary rewards can and cannot do: How to show employees the money. *Business Horizons, 56*(2), 241–249.

Argyle, M. (2013). *The psychology of happiness*. Routledge.

Argyle, M. & Henderson, M. (1984). The rules of friendship. *Journal of Social and Personal Relationships, 1*, 211–237.

Aron, A., Lewandowski, G. W. Jr., Mashek, D., & Aron, E. N. (2013). The self-expansion model of motivation and cognition in close relationships. In J. A. Simpson & L. Campbell (Eds.), *The Oxford handbook of close relationships* (pp. 90–115). Oxford University Press.

Arriaga, X. B., Kumashiro, M., Finkel, E. J., VanderDrift, L. E., & Luchies, L. B. (2014). Filling the void: Bolstering attachment security in committed relationships. *Social Psychological and Personality Science, 5*, 398–406.

Barber, N. (2003). Divorce and reduced economic and emotional interdependence: A cross-national study. *Journal of Divorce and Remarriage, 39*, 113–124.

Barker, E. (1946). *Aristotle: Politics*. Cambridge University Press.

Bar-On, R. (2004). The Bar-On emotional quotient inventory (EQ-i): Rationale, description, and summary of psychometric properties. In G. Geher (Ed.), *The measurement of emotional intelligence: Common ground and controversy* (pp. 115–145). Nova Science.

Bar-On, R. (2006). The Bar-On model of emotionalsocial intelligence (ESI). *Psicothema, 18*, 13–25.

Barry, R. A., Bunde, M., Brock, R. L., & Lawrence, E. (2009). Validity and utility of a multidimensional model of received support in intimate relationships. *Journal of Family Psychology, 23*, 48–57.

Bartholomew, K. (1990). Avoidance of intimacy: An attachment perspective. *Journal of Social and Personal Relationships, 7*, 147–178.

Baumeister, R. F., Bratslavsky, E., Finkenauer, C., & Vohs, K. D. (2001). Bad is stronger than good. *Review of General Psychology, 5*, 323–370.

Baumeister, R. F., Bratslavsky, E., Muraven, M., & Tice, D. M. (1998). Ego depletion: Is the active self a limited resource?. *Journal of Personality and Social Psychology, 74*, 1252–1265.

Baumeister, R. F. & Leary, M. R. (1995). The need to belong: Desire for interpersonal attachments as a fundamental human motivation. *Psychological Bulletin, 117*, 497–529.

Baumeister, R. F., Schmeichel, B. J., & Vohs, K. D. (2007). Self-regulation and the executive function: The self as controlling agent. In A. W. Kruglanski & E. T. Higgins (Eds.), *Social psychology: Handbook of basic principles* (pp. 516–539). Guilford.

Baumeister, R. F. & Vohs, K. D. (2016). Strength model of self-regulation as limited resource: Assessment, controversies, update. In M. O. James & P. Z. Mark (Eds.), *Advances in experimental social psychology* (pp. 67–127). Academic Press.

Beck, J. (2011). *Cognitive behavior therapy. Basics and beyond.* Guildford.

Becker, D. & Maracek, J. (2008). Positive psychology: History in the remaking?. *Theory and Psychology, 18*(5), 591–604.

Becker, E. (1973). *The denial of death.* Free Press.

Ben-Shahar, T. (2009). *The pursuit of perfect: How to stop chasing perfection and start living a richer, happier life.* McGraw Hill.

Berscheid, E. (1999). The greening of relationship science. *American Psychologist, 54*, 260–266.

Berscheid, E. & Walster, E. (1974). A little bit about love. In T. Huston (Ed.), *Foundations of interpersonal attraction* (pp. 355–381). Academic Press.

Biswas-Diener, R., Linley, P. A., Govindji, R., & Woolfston, L. (2011). Positive psychology as a force for social change. In K. M. Sheldon, T. B. Kashdan, & M. F. Steger (Eds.), *Designing positive psychology: Taking stock and moving forward* (pp. 410–420). Oxford University Press.

Biswas-Diener, R., Vittersø, J., & Diener, E. (2005). Most people are pretty happy, but there is cultural variation: The Inughuit, the Amish, and the Maasai. *Journal of Happiness Studies, 6*(3), 205–226.

Black, K. & Lobo, M. (2008). A conceptual review of family resilience factors. *Journal of Family Nursing, 14*(1), 33–55.

Blanchflower, D. G. & Oswald, A. J. (2008). Is well-being U-shaped over the life cycle? *Social Science & Medicine, 66*(8), 1733–1749.

Bolier, L. & Abello, K. M. (2014). State of the art and future directions. In A. C. Parks & S. Schueller (Eds.), *The Wiley Blackwell handbook of positive sychological interventions* (pp. 286–309). Wiley.

Bolier, L., Haverman, M., Westerhof, G., Riper, H., Smit, F., & Bohlmeijer, E. (2013). Positive psychology interventions: A meta-analysis of randomized controlled studies. *Bmc Public Health, 13,* 119.

Bonanno, G. A., Westphal, M., & Mancini, A. D. (2011). Resilience to loss and potential trauma. *Annual Review of Clinical Psychology, 7,* 511–535.

Boniwell, I. (2017). *Positive actions: Evidence based positive psychology intervention cards.* Paris: positron.

Bowlby, J. (1969). *Attachment and loss.* Basic Books.

Boyatzis, R. E., Goleman, D., & Rhee, K. (2000). Clustering competence in emotional intelligence: Insights from the Emotional Competency Inventory (ECI). In R. Bar-On & J. D. A. Parker (Eds.), *Handbook of emotional intelligence* (pp. 343–362). Jossey-Bass.

Brennan, K. A., Clark, C. L., & Shaver, P. R. (1998). Self-report measurement of adult attachment: An integrative overview. In J. A. Simpson & W. S. Rholes (Eds.), *Attachment theory and close relationships* (pp. 46–76). Guilford.

Brickman, P., Coates, D., & Janoff-Bulman, R. (1978). Lottery winners and accident victims: Is happiness relative?. *Journal of Personality and Social Psychology, 36,* 917–927.

Bridges, W. (2004). *Transitions: Making sense of life's changes.* Hachette.

Brock, R. L. & Lawrence, E. (2009). Too much of a good thing: Underprovision versus overprovision of partner support. *Journal of Family Psychology, 23,* 181–192.

Bryant, F. B. & Veroff, J. (2017). *Savoring: A new model of positive experience.* Psychology Press.

Burnett, S. (2011). *The happiness agenda: A modern obsession.* Springer.

Burton, C. M. & King, L. A. (2009). The health benefits of writing about positive experiences: The role of broadened cognition. *Psychology and Health, 24*(8), 867–879.

Butler, J. & Kern, M. L. (2016). The PERMA-Profiler: A brief multidimensional measure of flourishing. *International Journal of Wellbeing, 6*(3), 1–48.

Calhoun, L. G. & Tedeschi, R. G. (2013). *Posttraumatic growth in clinical practice.* Routledge.

Canary, D. J. & Lakey, S. (2013). *Strategic conflict.* Routledge.

Cann, A., Calhoun, L. G., Tedeschi, R. G., Taku, K., Vishnevsky, T., Triplett, K. N., & Danhauer, S. C. (2010). A short form of the Posttraumatic Growth Inventory. *Anxiety, Stress, & Coping, 23*(2), 127–137.

Cantril, H. (1965). *The pattern of human concerns.* Rutgers University Press.

Carver, C. S. & Scheier, M. F. (2001). *On the self-regulation of behavior.* Cambridge University Press.

Carver, C. S., Scheier, M. F., & Segerstrom, S. C. (2010). Optimism. *Clinical Psychology Review, 30*(7), 879–889.

Carver, C. S., Scheier, M. F., & Weintraub, J. K. (1989). Assessing coping strategies: A theoretically based approach. *Journal of Personality and Social Psychology, 56,* 267–283.

Carver, S. R. & Scheier, M. F. (2009). Optimism. In S. J. Lopez (Ed.), *The encyclopedia of positive psychology* (pp. 656–663). Blackwell.

Catalino, L. I., Algoe, S. B., & Fredrickson, B. L. (2014). Prioritizing positivity: An effective approach to pursuing happiness?. *Emotion, 14*(6), 1155–1161.

Cherniss, C. (2010). Emotional intelligence: Toward clarification of a concept. *Industrial and Organizational Psychology, 3*(2), 110–126.

Cloninger, C. R. (2006). The science of well-being: An integrated approach to mental health and its disorders. *World Psychiatry, 5*(2), 71–76.

Cohen, S. (1988). Perceived stress in a probability sample of the United States. In S. Spacapan & S. Oskamp (Eds.), *The Claremont symposium on applied social psychology. The social psychology of health* (pp. 31–67). Sage.

Cohen, S., Doyle, W. J., Skoner, D. P., Rabin, B. S., & Gwaltney, J. M. (1997). Social ties and susceptibility to the common cold. *Journal of American Medical Association, 277,* 1940–1944.

Cohen, S., Doyle, W. J., Turner, R. B., Alper, C. M., & Skoner, D. P. (2003). Emotional style and susceptibility to the common cold. *Psychosomatic Medicine, 65*, 652–657.

Collins, W. A. & Madsen, S. D. (2006). Personal relationships in adolescence and early adulthood. In D. Perlman & A. Vangelisti (Eds.), *Handbook of personal relationships* (pp. 191–209). Cambridge University Press.

Connor, K. M. & Davidson, J. R. T. (2003). Development of a new resilience scale: The Connor–Davidson Resilience Scale (CDRISC). *Depression and Anxiety, 18*, 76–82.

Coyne, J. C. & Tennen, H. (2010). Positive psychology in cancer care: Bad science, exaggerated claims, and unproven medicine. *Annals of Behavioral Medicine, 39*(1), 16–26.

Cropanzano, R. & Wright, T. A. (2001). When a "happy" worker is really a "productive" worker: A review and further refinement of the happy-productive worker thesis. *Consulting Psychology Journal: Practice and Research, 53*(3), 182.

Cross, M. P., Hofschneider, L., Grimm, M., & Pressman, S. D. (2018). Subjective well-being and physical health. In E. Diener, S. Oishi, & L. Tay (Eds.), *Handbook of well-being*. DEF Publishers.

Crumbaugh, J. C. & Maholick, L. T. (1964). An experimental study in existentialism: The psychometric approach to Frankl's concept of noogenic neurosis. *Journal of Clinical Psychology, 20*(2), 200–207.

Csikszentmihalyi, M. (2014). *Flow and the foundations of positive psychology: The collected works of Mihaly Csikszentmihalyi*. Springer.

Csikszentmihalyi, M. & Csikszentmihalyi, I. (1988). *Optimal experience. Psychological studies of flow in consciousness*. New York: Cambridge University Press.

Csikszentmihalyi, M. & Nakamura, J. (2011). Positive psychology: Where did it come from, where is it going?. In K. M. Sheldon, T. B. Kashdan, & M. F. Steger (Eds.), *Designing positive psychology* (pp. 3–8). Oxford University Press.

Damasio, A. & Dolan, R. J. (1999). The feeling of what happens. *Nature, 401*(6756), 847.

Danner, D. D., Snowdon, D. A., & Friesen, W. V. (2001). Positive emotions in early life and longevity: Findings from the nun study. *Journal of Personality and Social Psychology, 80*, 804–813.

Davis, M. H. & Begovic, E. (2014). Empathy-related interventions. In A. C. Parks & S. Schueller (Eds.), *The Wiley Blackwell handbook of positive psychological interventions* (pp. 111–134). Wiley.

de Jong Gierveld, J., van Tilburg, T., & Dykstra, P. A. (2006). Loneliness and social isolation. In A. Vangelisti & D. Perlman (Eds.), *Cambridge handbook of personal relationships* (pp. 485–500). Cambridge university pres.

Dell'Osso, B., Altamura, A. C., Allen, A., Marazziti, D., & Hollander, E. (2006). Epidemiologic and clinical updates on impulse control disorders: A critical review. *European Archives of Psychiatry and Clinical Neuroscience, 256*(8), 464–475.

Demir, M. & Weitekamp, L. A. (2007). I am so happy 'cause today I found my friend: Friendship and personality as predictors of happiness. *Journal of Happiness Studies, 8*(2), 181–211.

Diener, E. (2000). Subjective well-being: The science of happiness and a proposal for a national index. *American Psychologist, 55*(1), 34–43.

Diener, E. (2003). What is positive about positive psychology: The curmudgeon and Pollyanna. *Psychological Inquiry, 14,* 115–120.

Diener, E. & Diener, C. (1996). Most people are happy. *Psychological Science, 7,* 181–185.

Diener, E., Diener, C., Choi, H., & Oishi, S. (2018b). Revisiting "Most People Are Happy"—And discovering when they are not. *Perspectives on Psychological Science, 13*(2), 166–170.

Diener, E., Emmons, R. A., Larsen, R. J., & Griffen, S. (1985). The satisfaction with life scale. *Journal of Personality Assessment, 49,* 71–75.

Diener, E., Lucas, R. E., & Oishi, S. (2018a). Advances and open questions in the science of subjective well-being. *Collabra: Psychology, 4*(1), 15–19.

Diener, E. & Oishi, S. (2000). Money and happiness: Income and subjective well-being across nations. In E. Diener & E. M. Suh (Eds.), *Culture and subjective well-being* (pp. 185–218). MIT Press.

Diener, E., Seligman, M. E., Choi, H., & Oishi, S. (2018c). Happiest people revisited. *Perspectives on Psychological Science, 13*(2), 176–184.

Diener, E., Suh, E. M., Lucas, R. E., & Smith, H. L. (1999). Subjective well-being: Three decades of progress. *Psychological Bulletin, 125*(2), 276.

Diener, E., Suh, E. M., Smith, H., & Shao, L. (1995). National differences in reported subjective well-being: Why do they occur?. *Social Indicators Research, 34,* 7–32.

Diener, E., Wirtz, D., Tov, W., Kim-Prieto, C., Choi, D. W., Oishi, S., & Biswas-Diener, R. (2010). New wellbeing measures: Short scales to assess flourishing and positive and negative feelings. *Social Indicators Research, 97,* 143–156.

Dittmar, H., Bond, R., Hurst, M., & Kasser, T. (2014). The relationship between materialism and personal well-being: A meta-analysis. *Journal of Personality and Social Psychology, 107*(5), 879–924.

Donaldson, S. I., Dollwet, M., & Rao, M. A. (2015). Happiness, excellence, and optimal human functioning revisited: Examining the peer-reviewed literature linked to positive psychology. *The Journal of Positive Psychology, 10*(3), 185–195.

Donaldson, S. I., Lee, J. Y., & Donaldson, S. I. (2019). Evaluating positive psychology interventions at work: A systematic review and meta-analysis. *International Journal of Applied Positive Psychology, 4*(3), 113–134.

Doran, G. T. (1981). There's a S.M.A.R.T. way to write management's goals and objectives. *Management Review, 70*(11), 35–36.

Drigotas, S. M. (2002). The Michelangelo phenomenon and personal well-being. *Journal of Personality, 70*(1), 59–77.

Drigotas, S. M. & Rusbult, C. E. (1992). Should I stay or should I go? A dependence model of breakups. *Journal of Personality and Social Psychology, 62*(1), 62–87.

DuBois, C. M., Lopez, O. V., Beale, E. E., Healy, B. C., Boehm, J. K., & Huffman, J. C. (2015). Relationships between positive psychological constructs and health outcomes in patients with cardiovascular disease: A systematic review. *International Journal of Cardiology, 195,* 265–280.

Duckworth, A. L. (2016). *Grit: The power of passion and perseverance.* New York: Scribner.

Duckworth, A. L., Peterson, C., Matthews, M. D., & Kelly, D. R. (2007). Grit: Perseverance and passion for long-term goals. *Journal of Personality and Social Psychology, 92*(6), 1087–1101.

Dunn, E. & Norton, M. (2013). *Happy money: The science of happier spending.* Simon & Schuster.

Durkheim, E. (1963). *Suicide.* Original work published 1897 Free Press.

Easterlin, R. A. (1974). Does economic growth improve the human lot? Some empirical evidence. In P. A. David & W. R. Melvin (Eds.), *Nations and households in economic growth* (pp. 98–125). Stanford University Press.

Easterlin, R. A. (2005). Building a better theory of well-being. In L. Bruni & P. L. Porta (Eds.), *Economics and happiness: Framing the analysis* (pp. 29–64). Oxford University Press.

Ekman, P. (2003). *Emotions revealed.* Times Books.

Eldridge, K. A. & Baucom, B. (2012). Demand-withdraw communication in couples: Recent developments and future directions. In P. Noller & G. C. Karantzas (Eds.), *The Wiley-Blackwell handbook of couple and family relationships* (pp. 144–158). Wiley.

Elliot, A. J. (2006). The hierarchical model of approach-avoidance motivation. *Motivation and Emotion, 30*(2), 111–116.

Elliot, A. J. & Murayama, K. (2008). On the measurement of achievement goals: Critique, illustration, and application. *Journal of Educational Psychology, 100*(3), 613–628.

Elwert, F. & Christakis, N. A. (2008). The effect of widowhood on mortality by the causes of death of both spouses. *American Journal of Public Health, 98,* 2092–2098.

Emmons, R. A. (2003). Personal goals, life meaning, and virtue: Wellsprings of a positive life. In C. L. M. Keyes & J. Haidt (Eds.), *Flourishing: Positive psychology and the life well-lived* (pp. 105–128). APA.

Emmons, R. A. & Shelton, C. M. (2002). Gratitude and the science of positive psychology. In C. R. Snyder & S. J. Lopez (Eds.), *Handbook of positive psychology* (pp. 459–471). Oxford University Press.

Erbert, L. A. (2000). Conflict and dialectics: Perceptions of dialectical contradictions in marital conflict. *Journal of Social and Personal Relationships, 17,* 638–659.

Estrada, C. A., Isen, A. M., & Young, M. J. (1997). Positive affect facilitates integration of information and decreases anchoring in reasoning among physicians. *Organizational Behavior and Human Decision Processes, 72,* 117–135.

Everly, G. S. & Lating, J. M. (2019). *A clinical guide to the treatment of the human stress response.* Springer.

Fava, G. A. (2016). *Well-being therapy: Treatment manual and clinical applications.* Karger.

Fehr, B. (1996). *Friendship processes*. Sage.

Fehr, B. & Sprecher, S. (2013). Compassionate love: What we know so far. In M. Hojjat & D. Cramer (Eds.), *Positive psychology of love* (pp. 106–120). Oxford University Press.

Feldman, D. B. & Snyder, C. R. (2005). Hope and the meaningful life: Theoretical and empirical associations between goal–directed thinking and life meaning. *Journal of Social and Clinical Psychology*, *24*(3), 401–421.

Fletcher, G. J., Simpson, J. A., Campbell, L., & Overall, N. C. (2013). *The science of intimate relationships*. Wiley-Blackwell.

Fletcher, G. J. O., Tither, J. M., O'Loughlin, C., Friesen, M., & Overall, N. (2004). Warm and homely or cold and beautiful? Sex differences in trading off traits in mate selection. *Personality and Social Psychology Bulletin*, *30*, 659–672.

Folkman, S. & Lazarus, R. S. (1988). *Ways of coping questionnaire: Research edition*. Palo Alto, CA: Consulting Psychologists Press.

Folkman, S., Lazarus, R. S., Gruen, R. J., & DeLongis, A. (1986). Appraisal, coping, health status, and psychological symptoms. *Journal of Personality and Social Psychology*, *50*(3), 571–579.

Fordyce, M. W. (1983). A program to increase happiness: Further studies. *Journal of Counseling Psychology*, *30*(4), 483–498.

Forgeard, M. J. C. & Seligman, M. E. P. (2012). Seeing the glass half full: A review of the causes and consequences of optimism. *Pratiques Psychologiques*, *18*(2), 107–120.

Frankl, V. (1963). *Man's search for meaning*. Pocket Books.

Frankl, V. (1986). *The doctor and the soul: From psychotherapy to logotherapy*. Vintage Books.

Fredrickson, B. (2010). *Positivity*. Oneworld Publications.

Fredrickson, B. L. (2013a). *Love 2.0: Finding happiness and health in moments of connection*. Penguin.

Fredrickson, B. L. (2013b). Positive emotions broaden and build. In *Advances in experimental social psychology* (Vol. 47, pp. 1–53). Academic Press.

Fredrickson, B. L. & Cohn, M. A. (2008). Positive emotions. In M. Lewis, J. Haviland-Jones, & L. F. Barrett (Eds.), *Handbook of emotions* (3rd ed. ed., pp. 777–796). New York: Guilford.

Fredrickson, B. L. & Joiner, T. (2018). Reflections on positive emotions and upward spirals. *Perspectives on Psychological Science*, *13*(2), 194–199.

Fredrickson, B. L. & Losada, M. F. (2005). Positive affect and the complex dynamics of human flourishing. *American Psychologist, 60*(7), 678–686.

Fredrickson, B. L., Tugade, M. M., Waugh, C. E., & Larkin, G. R. (2003). What good are positive emotions in crises? A prospective study of resilience and emotions following the terrorist attacks on the United States on September 11th, 2001. *Journal of Personality and Social Psychology, 84*(2), 365–376.

Freud, S. (1966). *The ego and the mechanisms of defense.* International Universities Press.

Friborg, O., Hjemdal, O., Rosenvinge, J. H., & Martinussen, M. (2003). A new rating scale for adult resilience: What are the central protective resources behind health adjustment?. *International Journal of Methods in Psychiatric Research, 12*, 65–76.

Friese, M., Loschelder, D. D., Gieseler, K., Frankenbach, J., & Inzlicht, M. (2019). Is ego depletion real? An analysis of arguments. *Personality and Social Psychology Review, 23*(2), 107–131.

Frijda, N. H. (1986). *The emotions.* Cambridge University Press.

Frisch, M. B. (2006). *Quality of life therapy: Applying a life satisfaction approach to positive psychology and cognitive therapy.* Wiley.

Fromm, E. (1955). *The sane society.* Rinehart.

Gable, S. L., Gonzaga, G. C., & Strachman, A. (2006). Will you be there for me when things go right? Supportive responses to positive event disclosures. *Journal of Personality and Social Psychology, 91*(5), 904–917.

Gable, S. L. & Gosnell, C. L. (2011). The positive side of close relationships. In K. M. Sheldon, T. B. Kashdan, & M. F. Steger (Eds.), *Designing positive psychology* (pp. 265–279). Oxford University Press.

Gable, S. L. & Haidt, J. (2005). What (and why) is positive psychology?. *Review of General Psychology, 9*, 103–110.

Gardner, J. & Oswald, A. (2007). Money and mental wellbeing: A longitudinal study of medium-sized lottery wins. *Journal of Health Economics, 26*, 49–60.

Gee, L. K., Jones, J., & Burke, M. (2017a). Social networks and labor markets: How strong ties relate to job finding on facebook's social network. *Journal of Labor Economics, 35*(2), 485–518.

Gee, L. K., Jones, J. J., Fariss, C. J., Burke, M., & Fowler, J. H. (2017b). The paradox of weak ties in 55 countries. *Journal of Economic Behavior & Organization, 133*, 362–372.

Gerber, J. P., Wheeler, L., & Suls, J. (2018). A social comparison theory meta-analysis 60+ years on. *Psychological Bulletin, 144*(2), 177–197.

Gillham, J. (2000). *The science of optimism and hope.* Templeton.

Gillham, J. E., Abenavoli, R. M., Brunwasser, S. M., Linkins, M., Reivich, K. J., & Seligman, M. E. P. (2013). Resilience education. In S. A. David, I. Boniwell, & A. C. Ayers (Eds.), *The Oxford handbook of happiness* (pp. 609–630). Oxford University Press.

Gillham, J. E., Shatté, A. J., Reivich, K. J., & Seligman, M. E. P. (2001). Optimism, pessimism, and explanatory style. In E. C. Chang (Ed.), *Optimism & pessimism: Implications for theory, research, and practice* (pp. 53–75). APA.

Girme, Y. U., Overall, N. C., & Simpson, J. A. (2013). When visibility matters: Short-term versus long-term costs and benefits of visible and invisible support. *Personality and Social Psychology Bulletin, 39,* 1441–1454.

Goleman, D. (1995). *Emotional intelligence: Why it can matter more than IQ.* Bantam.

Goleman, D. (2001). An EI-based theory of performance. In C. Cerniss & D. Goleman (Eds.), *The emotionally intelligent workplace* (pp. 27–44). Jossey Bass.

Gollwitzer, P. M. (1990). Action phases and mind-sets. In E. T. Higgins & R. M. Sorrentino (Eds.), *Handbook of motivation and cognition* (pp. 53–92). Guilford.

Gollwitzer, P. M. & Sheeran, P. (2006). Implementation intentions and goal achievement: A meta-analysis of effects and processes. *Advances in Experimental Social Psychology, 38,* 69–119.

Goodman, F., Disabato, D., Kashdan, T., & Kauffman, S. (2017). Measuring well-being: A comparison of subjective wellbeing and PERMA. *The Journal of Positive Psychology,* 1–12.

Goodwin, S. A., Fiske, S. T., Rosen, L. D., & Rosenthal, A. M. (2002). The eye of the beholder: Romantic goals and impression biases. *Journal of Experimental Social Psychology, 38,* 232–241.

Gorchoff, S. M., John, O. P., & Helson, R. (2008). Contextualizing change in marital satisfaction during middle age: An 18 year longitudinal study. *Psychological Science, 19*(11), 1194–1200.

Gottfredson, M. R. & Hirschi, T. (1990). *A general theory of crime.* Stanford University Press.

Gottman, J. M. (1994). *Why marriages succeed or fail.* Simon & Schuster.

Gottman, J. M. (1999). *The marriage clinic.* Norton.

Gottman, J. M. (2014). *Principia amoris: The new science of love.* Routledge.

Gottman, J. M., Coan, J., Carrere, S., & Swanson, C. (1998). Predicting marital happiness and stability from newlywed interactions. *Journal of Marriage and the Family, 60,* 5–22.

Gottman, J. M. & Levenson, R. W. (1992). Marital processes predictive of later dissolution: Behavior, physiology, and health. *Journal of Personality and Social Psychology, 63,* 221–233.

Gottman, J. M. & Silver, N. (1999). *The seven principles for making marriage work.* Crown.

Gouin, J., Carter, S. C., Pournajafi-Nazarloo, H., Glaser, R., Malarkey, W. B., Loving, T. J., … Kiecolt-Glaser, J. (2010). Marital behavior, oxytocin, vasopressin, and wound healing. *Psychoneuroendocrinology, 35,* 1082–1090.

Granovetter, M. S. (1973). The strength of weak ties. *American Jouenal of Sociology, 78*(6), 1360–1380.

Grover, S. & Helliwell, J. F. (2019). How's life at home? New evidence on marriage and the set point for happiness. *Journal of Happiness Studies, 20*(2), 373–390.

Gruber, J., Mauss, I. B., & Tamir, M. (2011). A dark side of happiness? How, when, and why happiness is not always good. *Perspectives on Psychological Science, 6*(3), 222–233.

Hackney, C. H. & Sanders, G. S. (2003). Religiosity and mental health: A meta-analysis of recent studies. *Journal for the Scientific Study of Religion, 42,* 43–55.

Hall, J. A. (2012). Friendship standards: The dimensions of ideal expectations. *Journal of Social and Personal Relationships, 29,* 884–907.

Harker, L. & Keltner, D. (2001). Expressions of positive emotion in women's college yearbook pictures and their relationship to personality and life outcomes across adulthood. *Journal of Personality and Social Psychology, 80,* 112–124.

Harkin, B., Webb, T. L., Chang, B. P., Prestwich, A., Conner, M., Kellar, I., … Sheeran, P. (2016). Does monitoring goal progress promote goal attainment? A meta-analysis of the experimental evidence. *Psychological Bulletin, 142*(2), 198–229.

Hart, K. E. & Sasso, T. (2011). Mapping the contours of contemporary positive psychology. *Canadian Psychology, 52*(2), 82–92.

Hart, R., Ivtzan, I., & Hart, D. (2013). Mind the gap in mindfulness research: A comparative account of the leading schools of thought. *Review of General Psychology, 17*(4), 453–466.

Hatfield, E., Cacioppo, J. T., & Rapson, R. L. (1992). Primitive emotional contagion. In M. S. Clark (Ed.), *Emotion and social behavior* (pp. 151–177). Sage.

Hatfield, E. & Sprecher, S. (1986). Measuring passionate love in intimate relationships. *Journal of Adolescence, 9*, 383–410.

Haushofer, J. & Fehr, E. (2014). On the psychology of poverty. *Science, 344*(6186), 862–867.

Hawkley, L. C. & Cacioppo, J. T. (2010). Loneliness matters: A theoretical and empirical review of consequences and mechanisms. *Annals of Behavioral Medicine, 40*(2), 218–227.

Hawkley, L. C. & Cacioppo, J. T. (2013). Social connectedness and health. In C. Hazan & M. I. Campa (Eds.), *Human bonding: The science of affectional ties* (pp. 343–364). Guilford.

Hazan, C. & Shaver, P. (1987). Romantic love conceptualized as an attachment process. *Journal of Personality and Social Psychology, 52*, 511–524.

Hefferon, K., Grealy, M., & Mutrie, N. (2009). Post-traumatic growth and life threatening physical illness: A systematic review of the qualitative literature. *British Journal of Health Psychology, 14*(2), 343–378.

Heintzelman, S. J. & King, L. A. (2014). Life is pretty meaningful. *American Psychologist, 69*, 561–574.

Held, B. S. (2002). The tyranny of the positive attitude in America: Observation and speculation. *Journal of Clinical Psychology, 58*(9), 965–991.

Held, B. S. (2004). The negative side of positive psychology. *Journal of Humanistic Psychology, 44*, 9–46.

Held, B. S. (2005). The "virtues" of positive psychology. *Journal of Theoretical and Philosophical Psychology, 25*(1), 1–34.

Hendrick, S. & Hendrick, C. (1992). *Liking, loving and relating.* Brooks-Cole.

Hendriks, T., Warren, M. A., Schotanus-Dijkstra, M., Hassankhan, A., Graafsma, T., Bohlmeijer, E., & de Jong, J. (2019). How WEIRD are positive psychology interventions? A bibliometric analysis of randomized controlled trials on the science of well-being. *The Journal of Positive Psychology, 14*(4), 489–501.

Hill, P. L. & Turiano, N. A. (2014). Purpose in life as a predictor of mortality across adulthood. *Psychological Science, 25*(7), 1482–1486.

Hinde, R. A. (1979). *Towards understanding relationships*. Academic Press.

Hinde, R. A. (1997). *Relationships: A dialectical perspective*. Psychology Press.

Hofmann, S. G. & Kashdan, T. B. (2010). The affective style questionnaire: Development and psychometric properties. *Journal of Psychopathology and Behavioral Assessment, 32*(2), 255–263.

Hofmann, W. & Van Dillen, L. (2012). Desire: The new hot spot in self-control research. *Current Directions in Psychological Science, 21*, 317–322.

Hollenbeck, J. R., Klein, H. J., O'Leary, A. M., & Wright, P. M. (1989). Investigation of the construct validity of a self-report measure of goal commitment. *Journal of Applied Psychology, 74*, 951–956.

Holt-Lunstad, J., Smith, T. B., Baker, M., Harris, T., & Stephenson, D. (2015). Loneliness and social isolation as risk factors for mortality: A meta-analytic review. *Perspectives on Psychological Science, 10*, 227–237.

Holt-Lunstad, J., Smith, T. B., & Layton, J. (2010). Social relationships and mortality risk: A meta-analytic review. *PLoS Medicine, 7*(7), e1000316.

Holt-Lunstad, J. & Uchino, B. N. (2015). Social support and health. In K. Glanz, B. K. Rimer, & K. Viswanath (Eds.), *Health behavior: Theory, research, and practice* (pp. 183–204). Wiley.

Huppert, F. A. (2009). Psychological well-being: Evidence regarding its causes and consequences. *Applied Psychology, 1*(2), 137–164.

Huppert, F. A. (2014). The state of well-being science: Concepts, measures, interventions, and policies. In F. A. Huppert & C. L. Cooper (Eds.), *Interventions and policies to enhance well-being* (pp. 2–49). Wiley-Blackwell.

Huppert, F. A. & So, T. T. C. (2013). Flourishing across Europe: Application of a new conceptual framework for defining well-being. *Social Indicators Research, 110*(3), 837–861.

Huta, V. (2013). Pursuing eudaimonia versus hedonia: Distinctions, similarities, and relationships. In A. S. Waterman (Ed.), *The best within us: Positive psychology perspectives on eudaimonia* (pp. 139–158). APA Books.

Huta, V. (2016). Eudaimonic and hedonic orientations: Theoretical considerations and research findings. In J. Vittersø (Ed.), *Handbook of eudaimonic well-being* (pp. 215–231). Springer.

Huta, V. & Waterman, A. S. (2014). Eudaimonia and its distinction from hedonia: Developing a classification and terminology for understanding conceptual and operational definitions. *Journal of Happiness Studies*, *15*, 1425–1456.

Ivtzan, I., Lomas, T., Hefferon, K., & Worth, P. (2015). *Second wave positive psychology*. Routledge.

Izard, C. E. (2009). Emotion theory and research: Highlights, unanswered questions, and emerging issues. *Annual Review of Psychology*, *60*, 1–25.

James, W. (1890/1950). *The principles of psychology*. Dover.

Janoff-Bulman, R. (1992). *Shattered assumptions*. Free Press.

Janoff-Bulman, R. (2004). Posttraumatic growth: Three explanatory models. *Psychological Inquiry*, *15*(1), 30–34.

Johnson, K. J., Waugh, C. E., & Fredrickson, B. L. (2010). Smile to see the forest: Facially expressed positive emotions broaden cognition. *Cognition and Emotion*, *24*(2), 299–321.

Joseph, S. (2013). *What doesn't kill us*. Basic Books.

Joseph, S. & Linley, P. A. (2006). Growth following adversity: Theoretical perspectives and implications for clinical practice. *Clinical Psychology Review*, *26*(8), 1041–1053.

Kabat-Zinn, J. (2003). Mindfulness-based interventions in context: Past, present, and future. *Clinical Psychology*, *10*(2), 144–156.

Kahneman, D. (2011). *Thinking fast and slow*. Straus and Giroux.

Kahneman, D., Krueger, A. B., Schkade, D. A., Schwarz, N., & Stone, A. A. (2004). A survey method for characterizing daily life experience: The day reconstruction method. *Science*, *306*, 1776–1780.

Kahneman, D. & Tversky, A. (1996). On the reality of cognitive illusions. *Psychological Review*, *103*(3), 582–591.

Karasu, T. B. (1992). *Wisdom in the practice of psychotherapy*. Basic Books.

Kashdan, T. B. & Steger, M. F. (2011). Challenges, pitfalls and aspirations for positive psychology. In K. M. Sheldon, T. B. Kashdan, & M. F. Steger (Eds.), *Designing positive psychology* (pp. 3–8). Oxford University Press.

Kelley, H. H. (1983). Love and commitment. In H. H. Kelley, E. Berscheid, A. Christensen, J. H. Harvey, T. L. Huston, G. Levinger, … D. P. Peterson (Eds.), *Close relationships* (pp. 265–314). Freeman.

Keltner, D., Sauter, D., Tracy, J., & Cowen, A. (2019). Emotional expression: Advances in basic emotion theory. *Journal of Nonverbal Behavior*, 1–28.

Keyes, C. L. (2005). Mental illness and/or mental health? Investigating axioms of the complete state model of health. *Journal of Consulting and Clinical Psychology, 73*(3), 539–548.

Keyes, C. L. M. (1998). Social well-being. *Social Psychology Quarterly, 61*, 121–140.

Keyes, C. L. M. (2002). The mental health continuum: From languishing to flourishing in life. *Journal of Health and Social Research, 43*, 207–222.

Keyes, C. L. M. (2003). Complete mental health: An agenda for the 21st century. In C. L. M. Keyes & J. Haidt (Eds.), *Flourishing: Positive psychology and the life well-lived* (pp. 293–290). APA.

Keyes, C. L. M. & Shapiro, A. D. (2004). Social well-being in the United States: A descriptive epidemiology. In O. G. Brim, C. D. Ryff, & R. C. Kessler (Eds.), *How healthy are we? A national study of well-being at midlife* (pp. 350–372). University of Chicago Press.

Kim, H., Doiron, K., Warren, M., & Donaldson, S. (2018). The international landscape of positive psychology research: A systematic review. *International Journal of Wellbeing, 8*(1), 50–70.

King, L. A. (2001). The health benefits of writing about life goals. *Personality and Social Psychology Bulletin, 27*, 798–807.

King, L. A., Heintzelman, S. J., & Ward, S. J. (2016). Beyond the search for meaning: A contemporary science of the experience of meaning in life. *Current Directions in Psychological Science, 25*(4), 211–216.

Koestner, R., Powers, T. A., Carbonneau, N., Milyavskaya, M., & Chua, S. N. (2012). Distinguishing autonomous and directive forms of goal support: Their effects on goal progress, relationship quality, and subjective well-being. *Personality and Social Psychology Bulletin, 38*, 1609–1620.

Koltko-Rivera, M. E. (2006). Rediscovering the later version of Maslow's hierarchy of needs: Self-transcendence and opportunities for theory, research, and unification. *Review of General Psychology, 10*(4), 302–317.

Koydemir, S., Sökmez, A. B., & Schütz, A. (2020). A meta-analysis of the effectiveness of randomized controlled positive psychological interventions on subjective and psychological well-being. *Applied Research in Quality of Life*, 1–41.

Kubler-Ross, E. & Kessler, D. (2014). *On grief and grieving*. Simon and Schuster.

Lakey, B. (2013). Perceived social support and happiness: The role of personality and relational processes. In S. A. David, I. Boniwell, & A. C. Ayers (Eds.), *The Oxford handbook of happiness* (pp. 847–859). Oxford University Press.

Landry, A. T., Kindlein, J., Trépanier, S. G., Forest, J., Zigarmi, D., Houson, D., & Brodbeck, F. C. (2016). Why individuals want money is what matters: Using self-determination theory to explain the differential relationship between motives for making money and employee psychological health. *Motivation and Emotion, 40*(2), 226–242.

Larsen, J. T., McGraw, A. P., & Cacioppo, J. T. (2001). Can people feel happy and sad at the same time?. *Journal of Personality and Social Psychology, 81*(4), 684–696.

Latham, G. P., Ganegoda, D. B., & Locke, E. A. (2011). A state theory, but related to traits. In T. Chamorro-Premuzic, S. von Stumm, & A. Furnham (Eds.), *The Wiley-Blackwell handbook of individual differences* (pp. 579–587). Willey-Blackwell.

Lauer, R. H., Lauer, J. C., & Kerr, S. T. (1990). The long-term marriage: Perceptions of stability and satisfaction. *International Journal of Aging and Human Development, 31*, 189–195.

Laurenceau, J., Rivera, L. M., Schaffer, A. R., & Pietromonaco, P. R. (2004). Intimacy as an interpersonal process: Current status and future directions. In D. J. Mashek & A. Aron (Eds.), *Handbook of closeness and intimacy* (pp. 81–101). Erlbaum.

Lawless, N. M. & Lucas, R. E. (2011). Predictors of regional well-being: A county level analysis. *Social Indicators Research, 101*, 341–357.

Layous, K. & Lyubomirsky, S. (2014). The how, why, what, when, and who of happiness. In J. Gruber & J. T. Moskowitz (Eds.), *Positive emotion: Integrating the light sides and dark sides* (pp. 473–495). Oxford University Press.

Layous, K., Sheldon, K. M., & Lyubomirsky, S. (2015). The prospects, practices, and prescriptions for the pursuit of happiness. In P. A. Linley & S. Joseph (Eds.), *Positive psychology in practice* (pp. 183–206). Wiley.

Lazarus, R. S. (2003). Does the positive psychology movement have legs?. *Psychological Inquiry, 14*, 93–109.

Lazarus, R. S. & Folkman, S. (1984). *Stress, appraisal, and coping.* Springer.

Lepore, S. J. & Revenson, T. A. (2006). Resilience and posttraumatic growth: Recovery, resistance, and reconfiguration. In L. G. Calhoun & R. G. Tedeschi (Eds.), *Handbook of posttraumatic growth: Research & practice* (pp. 24–46). Lawrence Erlbaum.

Lewis, M. K. (2002). *Multicultural health psychology*. Allyn and Bacon.

Linley, P. A. & Joseph, S. (2004a). Toward a theoretical foundation for positive psychology in practice. In P. A. Linley & S. Joseph (Eds.), *Positive psychology in practice* (pp. 713–731). Wiley.

Linley, P. A. & Joseph, S. (2004b). Applied positive psychology: A new perspective for professional practice. In P. A. Linley & S. Joseph (Eds.), *Positive psychology in practice* (pp. 3–12). Wiley.

Linley, P. A., Joseph, S., Harrington, S., & Wood, A. M. (2006). Positive psychology: Past, present, and (possible) future. *The Journal of Positive Psychology, 1*(1), 3–16.

Leppin, A. L., Bora, P. R., Tilburt, J. C., Gionfriddo, M. R., Zeballos-Palacios, C., Dulohery, M. M., … Montori, V. M. (2014). The efficacy of resiliency training programs: a systematic review and meta-analysis of randomized trials. *PloS one, 9*(10), e111420.

Locke, E. A. & Latham, G. P. (2013). Goal-setting theory: The current state. In E. A. Locke & G. P. Latham (Eds.), *New developments in goal setting and task performance* (pp. 623–630). Routledge.

Lomas, T., Froh, J. J., Emmons, R. A., Mishra, A., & Bono, G. (2014b). Gratitude interventions. In A. C. Parks & S. Schueller (Eds.), *The Wiley Blackwell handbook of positive psychological interventions* (pp. 3–19). Wiley.

Lomas, T., Hefferon, K., & Ivtzan, I. (2014a). *Applied positive psychology: Integrated positive practice*. Sage.

Lomas, T. & Ivtzan, I. (2016). Professionalising positive psychology: Developing guidelines for training and regulation. *International Journal of Wellbeing, 6*(3), 96–112.

Long, K. & Bonanno, G. A. (2018). An integrative temporal framework for psychological resilience. In J. G. Noll & I. Shalev (Eds.), *The biology of early life stress* (pp. 121–146). Springer.

Lovallo, D. & Kahneman, D. (2003). Delusions of success: How optimism undermines executives' decisions. *Harvard Business Review*, 56–63.

Lovallo, W. R. (2015). *Stress and health*. Sage Publications.

Lucas, R. E. (2007). Long-term disability is associated with lasting changes in subjective well-being: Evidence from two nationally representative longitudinal studies. *Journal of Personality and Social Psychology, 92,* 717–730.

Lucas, R. E., Clark, A. E., Georgellis, Y., & Diener, E. (2003). Reexamining adaptation and the set point model of happiness: Reactions to changes in marital status. *Journal of Personality and Social Psychology, 84,* 527–539.

Lucas, R. E., Clark, A. E., Georgellis, Y., & Diener, E. (2004). Unemployment alters the set point for life satisfaction. *Psychological Science, 15,* 8–13.

Luhmann, M., Hofmann, W., Eid, M., & Lucas, R. E. (2012). Subjective well-being and adaptation to life events: A meta-analysis. *Journal of Personality and Social Psychology, 102,* 592–615.

Lyengar, S. S. & Lepper, M. R. (2000). When choice is demotivating: Can one desire too much of a good thing? *Journal of Personality and Social Psychology, 79*(6), 995–1006.

Lykken, D. & Tellegen, A. (1996). Happiness is a stochastic phenomenon. *Psychological Science, 7,* 186–189.

Lyubomirsky, S. (2011). *The how of happiness.* Penguin.

Lyubomirsky, S. (2014). *The myths of happiness.* Penguin.

Lyubomirsky, S., King, L., & Diener, E. (2005b). The benefits of frequent positive affect: Does happiness lead to success? *Psychological Bulletin, 131,* 803–855.

Lyubomirsky, S. & Lepper, H. S. (1999). A measure of subjective happiness: Preliminary reliability and construct validation. *Social Indicators Research, 46,* 137–155.

Lyubomirsky, S., Sheldon, K. M., & Schkade, D. (2005a). Pursuing happiness: The architecture of sustainable change. *Review of General Psychology, 9*(2), 111–131.

Macaskill, A. (2016). Review of positive psychology applications in clinical medical populations. *Healthcare, 4*(3), 66. Multidisciplinary Digital Publishing Institute.

MacDonald, M. J., Wong, P. T., & Gingras, D. T. (2012). Meaning-in-life measures and development of a brief version of the Personal Meaning Profile. In P. T. Wong (Ed.) *The human quest for meaning: Theories, research, and applications* (pp. 357–382). Routledge.

Maddux, J. E. (2005). Stopping the "madness": Positive psychology and the deconstruction of the illness ideology and the DSM. In C. R. Snyder & S. J. Lopez (Eds.), *Handbook of positive psychology* (pp. 13–25). Oxford University Press.

Maslow, A. H. (1987). *Motivation and personality*. Pearson Education.

Masten, A. S. (2015). *Ordinary magic: Resilience in development*. Guilford.

Mattingly, V. & Kraiger, K. (2019). Can emotional intelligence be trained? A meta-analytical investigation. *Human Resource Management Review, 29*(2), 140–155.

Mayer, J. D., Caruso, D. R., & Salovey, P. (1999). Emotional intelligence meets traditional standards for an intelligence. *Intelligence, 27,* 267–298.

Mayer, J. D., Salovey, P., Caruso, D. R., & Sitarenios, G. (2003). Measuring emotional intelligence with the MSCEIT V2.0. *Emotion, 3,* 97–105.

McCarthy, V. L., Ling, J., & Carini, R. M. (2013). The role of self-transcendence: A missing variable in the pursuit of successful aging?. *Research in Gerontological Nursing, 3*(6), 178–186.

McEwen, B. S. (2005). Stressed or stressed out: What is the difference?. *Journal of Psychiatry and Neuroscience, 30*(5), 315–318.

McKee-Ryan, F., Song, Z., Wanberg, C. R., & Kinicki, A. J. (2005). Psychological and physical well-being during unemployment: A meta-analytic study. *Journal of Applied Psychology, 90*(1), 53–76.

McMahan, E. A. & Estes, D. (2011). Hedonic versus eudaimonic conceptions of well-being: Evidence of differential associations with experienced well-being. *Social Indicators Research, 103,* 93–108.

McMain, S., Newman, M. G., Segal, Z. V., & DeRubeis, R. J. (2015). Cognitive behavioral therapy: Current status and future research directions. *Psychotherapy Research, 25*(3), 321–329.

Meyers, M. C., van Woerkom, M., & Bakker, A. B. (2013). The added value of the positive: A literature review of positive psychology interventions in organizations. *European Journal of Work and Organizational Psychology, 22*(5), 618–632.

Michalos, A. C. (2008). Education, happiness and wellbeing. *Social Indicators Research, 87,* 347–366.

Mikucka, M. (2016). The life satisfaction advantage of being married and gender specialization. *Journal of Marriage and Family, 78*(3), 759–779.

Mill, J. S. & Bentham, J. (1987). *Utilitarianism and other essays*. Penguin.

Miller, A. (2008). A critique of positive psychology—Or 'the new science of happiness'. *Journal of Philosophy of Education, 42*(3–4), 591–608.

Miller, R. (2015). *Intimate relationships*. McGraw-Hill Education.

Miller, R. S. & Lefcourt, H. M. (1982). The assessment of social intimacy. *Journal of Personality Assessment, 46*(5), 514–518.

Milyavskaya, M. & Werner, K. M. (2018). Goal pursuit: Current state of affairs and directions for future research. *Canadian Psychology, 59*(2), 163–184.

Mischel, W., Ayduk, O., Berman, M. G., Casey, B. J., Gotlib, I. H., Jonides, J., … Shoda, Y. (2010). Willpower over the life span: Decomposing self-regulation. *Social Cognitive and Affective Neuroscience, 6*(2), 252–256.

Mischel, W., Shoda, Y., & Rodriguez, M. I. (1989). Delay of gratification in children. *Science, 244*(4907), 933–938.

Nakamura, J. & Csikszentmihalyi, M. (2002). The concept of flow. In C. R. Snyder & S. J. Lopez (Eds.), *Handbook of positive psychology* (pp. 89–105). Oxford University Press.

Nelson, S. K., Kushlev, K., & Lyubomirsky, S. (2014). The pains and pleasures of parenting: When, why, and how is parenthood associated with more or less well-being?. *Psychological Bulletin, 140*(3), 846–895.

Nes, R. B. & Roysamb, E. (2015). The heritability of subjective well-being: Review and meta-analysis. In M. Pluess (Ed.), *The genetics of psychological well-being* (pp. 75–96). Oxford University Press.

Niemiec, R. M. (2017). *Character strenghts interventions*. Hogrefe.

Norem, J. K. (2001). Defensive pessimism, optimism, and pessimism. In E. C. Chang (Ed.), *Optimism and pessimism* (pp. 77–100). APA.

Norem, J. K. & Cantor, N. (2005). Anticipatory and post hoc cushioning strategies: Optimism and defensive pessimism in "risky" situations. *Cognitive Therapy and Research, 10*(3), 347–362.

Norem, J. K. & Chang, E. C. (2002). The positive psychology of negative thinking. *Journal of Clinical Psychology, 58*(9), 993–1001.

North, R. J., Holahan, C. J., Moos, R. H., & Cronkite, R. C. (2008). Family support, family income, and happiness: A 10-year perspective. *Journal of Family Psychology, 22*, 475–483.

Oatley, K. & Johnson-Laird, P. N. (2014). Cognitive approaches to emotions. *Trends in Cognitive Sciences, 18*(3), 134–140.

OECD. (2017). *How's life? Measuring well-being*. OECD.

Oishi, S. & Kurtz, J. L. (2011). The positive psychology of positive emotions: An avuncular view. In K. M. Sheldon, T. B. Kashdan, & M. F. Steger (Eds.), *Designing positive psychology* (pp. 101–114). Oxford University Press.

ONS. (2016). *Marriages in England and Wales*. ONS.

ONS. (2019). *Measuring national well-being in the UK*. ONS.

Palmer, B. W. (Ed.) (2015). *Positive psychiatry: A clinical handbook*. American Psychiatric Pub.

Papp, L. M., Cummings, E. M., & Goeke-Morey, M. C. (2009). For richer, for poorer: Money as a topic of marital conflict in the home. *Family Relations, 58*(1), 91–103.

Papp, L. M., Danielewicz, J., & Cayemberg, C. (2012). "Are we Facebook official?" Implications of dating partners' Facebook use and profiles for intimate relationship satisfaction. *Cyberpsychology, Behavior, and Social Networking, 15*, 85–90.

Parks, A. C. & Biswas-Diener, R. (2013). Positive interventions: Past, present and future. In T. B. Kashdan & J.V. Ciarrochi (Eds.), *Mindfulness, acceptance, and positive psychology* (pp. 140–165). New Harbinger Publications.

Parks, A. C. & Schueller, S. (2014). *The Wiley Blackwell handbook of positive psychological interventions*. Wiley-Blackwell.

Pavot, W. (2018). The cornerstone of research on subjective well-being: Valid assessment methodology. In E. Diener, S. Oishi, & L. Tay (Eds.), *Handbook of well-being*. DEF Publishers.

Pavot, W. & Diener, E. (2004). Findings on subjective well-being: Applications to public policy, clinical interventions, and education. In P. A. Linley & S. Joseph (Eds.), *Positive psychology in practice* (pp. 679–692). Wiley.

Pawelski, J. O. (2016). Defining the 'positive'in positive psychology: Part II. A normative analysis. *The Journal of Positive Psychology, 11*(4), 357–365.

Pennebaker, J.W. & Chung, C.K. (2011). Expressive writing: Connections to physical and mental health. In H. S. Friedman (Ed.), *Oxford handbook of health psychology* (pp. 417–437). Oxford University Press.

Peterson, C. (2000). The future of optimism. *American Psychologist, 55*, 44–55.

Peterson, C. (2005). Forward. In C. R. Snyder & S. J. Lopez (Eds.), *Handbook of positive psychology* (pp. xxiii–xxiv). Oxford University Press.

Peterson, C. (2006). *A primer in positive psychology*. Oxford University Press.

Peterson, C. & Park, N. (2003). Positive psychology as the evenhanded positive psychologist views it. *Psychological Inquiry, 14*(2), 143–147.

Peterson, C. & Park, N. (2009). Classifying and measuring strengths of character. In S. J. Lopex & C. R. Snyder (Eds.), *Oxford handbook of positive psychology* (pp. 25–34). Oxford University Press.

Peterson, C., Schulman, P., Castellon, C., & Seligman, M. E. P. (1992). CAVE: Content analysis of verbatim explanations. In C. P. Smith (Ed.), *Motivation and personality: Handbook of thematic content analysis* (pp. 383–392). Cambridge University Press.

Peterson, C. & Seligman, M. E. P. (1984). Causal explanations as a risk factor for depression: Theory and evidence. *Psychological Review, 91,* 347–374.

Peterson, C. & Seligman, M. E. P. (2004). *Character strengths and virtues.* APA.

Peterson, C., Semmel, A., von Baeyer, C., Abramson, L. Y., Metalsky, G. I., & Seligman, M. E. P. (1982). The attributional style questionnaire. *Cognitive Therapy and Research, 6,* 287–299.

Peterson, D. R. (2002). Conflict. In H. H. Kelley, E. Berscheid, A. Christensen, J. H. Harvey, T. L. Huston, G. Levinger, E. McClinton, L. A. Peplau & D. R. Peterson, (Eds.), *Close relationships* (pp. 265–314). Percheron.

Petrides, K. V. (2009). *Technical manual for the Trait Emotional Intelligence Questionnaires (TEIQue).* London Psychometric Laboratory.

Petrides, K. V., Pita, R., & Kokkinaki, F. (2007). The location of trait emotional intelligence in personality factor space. *British Journal of Psychology, 98,* 273–289.

Pietromonaco, P. R. & Collins, N. L. (2017). Interpersonal mechanisms linking close relationships to health. *American Psychologist, 72*(6), 531–542.

Plutchik, R. (2001). The nature of emotions: Human emotions have deep evolutionary roots, a fact that may explain their complexity and provide tools for clinical practice. *American Scientist, 89*(4), 344–350.

Prager, K. J. & Roberts, L. J. (2004). Deep intimate connection: Self and intimacy in couple relationships. In D. J. Mashek & A. Aron (Eds.), *Handbook of closeness and intimacy* (pp. 43–60). Erlbaum.

Prochaska, J. & DiClemente, C. (1992). The transtheoretical approach. In J. C. Norcross & M. R. Goldfield (Eds.), *Handbook of psychotherapy integration* (pp. 147–171). Basic Books.

Prochaska, J. O., Redding, C. A., & Evers, K. E. (2015). The transtheoretical model and stages of change. In K. Glantz, B. K.

Rimer, & K.Viswanath (Eds.), *Health behavior: Theory, research, and practice* (pp. 125–148). Josey Bass.

Rashid, T. & Seligman, M. P. (2018). *Positive psychotherapy: Clinician manual.* Oxford University Press.

Rath, T. & Harter, J. (2010). *Wellbeing: The five essential elements.* Simon and Schuster.

Reis, H. T. (1998). Gender differences in intimacy and related behaviors: Context and process. In D. J. Canary & K. Dindia (Eds.), *Sex differences and similarities in communication* (pp. 203–234). Erlbaum.

Reis, H. T. (2012). A history of relationship research in social psychology. In A. W. Kruglanski & W. Stroebe (Eds.), *Handbook of the history of social psychology* (pp. 363–382). Psychology Press.

Reis, H. T. & Gable, S. L. (2003). Toward a positive psychology of relationships. In C. L. M. Keyes & J. Haidt (Eds.), *Flourishing: Positive psychology and the life well-lived* (pp. 129–159). APA.

Reis, H. T., Smith, S. M., Carmichael, C. L., Caprariello, P. A., Tsai, F. F., Rodrigues, A., & Maniaci, M. R. (2010). Are you happy for me? How sharing positive events with others provides personal and interpersonal benefits. *Journal of Personality and Social Psychology, 99*(2), 311–329.

Reivich, K. J., Seligman, M. E., & McBride, S. (2011). Master resilience training in the US Army. *American Psychologist, 66*(1), 25–34.

Richins, M. L. & Dawson, S. (1992). A consumer values orientation for materialism and its measurement: Scale development and validation. *Journal of Consumer Research, 19*(3), 303–316.

Riley, J. R. & Masten, A. S. (2005). Resilience in context. In R. Peters, R, B Leadbeater, & R. McMahon (Eds.), *Resilience in children, families, and communities* (pp. 13–25). Springer.

Rogers, C. R. (1963). The concept of the fully functioning person. *Psychotherapy: Theory, Research, and Practice, 1*, 17–26.

Romal, J. B. & Kaplan, B. J. (1995). Difference in self-control among spenders and savers. *Psychology—A Quarterly Journal of Human Behavior, 32*, 8–17.

Romas, J. A. & Sharma, M. (2017). *Practical stress management.* Academic Press.

Røysamb, E. & Nes, R. B. (2018). The genetics of wellbeing. In E. Diener, S. Oishi, & L. Tay (Eds.), *Handbook of well-being.* DEF Publishers.

Rozanski, A., Bavishi, C., Kubzansky, L. D., & Cohen, R. (2019). Association of optimism with cardiovascular events and all-cause mortality: A systematic review and meta-analysis. *JAMA Network Open, 2*(9), e1912200–e1912200.

Ruberton, P. M., Gladstone, J., & Lyubomirsky, S. (2016). How your bank balance buys happiness: The importance of "cash on hand" to life satisfaction. *Emotion, 16*(5), 575–580.

Ruini, C. (2017). *Positive psychology in the clinical domains*. Springer.

Rusk, R. D. & Waters, L. E. (2013). Tracing the size, reach, impact, and breadth of positive psychology. *The Journal of Positive Psychology, 8*(3), 207–221.

Russell, D. W. (1996). UCLA Loneliness Scale: Reliability, validity, and factor structure. *Journal of Personality Assessment, 66*(1), 20–40.

Ryan, R. M. & Deci, E. L. (2000). Self-determination theory and the facilitation of intrinsic motivation, social development, and well-being. *American Psychologist, 55*(1), 68–78.

Ryan, R. M. & Deci, E. L. (2017). *Self-determination theory*. Guilford Publications.

Ryff, C. D. (1989). Happiness is everything, or is it? Explorations on the meaning of psychological well-being. *Journal of Personality and Social Psychology, 57*, 1069–1081.

Ryff, C. D. (2014). Psychological well-being revisited: Advances in the science and practice of eudaimonia. *Psychotherapy and Psychosomatics, 83*(1), 10–28.

Ryff, C. D. (2018). Eudaimonic well-being: Highlights from 25 years of inquiry. In K. Shigemasu, S. Kuwano, T. Sato, & T. Matsuzawa (Eds.), *Diversity in harmony–insights from psychology* (pp. 375–395). Wiley.

Ryff, C. D. & Singer, B. (1996). Psychological well-being: Meaning, measurement, and implications for psychotherapy research. *Psychotherapy and Psychosomatics, 65*(1), 14–23.

Salovey, P. & Mayer, J. (1990). Emotional intelligence. *Imagination, Cognition, and Personality, 9*, 185–211.

Satici, S. A. & Uysal, R. (2015). Well-being and problematic Facebook use. *Computers in Human Behavior, 49*, 185–190.

Sbarra, D. A. & Nietert, P. J. (2009). Divorce and death: Forty years of the Charleston Heart Study. *Psychological Science, 20*, 107–113.

Scheier, M. F. & Carver, C. S. (1985). Optimism, coping and health: Assessment and implications of generalized outcome expectancies. *Health Psychology, 4*, 219–247.

Scheier, M. F. & Carver, C. S. (1992). Effects of optimism on psychological and physical well-being: Theoretical overview and empirical update. *Cognitive Therapy and Research, 16,* 201–228.

Scheier, M. F. & Carver, C. S. (2018). Dispositional optimism and physical health: A long look back, a quick look forward. *American Psychologist, 73*(9), 1082–1094.

Scheier, M. F., Carver, C. S., & Bridges, M. W. (1994). Distinguishing optimism from neuroticism: A re-evaluation of the Life Orientation Test. *Journal of Personality and Social Psychology, 67,* 1063–1078.

Schkade, D. A. & Kahneman, D. (1998). Does living in California make people happy? A focusing illusion in judgments of life satisfaction. *Psychological Science, 9*(5), 340–346.

Schueller, S. M. & Seligman, M. E. (2011). Optimism and pessimism. In K. S. Dobson & D. J. Dozois (Eds.), *Risk factors in depression* (pp. 171–194). Elsevier.

Segal, Z. V. & Teasdale, J. (2018). *Mindfulness-based cognitive therapy for depression.* Guilford.

Seligman, M. (2018). PERMA and the building blocks of well-being. *The Journal of Positive Psychology, 13*(4), 333–335.

Seligman, M. E. (2006). *Learned optimism.* Vintage.

Seligman, M. E., Parks, A. C., & Steen, T. (2004). A balanced psychology and a full life. *Philosophical Transactions of the Royal Society of London. Series B: Biological Sciences, 359*(1449), 1379–1381.

Seligman, M. E. P. (1999). The president's address. *American Psychologist, 54,* 559–562.

Seligman, M. E. P. (2002). *Authentic happiness.* Free Press.

Seligman, M. E. P. (2005). Positive psychology, positive prevention, and positive therapy. In C. R. Snyder & S. J. Lopez (Eds.), *Handbook of positive psychology* (pp. 3–9). Oxford University Press.

Seligman, M. E. P. (2011). *Flourish.* Free Press.

Seligman, M. E. P. & Csikszentmihalyi, M. (2000). Positive psychology: An Introduction. *American Psychologist, 55,* 5–14.

Selye, H. (1993). History of the stress concept. In L. Goldberger & S. Breznitz (Eds.), *Handbook of stress: Theoretical and clinical aspects* (pp. 7–17). Free Press.

Sharot, T. (2011). *The optimism bias.* Alfred Knopf.

Sharot, T., Korn, C. W., & Dolan, R. J. (2011). How unrealistic optimism is maintained in the face of reality. *Nature Neuroscience,* 1475–1479.

Sharot, T., Riccardi, A. M., Raio, C. M., & Phelps, E. A. (2007). Neural mechanisms mediating optimism bias. *Nature, 450*(1), 102–106.

Shaver, P. R. & Mikulincer, M. (2013). Patterns of relating and of thinking about relationships: Conceptualizing and measuring individual differences in the adult attachment system. In C. Hazan & M. I. Campa (Eds.), *Human bonding* (pp. 251–280). Guilford.

Sheldon, K. M. & Elliot, A. J. (1999). Goal striving, need satisfaction, and longitudinal well-being: The self-concordance model. *Journal of Personality and Social Psychology, 76*(3), 482–497.

Sheldon, K. M., Elliot, A. J., Kim, Y., & Kasser, T. (2001). What is satisfying about satisfying events? Testing 10 candidate psychological needs. *Journal of Personality and Social Psychology, 80*(2), 325–339.

Sheldon, K. M. & Lyubomirsky, S. (2019). Revisiting the sustainable happiness model and pie chart: Can happiness be successfully pursued?. *The Journal of Positive Psychology*, 1–10.

Sherman, D. K. & Cohen, G. L. (2006). The psychology of self-defense: Self-affirmation theory. *Advances in Experimental Social Psychology, 38*, 183–242.

Sin, N. L. & Lyubomirsky, S. (2009). Enhancing well-being and alleviating depressive symptoms with positive psychology interventions: A practice-friendly meta-analysis. *Journal of Clinical Psychology, 65*(5), 467–487.

Sinclair, E., Hart, R., & Lomas, T. (2020). Can positivity be counterproductive when suffering domestic abuse?: A narrative review. *International Journal of Wellbeing, 10*(1), 26–53.

Skinner, E. A. & Zimmer-Gembeck, M. J. (2007). The development of coping. *Annual Review of Psychology, 58*, 119–144.

Snyder, C. R. (1994). *The psychology of hope*. Free Press.

Snyder, C. R., Irving, L., & Anderson, J. R. (1991). Hope and health: Measuring the will and the ways. In C. R. Snyder & D. R. Forsyth (Eds.), *Handbook of social and clinical psychology: The health perspective* (pp. 285–305). Pergamon.

Snyder, C. R., Lopez, S. J., & Pedrotti, J. T. (2011). *Positive psychology*. Sage.

Snyder, C. R., Rand, K. L., & Sigmon, D. R. (2005). Hope theory. In C. R. Snyder & S. J. Lopez (Eds.), *Handbook of positive psychology* (pp. 257–276). Oxford University Press.

Solomon, R. C. (2008). The philosophy of emotions. In M. Lewis, J. Haviland-Jones, & L. F. Barrett (Eds.), *Handbook of emotions* (pp. 3–15). Guilford.

Spector, P. E. & Johnson, H. M. (2006). Improving the definition, measurement, and application of emotional intelligence. In K. R. Murphy (Ed.), *A critique of emotional intelligence* (pp. 325–344). Lawrence Erlbaum.

Sprecher, S. & Metts, S. (2013). Logging on, hooking up: The changing nature of romantic relationship initiation and romantic relating. In C. Hazan & M. I. Campa (Eds.), *Human bonding: The science of affectional ties* (pp. 197–225). Guilford.

Steger, M. F. (2012). Making meaning in life. *Psychological Inquiry, 23*(4), 381–385.

Steger, M. F. (2017). Meaning in life and wellbeing. In M. Slade, L. Oades, & A. Jarden (Eds.), *Wellbeing, recovery and mental health* (pp. 75–85). Cambridge University Press.

Steger, M. F., Frazier, P., Oishi, S., & Kaler, M. (2006). The meaning in life questionnaire: Assessing the presence of and search for meaning in life. *Journal of Counseling Psychology, 53*(1), 80–93.

Steptoe, A. (2019). Happiness and health. *Annual Review of Public Health, 40*, 339–359.

Steptoe, A., Deaton, A., & Stone, A. A. (2015). Subjective wellbeing, health, and ageing. *The Lancet, 385*(9968), 640–648.

Sternberg, R. J. (1987). *The triangle of love: Intimacy, passion, commitment.* Basic Books.

Sternberg, R. J. (2006). A duplex theory of love. In R. J. Sternberg & K. Weis (Eds.), *The new psychology of love* (pp. 184–199). Yale University Press.

Stutzer, A. & Frey, B. S. (2008). Stress that doesn't pay: The commuting paradox. *Scandinavian Journal of Economics, 110*, 339–366.

Tangney, J. P., Baumeister, R. F., & Boone, A. L. (2004). High self-control predicts good adjustment, less pathology, better grades, and interpersonal success. *Journal of Personality, 72*, 271–322.

Tay, L., Li, M., Myers, D., & Diener, E. (2014). Religiosity and subjective well-being: An international perspective. In C. Kim-Prieto (Ed.), *Religion and spirituality across cultures* (pp. 163–175). Springer.

Tay, L., Zyphur, M., & Batz, C. L. (2018). Income and subjective well-being: Review, synthesis, and future research. In E. Diener, S. Oishi, & L. Tay (Eds.), *Handbook of well-being.* DEF Publishers.

Taylor, E. (2001). Positive psychology and humanistic psychology: A reply to Seligman. *Journal of Humanistic Psychology*, *41*(1), 13–29.

Taylor, S. E. (1989). *Positive illusions*. Basic Books.

Taylor, S. E. & Brown, J. D. (1988). Illusions and well-being: A social psychological perspective on mental health. *Psychological Bulletin*, *103*(2), 193–210.

Taylor, S. E. & Brown, J. D. (1994). Positive illusions and well-being revisited: Separating fact from fiction. *Psychological Bulletin*, *116*(1), 21–27.

Tedeschi, R. G. & Calhoun, L. G. (1996). The Posttraumatic Growth Inventory: Measuring the positive legacy of trauma. *Journal of Traumatic Stress*, *9*, 455–471.

Tedeschi, R. G. & Calhoun, L. G. (2004). Posttraumatic growth: Conceptual foundations and empirical evidence. *Psychological Inquiry*, *15*(1), 1–18.

Tedeschi, R. G., Cann, A., Taku, K., Senol-Durak, E., & Calhoun, L. G. (2017). The posttraumatic growth inventory: A revision integrating existential and spiritual change. *Journal of Traumatic Stress*, *30*(1), 11–18.

Tedeschi, R. G., Shakespeare-Finch, J., Taku, K., & Calhoun, L. G. (2018). *Posttraumatic growth*. Routledge.

Tokunaga, R. S. (2011). Friend me or you'll strain us: Understanding negative events that occur over social networking sites. *Cyberpsychology, Behavior, and Social Networking*, *14*, 425–432.

Tran, S., Simpson, J. A., & Fletcher, G. J. O. (2008). The role of ideal standards in relationship initiation processes. In S. Sprecher, A. Wenzel, & J. Harvey (Eds.), *Handbook of relationship initiation* (pp. 487–498). Psychology Press.

Valkenburg, P. M. & Peter, J. (2009). The effects of instant messaging on the quality of adolescents' existing friendships: A longitudinal study. *Journal of Communication*, *59*, 79–97.

Van Lange, P. A. M. & Rusbult, C. E. (2012). Interdependence theory. In P. Van Lange, A. Kruglanski, & E. T. Higgins (Eds.), *Handbook of theories of social psychology* (pp. 251–272). Sage.

Van Zalk, M. H. W., Branje, S. J. T., Denissen, J., Van Aken, M. A. G., & Meeus, W. H. J. (2011). Who benefits from chatting, and why? The roles of extraversion and supportiveness in online chatting and emotional adjustment. *Personality and Social Psychology Bulletin*, *37*, 1202–1215.

Vohs, K. D., Mead, N. L., & Goode, M. R. (2008). Merely activating the concept of money changes personal and interpersonal behavior. *Current Directions in Psychological Science, 17*(3), 208–212.

Walsh, F. (2012). The new normal: Diversity and complexity in 21st-century families. In F. Walsh (Ed.), *Normal family processes: Growing diversity and complexity* (pp. 3–24). Guilford.

Walsh, L. C., Boehm, J. K., & Lyubomirsky, S. (2018). Does happiness promote career success? Revisiting the evidence. *Journal of Career Assessment, 26*(2), 199–219.

Ward, S. J. & King, L. A. (2016). Poor but happy? Income, happiness, and experienced and expected meaning in life. *Social Psychological and Personality Science, 7*(5), 463–470.

Warr, P. (2007). *Work, happiness, and unhappiness.* Lawrence Erlbaum.

Warren, M. A., Donaldson, S. I., & Lee, J. Y. (2017). Applying positive psychology to advance relationship science. In M. A. Warren & S. I. Donaldson (Eds.), *Toward a positive psychology of relationships* (pp. 9–34). Praeger.

Waterman, A. S. (1990). The relevance of Aristotle's conception of eudaimonia for the psychological study of happiness. *Theoretical & Philosophical Psychology, 10*(1), 39–44.

Waterman, A. S. (2013). The humanistic psychology–positive psychology divide: Contrasts in philosophical foundations. *American Psychologist, 68*(3), 124–133.

Watson, D., Clark, L. A., & Tellegen, A. (1988). Development and validation of brief measures of positive and negative affect: The PANAS scales. *Journal of Personality and Social Psychology, 54*, 1063–1070.

Weiss, L. A., Westerhof, G. J., & Bohlmeijer, E. T. (2016). Can we increase psychological well-being? The effects of interventions on psychological well-being: A meta-analysis of randomized controlled trials. *PloS One, 11*, 6.

Werner, E. E. (1993). Risk, resilience, and recovery: Perspectives from the Kauai longitudinal study. *Development and Psychopathology, 5*(4), 503–515.

White, C. A., Uttl, B., & Holder, M. D. (2019). Meta-analyses of positive psychology interventions: The effects are much smaller than previously reported. *PloS One, 14*, 5.

World Health Organisation. (2001). *The world health report—Mental health.* WHO.

Wilson, T. D. & Gilbert, D. T. (2005). Affective forecasting: Knowing what to want. *Current Directions in Psychological Science*, *14*(3), 131–134.

Wolfinger, N. H. (2005). *Understanding the divorce cycle*. Cambridge University Press.

Wong, P. T. (2010). What is existential positive psychology?. *International Journal of Existential Psychology and Psychotherapy*, *3*(1), 1–10.

Wong, P. T. (2012a). Toward a dual-systems model of what makes life worth living. In P. Wong (Ed.), *The human quest for meaning* (pp. 3–23). Routledge.

Wong, P. T. (2012b). From logotherapy to meaning-centered counseling and therapy. In P. Wong (Ed.), *The human quest for meaning* (pp. 619–647). Routledge.

Wong, P. T. P. (1998). Implicit theories of meaningful life and the development of the personal meaning profile. In P. T. P. Wong & P. S. Fry (Eds.), *The human quest for meaning*. Lawrence Erlbaum.

Wong, P. T. P. (2011). Positive psychology 2.0: Towards a balanced interactive model of the good life. *Canadian Psychology*, *52*(2), 69–81.

Worthington Jr, E. L., Wade, N. G., & Hoyt, W. T. (2014). Positive psychological interventions for promoting forgiveness: History, present status, and future prospects. In A. C. Parks & S. Schueller (Eds.), *The Wiley Blackwell handbook of positive psychological interventions* (pp. 20–41). Wiley.

Wright, P. H. (1982). Men's friendships, women's friendships and the alleged inferiority of the latter. *Sex Roles*, *8*, 1–20.

Yalom, I. (1980). *Existential psychotherapy*. Basic Books.

Youngman, H. (1998). *Take my wife, please!: Henny Youngman's giant book of jokes*. Citadel.

Zautra, A. J., Hall, J. S., & Murray, K. E. (2010). Resilience: A new definition of health for people and communities. In J. W. Reich, A. J. Zautra, & J. S. Hall (Eds.), *Handbook of adult resilience* (pp. 3–34). Guilford.

Zuckerman, M., Li, C., & Diener, E. (2017). Societal conditions and the gender differences in well-being: Testing a 3-stage model. *Personality and Social Psychology Bulletin*, *43*, 329–336.

INDEX